CRISIS COMMUNICATION CASES FROM ASIA

This book analyzes crisis communication in Asia, focusing on how culture (broadly defined) plays a central role in the way a crisis develops and is resolved.

Using the case study method, this book offers the reader glimpses of the variety of cultures in the continent, displaying the complexity of the cross-cultural process of conducting crisis communication in this diverse environment. Each of these cases addresses the onset, evolution, and resolution of the crisis. The contributors are practitioners who have done crisis communication work in this continent and have used the same framework of five environmental variables that define culture in this book: political culture, economic systems, societal culture, media systems, and activist environments.

This edited volume is ideal for scholars and advanced students in public relations and strategic communication generally and crisis communication specifically.

Krishnamurthy Sriramesh is a Professor of Public Relations in the College of Media, Communication, and Information at the University of Colorado, Boulder, USA.

Su Lin Yeo is an Associate Professor in the Lee Kong Chian School of Business at Singapore Management University.

"*Crisis Communication Cases from Asia* is a book that fills a void in the marketplace which will be welcomed by both students and practitioners interested in learning more about Crisis Communication in Asia. The editors of the book, Prof. Krishnamurthy Sriramesh and Associate Professor Yeo Su Lin, are well-known scholars in the field of Crisis Communication who worked closely with practitioners from both the private and public sectors in Asia in writing the book. The book incorporates a cultural perspective to crisis communication and includes a wide range of cases from different countries in the region, as well as different types of crises."

Daniel Laufer, *Victoria University of Wellington, New Zealand*

"This book pushes the boundaries of theory and practice in crisis communication by incorporating a cultural perspective. Each case is examined through a socio-political lens including societal, organizational, political, economic, media and activist cultures. Such a perspective is novel to crisis communication scholarship, a welcome addition to advance knowledge. Notably, the book does not treat Asia as a homogeneous whole, but as a tapestry of widely divergent cultures. This book fills a glaring lacuna in crisis communication research by offering a rich compilation of crisis cases from nine Asian countries written by practitioners using the same conceptual framework for analysis."

Ganga Dhanesh, *University of Maryland, USA*

CRISIS COMMUNICATION CASES FROM ASIA

A Cultural Approach

Edited by Krishnamurthy Sriramesh and Su Lin Yeo

Routledge
Taylor & Francis Group
NEW YORK AND LONDON

Designed cover image: Blue glowing Earth [Lower Asia] - stock photo.
fpm via Getty Images.

First published 2025
by Routledge
605 Third Avenue, New York, NY 10158

and by Routledge
4 Park Square, Milton Park, Abingdon, Oxon, OX14 4RN

Routledge is an imprint of the Taylor & Francis Group, an informa business

Library of Congress Cataloging-in-Publication Data
Names: Yeo, Su Lin, editor. | Sriramesh, Krishnamurthy, editor.
Title: Crisis communication cases from Asia : a cultural approach / edited by Krishnamurthy Sriramesh and Su Lin Yeo.
Description: New York, NY : Routledge, 2025. | Includes bibliographical references and index.
Identifiers: LCCN 2024029603 (print) | LCCN 2024029604 (ebook) |
ISBN 9781032533896 (hardback) | ISBN 9781032533889 (paperback) |
ISBN 9781032637679 (ebook) | ISBN 9781040151365 (adobe pdf) |
ISBN 9781040151419 (epub)
Subjects: LCSH: Communication in crisis management--Asia--Case studies. | Corporations--Public relations--Asia--Case studies. | Intercultural communication--Asia--Case studies.
Classification: LCC HD49.3 .C77 2025 (print) | LCC HD49.3 (ebook) |
DDC 658.4/5095--dc23/eng/20240709
LC record available at https://lccn.loc.gov/2024029603
LC ebook record available at https://lccn.loc.gov/2024029604

ISBN: 978-1-032-53389-6 (hbk)
ISBN: 978-1-032-53388-9 (pbk)
ISBN: 978-1-003-41180-2 (ebk)

DOI: 10.4324/9781003411802

Typeset in Times New Roman
by KnowledgeWorks Global Ltd.

Respectfully and Lovingly Dedicated

To my dearest parents

मातृदेवो भव।
MaatruDevo Bhava

[May the mother be, to thee, a God] – Taittiriya Upanishad (1:11:2)

For instilling in me good values and overlooking all my shortcomings and being most understanding of my absence and neglecting your needs while I selfishly worked on this and other professional projects

पितृदेवो भव।
PitruDevo Bhava

[May the father be, to thee, a God] – Taittiriya Upanishad (1:11:2)

For teaching me the values of life and scholarship as well as teaching me English grammar early in life thus equipping me to complete my many writing projects

Krishnamurthy Sriramesh

CONTENTS

LIST OF FIGURE AND TABLE

Figure

Table

EDITOR BIOGRAPHIES

Krishnamurthy Sriramesh is a Professor of Public Relations at the University of Colorado. His rich teaching experience includes teaching a range of courses in 10 universities in North America, Asia, Australasia, and Europe while also delivering seminars/talks in over 40 countries. He is recognized for his scholarship on global public relations, culture and public relations, corporate social responsibility (CSR), and public relations for development. His program of research has resulted in 8 edited or co-edited books, over 120 articles and book chapters, and over 120 conference papers and other presentations around the world. A recent bibliometric analysis published in *Public Relations Review* placed him among the top five cited global public relations scholars. In 2004, the Institute of Public Relations (USA) recognized his scholarship by honoring him with the prestigious Pathfinder Award for "*original scholarly research contributing to the public relations body of knowledge*." He has won several other awards for scholarship including two PRIDE awards (2003 and 2020) from the National Communication Association (NCA), the Faculty Research Award and the Golden Gator Award (University of Florida). His teaching excellence has also been recognized with awards such as the Charles W. Redding Award (Purdue University) and the Teacher of the Year (University of Florida). Purdue University appointed him as a University Faculty Scholar from 2012–2017. In 2018, he was also Faculty Fellow of Purdue Institute for Civic Communication (PICC) at Purdue University. He received the Page Legacy Scholar award from the Arthur W. Page Society in 2016. From 2012–2016, he served as a member of the Independent Advisory Committee of *Humidtropics*, a project operated by the International Institute of Tropical Agriculture (IITA), Ibadan, Nigeria under the aegis of the CGIAR – a global partnership for global food security. He has served as Assistant Editor of *Public Relations Review* (2004 – 2013), Associate Editor of *Journal of Communication Management* (2002 – 2016), and is currently a member of the editorial boards of a number of journals including *Journalism & Mass Communication Quarterly, Management Communication Quarterly,* and *Public Relations Review.*

Su Lin Yeo is an Associate Professor of Communication Management (Practice) and full-time faculty in the Lee Kong Chian School of Business at the Singapore Management University (SMU). She serves on the SMU Faculty Senate and several university task force committees and additionally sits on national health boards as an advisor on stakeholder engagement and communication. Regionally and internationally, she is the Director for the SMU-IPR Alliance (Southeast Asia) and an appointed Board Trustee at the Institute for Public Relations (USA) respectively. She teaches a range of full-credit communication modules from undergraduate to postgraduate programmes including the MBA and EMBA. Since joining SMU in 2014, she has been placed yearly on the Dean's Teaching Honor List from 2015 to 2023. She further conducts executive education workshops for C-suite and business leaders from different industries in Asia. Her primary research interests focus primarily on Corporate Reputation, Crisis Communication, and Public Health Communication. She received the prestigious Robert Heath Award for Top Faculty Paper for Public Relations at the International Communication Association in San Diego (USA) in 2017, and the New Researcher Award at the World Public Relations Forum in Toronto (Canada) in 2016, among other paper awards. She is an editorial board member of the Journal of Communication Management and publishes in top communication journals, including Communication Research, Public Relations Review, and the International Journal of Strategic Communication. Prior to receiving her PhD in Communication Studies from Nanyang Technological University in Singapore, she spent 12 years managing corporate communication and investor relations in the banking and financial services sectors, where she was instrumental in strategizing communication and reputation-enhancing initiatives that drove business outcomes for her organizations in Asia.

CONTRIBUTOR BIOGRAPHIES

Sam Ahmed is a senior banker in Asia who has spent the past 26 years working in global banks across Sydney, Tokyo, and Singapore in areas such as trading, sales, and risk in financial markets. As Managing Director of Deriv Asia, he has worked with both governments in Thailand, Korea, and Indonesia as well as banks across Singapore, HK, and Japan to help them build new businesses and financial infrastructures. He is a familiar face in the regional media and has also published articles and thought leadership papers in *The Asian Banker*, *The Straits Times*, *The Asset*, *Asian Investor* along with making frequent media appearances on *BBC* and *Bloomberg*.

Shabbir Akhtar is a seasoned content, creative, and communication strategist with experience spanning over a decade. He currently serves as the Head - Marketing & Communication at Globsyn Group. Specializing in guiding brands to establish their unique voices within the dynamic digital landscape, he excels in merging technical acumen with storytelling finesse. Through a journey that seamlessly transitioned from technology journalism and digital marketing to comprehensive strategic content, creative, and communication roles, he crafts narratives that resonate, captivate, and endure to help companies unlock their brand potential.

Hannah Luz Awitan is an experienced market research professional and storyteller. She has previously worked for ABS-CBN Corporation, a leading media and entertainment company in the Philippines, to better understand Filipino consumers.

Lois Bastiaan is head of finance in her family company in Indonesia. She is interested in the interdisciplinary discourse between strategic communications, branding, and designs. She has always been interested in the details and behind-the-scenes of maintaining a positive and memorable corporate image while responding to the dynamic interactions between corporates and shareholders in a fast-paced business environment. Although she oversees finance, she is proactively involved in the design and branding process of building her family company's corporate image.

Ivan Chan is a digital communications platform manager at Great Eastern Life. His work experience spanned the finance and technology sectors. Prior to his current role, he worked as a product business partner at TikTok and as a strategic initiatives manager at the Development Bank of Singapore.

Soe Honey Cho is a marketing communications lead at Bayer Singapore, where she drives digital communication initiatives to transform and digitalize the agricultural industry across the Asia-Pacific region. With experience spanning eight years in country and regional roles across diverse industries from mobile and technology to telecoms, consumer goods, and FinTech, she excels in corporate communication, public relations, and influencer management. She thrives on conceptualizing creative ideas to elevate communication in a fast-paced environment.

Subhas Gopalakrishnan is a defense relations officer in Singapore's Armed Forces. Having served in the military for 23 years, he had varied portfolios, including working in the Army's Corporate Communications branch. Overall, he is responsible for internal communication and stakeholder management, and his work focuses primarily on people management and organizational skills. A motivating leader, and collaborative team player, he is task-driven with a passion for the outdoors and history.

Kritika Gupta is a consultant at MSL Group, an integrated communications agency. Partnering closely with corporate clients across the Asia-Pacific region to execute and elevate regional communications, she was responsible for accounts such as Meta, Coca-Cola, P&G, Standard Chartered Bank, and Bacardi, among others. She has led the launch of products and campaigns for reputed global brands and devised campaign strategies for marquee properties such as BACARDI NH7 Weekender, Coke Studio, and Coca-Cola's FIFA World Cup Trophy Tour.

Elle Ning Jin is an assistant manager at the National University of Singapore. Her eight years of industry experience included creating integrated communication strategies for global clients such as Google, Adobe, Netapp, and Lenovo.

Her expertise lies in hub management in Asia-Pacific, where she conducted periodic analyses of performance indicators across earned and paid media channels in the development of PR reports to C-Suite. She has devised campaigns to enhance the clients' reputation and increase brand visibility through content strategies such as thought leadership bylines, executive profiling, and social media engagement.

Nicole Lee holds a strategic partnership role in the Google and Infocomm Media Development Authority Singapore's SISG program. Her professional experience spans from trade communication in consumer-packaged goods to business development and digital user acquisition on a global scale. Her experience in working with global teams and diverse customer segments, along with involvement in scaled initiatives, has provided her with a nuanced understanding of how precisely tailored communication strategies can effectively mold and influence diverse corporate ecosystems.

Isreya Liangkobkit is the chief sales officer and co-founder of innovation food company Eatvolution Co Ltd in Thailand. An enterprising and strategic planning consultant with more than 10 years' experience in communication, he is inspired by the deep roots of local discipline and context as well as their way of life. He believes that learning is a lifelong journey and that the diversity that life brings along the way will not only help broaden world perspectives but also enlighten every initiative through strategic communication.

Jotham Tobiah Lim is a fundraising and development senior specialist for the largest public healthcare group in Singapore. Responsible for its fundraising efforts, he manages communications activities, external stakeholder communication, and donor engagement at the group level. In addition, he is an award-winning live-commerce communicator, a permanent key opinion leader for Shopee's official channel, and oversees the e-commerce live-streaming platforms for Singapore's top homegrown tech companies such as Prism+, AfterShock PC, Omnidesk, and Sterra.

Ryan Lim is a Senior Analyst at Edelman Global Advisory. Covering projects in India, Japan, and Thailand, he works across several industry sectors, including agri-food, medical aesthetics, and mining. Formerly with Edelman Singapore, he was awarded the gold and bronze honors at the PR Awards Southeast Asia 2022 for his work, *SingapoReimagine Global Conversations*. His expertise was further recognized for the *UseYourRoadSense* campaign, which won him two additional silver awards. He co-presented a paper on former US President Donald Trump's image repair strategies after the 2021, January 6 Capitol Hill Riots at an international forum.

Pui Fong Loh is the assistant director of human resource (HR) division in the Ministry of Home Affairs (MHA) Singapore. Her portfolio involves reviewing HR policies, salaries, and compensation packages to ensure the continued attractiveness and competitiveness of MHA schemes. She also develops communication messages targeted at employees and works with HR stakeholders to implement changes to internal policies and compensation strategies for the ministry.

Fiona Hui Ling Loi is an assistant director in the information plans branch in the Singapore Armed Forces, where she leads a team to develop, drive, and oversee information policies, strategies, and campaign plans for the Digital Intelligence Service. Having spent 14 years in the government sector working on various portfolios, she was responsible for communication and information policy, media relations, and new media strategy and planning.

Quelle Audris Loo is the vice president of corporate communications in a local oil and gas company. She pioneered the communication efforts and activities of the organization and now oversees the development and execution of the company's branding, media relations, ESG initiatives, and stakeholder engagement strategies. In this homegrown company, she works with staff from different countries and seeks to establish worldwide partnerships and effective cross-cultural communication in her role.

Jia Ning Neo is an account manager in a public relations consultancy firm in Singapore. She looks after different client accounts ranging from engineering, technology, healthcare, transport, F&B to lifestyle. She enjoys the multi-faceted role as a communication practitioner and strives to contribute out-of-the-box ideas to bring the communications profession to the next level in a dynamic, challenging, and fast-paced environment in Asia. She enjoys her stakeholder-centric role, where strategic communication, management, and engagement are key.

Stephanie Ai Ling Ng is a senior manager at the Land Transport Authority Singapore. Responsible for internal and external stakeholder communications, she further oversees the publicity for a range of portfolios and facilitates the implementation of digital services and systems related to land transport. Her two-decade communication career in the public service sector included marketing, events, corporate communication, employee communication, and strategic project management.

Mae Nguyen is the marketing communication manager at Calderys Group. She plays a vital role in the global communication team, overseeing and shaping the group's marketing communication initiatives in the Asia-Pacific (APAC) region. Her expertise includes marketing management, business-to-business communication, digital marketing, and developing strategic marketing communication campaigns for various stakeholders in different countries. Through her seven-year engagement in multinational contexts, she has honed her communication skills and nurtured an unwavering passion in the field. As a member of the Public Relations and Communications Association Asia Pacific (PRCA), she was invited to be part of the judging panel for the prestigious PRCA-APAC Awards in 2023.

Yuri Okutsu is the Asia-Pacific marketing communications manager for an American multinational company in the financial services sector headquartered in Boston. A Japanese national, she is based in its regional headquarters in Singapore and oversees media relations, events, and other marketing and communication strategies and activities in the region. With 12 years of previous work experience in Japan's biggest trading house in Tokyo, her expertise ranges from marketing, corporate communications to investor relations.

Angeline Onasis is the media service manager for an in-flight entertainment company. Originally from Indonesia, she has lived in Singapore for the last 10 years. Her primary areas of expertise include business-to-business communication, stakeholder management, and the development of effective communication strategies to engage with vendors, as well as clients.

Natawan Panachuenvongsakul is a chief creative officer and co-founder of Eatvolution Co Ltd. Her role in communications has motivated and inspired her to challenge herself in entrepreneurship, where she can better appreciate and incorporate value and importance to communications. She is fascinated by the interdisciplinary facets and diverse perspectives of communications and is challenged by the fast-paced and ever-changing dynamic of today's business environment.

Zi Xiang Phoon is a business consultant for a multinational firm that mainly provides services in tax and accounting. He has handled multiple engagements in areas of business transformation, technology implementation, and customer experience for both local and global clients. Prior to his current position, he spent four years in the agritech and sustainability sector handling key accounts and media-related duties.

Celest Quek is the head of marketing and communications for Asia in The Travel Corporation, where she oversees six travel brands in the region. She has over 14 years of working experience and has held marketing and communications positions in both local and global companies, leading teams across Southeast Asia and India. She works collaboratively with global stakeholders from different parts of the world, applying strategic solutions that address cultural nuances for different markets.

Himesh Sharma is a digital marketing manager at One World International School in Singapore, where he is responsible for the institution's online marketing and communication content and activities. Trained in electrical and electronics engineering, he had previously worked in performance and digital marketing at Xiaomi Technologies Pte Ltd and the Landmark group. He is a great storyteller with an eye for numbers and history.

Clement Sim is a global brand manager at Unilever and is part of the company's Global Brand Team. Exposed to multiple markets across the globe, he works on diverse cultural nuances to ensure effective communication for brands operating in different and varied markets. His work, which focuses primarily on Indonesia, Türkiye, Vietnam, Bangladesh, China, and Thailand, challenges him to use consumer insights to craft ideas in a way that is culturally relevant while being a guardian to a brand's core identity. He is passionate about understanding the psyche of other people, and to be able to leverage that to establish win-win situations.

Emmeline Jie Yi Tan is a senior manager of the International Cyber Policy Office in the Cyber Security Agency of Singapore (CSA). Her responsibilities include managing Singapore's international cyber relations and engaging international stakeholders on related issues. She had previously worked at the Smart Nation and Digital Government Office to develop and implement communications and engagement strategies for the adoption of digital government services in the city-state. Having also worked in Japan, where she collaborated with individuals of diverse nationalities to curate events aimed at fostering cross-cultural understanding, her international experience made her adept at reaching audiences across varied geographical regions.

Malcolm Teo provides expertise to start-ups and is a deals and advisory consultant. His exposure to various projects gives him a breadth of knowledge across many industries, while his depth of experience in carve outs and integrations gives him an understanding of the complexities of human resources and operations. Having collaborated with clients and colleagues across North America, Europe, and Asia, he excels at bridging cultural differences and navigating the complexities of stakeholder management.

Rahmatina Widyarini is a digital product designer at SGCARMART, Singapore's largest online car auction platform. She has a deep passion for architectural design and focuses on studying behavioral changes in people. Her work experience is concentrated primarily in digital media and architectural design.

Nikole Wong is a Program Manager at Edelman Global Advisory. Specializing in policy and strategic communications, she is involved in advocacy, strategy, and policy communications. She has advised multinational corporations on global, regional, and local projects across agri-food, healthcare, trade, tourism, supply chain and logistics, and crypto sectors. Her award-winning work for her client, FrieslandCampina, won her an international Gold Standard Award at the Public Relations and Communications Association Asia Pacific in June 2022. The communication piece showcased a suite of sustainability-related policy communication tools and narratives.

Daphne Zhiying Xu is the deputy director of the information policy and plans department in the Information Policy and Strategy Office at Singapore's Ministry of Defense Communications Organization. She leads a communication team that provides centralized guidance and oversight of the strategic communications policies, in addition to strategizing plans across a spectrum of issues. She has been in the government service for 15 years and her work experience spanned from managing strategic communications, national education and policy communication, and leadership development.

Ju Young Yoon is a consultant with a globally renowned consulting firm. A South Korean national and trained in information systems, he has successfully spearheaded transformative IT implementations in his area of work. Having spent and lived 15 formative years in South Korea and a decade between the vibrant landscapes of Singapore and Indonesia, his international journey has kindled a fervent passion for Korean history, national affairs, and events. With expertise in software development, he adeptly navigates and offers insights in the intersections of technology and culture.

Kathy Chengshuang Zhang, DBA, is an adjunct faculty at the Singapore Management University. She co-founded Financial PR in 2001 and was the firm's Chairperson and CEO for two decades, during which her company established a notable presence in Singapore, Hong Kong, Taipei, Beijing, Shanghai, and Shenzhen. She is also co-author of *Achieving Billion Dollar Market Capitalization through Performance Investor Relations*. The book, published in Mandarin, offers insights on how listed companies in Asia strategically enhanced value for their shareholders.

FOREWORD

Big businesses and big countries often suffer from cultural myopia. Being short-sighted enables them to fearlessly move fast and wide. And more often then not, it gets them into trouble. When one gets into a crisis, seeing and understanding others through their own eyes becomes essential. This is a sort of literacy, like an ability to read and write, like digital literacy is an ability to live, learn, and work in a society dependent on information technology and the Internet; cultural literacy is an ability to live, learn, and work with and in other cultures. Successful crisis communication presupposes a threshold level of cultural literacy.

Asia is the largest continent on the planet Earth: it accounts for approximately 60 percent of global population, 40 percent of the global GDP, and 30 percent of Earth's total land area. Not only that, but Asia is also politically, economically, socially, and technologically developing and growing fast and gaining its rightful place in all areas of life. Businesses and other organizations entering and operating in Asian countries must learn its multitude of cultures. Cultural literacy is important not only for crisis management; many, if not the majority of crises could be avoided or at least contained if corporate actors could envision potential consequences of their actions and words.

For this reason, *Crisis Communication Cases from Asia: A Cultural Approach*, edited by Professor Krishnamurthy Sriramesh from the University of Colorado, USA, and Professor Su Lin Yeo from Singapore Management University, Singapore, is a valuable reading for everybody interested in how are crises enabled and shaped by different cultures of Asia. We all were born in" our" cultures which we not only perceive, but bodily experience as "normal" (for us, of course). Entering into relation with another culture, we can easily make a *faux pas* or worse. Reading about others' mistakes is an intelligent way of learning. Here are nine cases to consider, analyze, and evaluate: how could things be done differently, and how should I strategize in a similar situation?

This book is the first book on crisis communication in Asia. Through nine case studies, it presents a unique perspective of crisis communication in Asia considering socio-economic factors affecting cultures and their peculiarities. Cases were written by country-specific authors who are all practitioners working in the private and public sectors in Asia, using the same conceptual framework to critique each of the nine cases from nine Asian countries. This unique approach connects theory with practice. It elaborates how culture affects crisis communication. It takes a more expansive definition of *culture* that goes beyond the anthropological notion of the concept to include political, economic, media, and activist cultures because each of these variables has a significant impact on crisis communication. No other book currently takes this perspective to crisis communication.

Communication is what brings and keeps us into relationships. We all come with our cultures, and together, we develop new cultures. Crisis communication literacy helps us smooth our intercourse and achieve our goals. Developing our crisis communication competence makes pure business sense.

Dr. Dejan Verčič,
Partner and Knowledge Director in Herman & Partnerji, and Professor at the University of Ljubljana, Slovenia

INTRODUCTION

Krishnamurthy Sriramesh

As a practice, one could say crises are as old as humanity. By extension, crisis communication has also been used by humans over millennia. However, the frequency of crises has increased in recent times due to a variety of factors, with technology being the catalyst at times and perhaps *the* crisis as well. Despite the much longer history of the practice, crisis communication scholarship has come of age in the past three decades. As laudable as that development is, it is hard to deny that the body of knowledge of crisis communication is ethnocentric in many ways. The most glaring lacuna I see in extant scholarship is its "silence" about the role of culture – aptly referred to as the *silent language* by anthropologist Edward T. Hall.

I contend that research in crisis communication is ripe for the next phase of its development, built on a strong foundation laid over the past three decades. I envision this next phase to be one that will involve increasing both the *depth* and *breadth* of the body of knowledge. This, I posit, is possible only when we integrate experience from diverse socio-political environments into our conceptualization. After all, crisis communication is global in nature in every way – it is needed in every region of the world, its players hail from every region of the world, and its consequences are also global in nature. One needs to look around us currently with two wars waging in Europe and the Middle-East that have involved practically every nation of the world in some way.

With that goal in mind, I propose that the socio-cultural variables used in three editions of *The Global Public Relations Handbook: Theory, Research, and Practice* could be integrated to crisis communication research as well. After all, communication is the basis for public relations as well as for crisis communication. Among other things, both public relations and crisis communication occur ***in*** socio-cultural environments, are influenced ***by*** socio-cultural environments,

DOI: 10.4324/9781003411802-1

and have a direct impact ***on*** diverse socio-cultural environments. Therefore, it is a logical extension to apply the global public relations framework to expand the horizons of crisis communication scholarship and practice.

Based on that rationale, nearly six years ago, I conceptualized a case study analysis of Nestle India's crisis surrounding its very popular and profitable Maggi Instant Noodles brand in India (Dhanesh & Sriramesh, 2018). That study was well-received by fellow researchers, which spurred me on to continue to build on that conceptualization. We refined the theorizing and linkage between the five socio-cultural variables and crisis communication (Sriramesh & Dhanesh, in press). Given the complexity of studying culture and linking it to an equally complex topic – crisis communication – I am convinced that the case study methodology is ideal during these initial stages of linking culture with crisis communication. I discussed this idea with Dr. Su Lin Yeo, and it resulted in this book of nine case studies from Asia.

All nine cases are authored by full-time practitioners with advanced degrees, which I think adds value to the information provided and analysis. Asia is as culturally diverse as any region of the world, and given its size (both area and population), diversity adds to the complexity. It is my hope that readers will get a sense of the breadth and depth of this diversity, even if only nine nations are covered. In my view, that reality lends further credence to my assertion that there is a dire need to incorporate socio-cultural variables into crisis communication theorizing. The Chapter on Vietnam highlights how a mistake in translating advertising slogans from English to the local language caused a big crisis for Coca-Cola. Instead of the intended boost to the national football team prior to a tournament, the advertisement was perceived as negative and even obscene to some landing the corporation in hot water. One glaring lesson from this case is that MNCs should not rely only on literal translations but also need to be very sensitive to *cultural* translations. The impact of digital and social media – sans journalistic gatekeepers – is seen in this and every one of the cases presented in this book.

Religion – an integral part of societal culture – is often overlooked by crisis communication scholarship. Neglecting the role that religion plays in society has cost many a corporation dearly as we see in Chapter 3. McDonald's India ran into hot water when it responded in the affirmative to a customer's question whether the meat it served was "halal" – a particular way of slaughtering required by devout Islamic tradition. The customer may have been satisfied, but this led to activism against the corporation from Hindus, resulting in a crisis for the fast food giant. It is ironic that the corporation, which has been in India for decades, could not predict the reaction leading to the crisis.

Activism, one of the five socio-cultural variables in the framework, was highlighted in the case from Malaysia, as in several cases presented in this book. Environmental activists conducted a lengthy, and persuasive, campaign against an Australian mining company that had been licensed by the Malaysian government to process rare earth minerals in the country. They were angered that there was scant information or transparency about the radioactive waste generated by the process that would obviously pollute the land for decades to come – long after the corporation returned to its home base with profits. The government (political system) had its own priorities including economic development (economic system) and was willing to overlook the environmental damage. This case again highlights the complex role that socio-cultural variables play in spawning crises. Crisis communication is not simply about strategizing how to communicate during crises but also to avoid crises in the first place through culturally sensitive strategies.

The case from Singapore presents how employee communication can be a source of crisis for a corporation. Singapore's government is friendly to multinational corporations (MNCs) because of the economic impact they have had on society. As an island city-state, it has to depend on international exchanges more than most nations. However, there has been pushback from locals for over two decades against too much reliance on especially white-collar foreign workers. In this case, a multinational corporation (MNC) and its local subsidiary were caught in the crossfire when they terminated employees in violation of Singaporean employee protocols and traditions. The umbrella trade union organization NTUC stepped in to protect the interests of Singaporeans. The next case from Japan again involves the negative consequences from advertisements deemed controversial. Nike ran an anti-racism and anti-bullying advertising campaign in the country with all good intentions. However, the locals found it to be too provocative in a society that prefers much more muted public discussions in general but certainly about controversial topics. They felt a foreign brand was deliberately castigating Japan in a negative light for the world as the advertisement went viral on digital and social media. This case provides another example of how cultural idiosyncrasies, the media, and activism combine to challenge communication by organizations.

The next case is from China, where several international brands criticized the government for human rights abuses in Xinjiang province, home to Uyghurs. In particular, H&M Corporation spoke out against forced labor of the Uyghur population for handpicking cotton. Not only did the corporation face the wrath of the government and state-owned media, but it also faced boycotts by Chinese consumers – a significantly large market. As a result, the corporation was forced to close about 120 of 500 stores. In the next case, we again see religious sentiments and cultural norms at the center of a crisis. The majority Muslim populace took exception to Starbucks' support of LGBTQ+ lifestyle and initiated a consumer boycott. Interestingly, the "offensive" comment by CEO Shultz was made in 2013, but it became a crisis only four years later when the comment came to the attention of a politician and influential religious leader who called for a consumer boycott while also pressuring the government to revoke the license of the corporation.

The case from Thailand showcases how the political system of a country can spawn a crisis. For several years, Thai society has witnessed popular pro-democracy movements. Against that backdrop, a food delivery service faced consumer wrath and boycotts when it tweeted against the action of one of its delivery drivers who publicly burnt the portrait of the king. The strict Lèse-majesté laws of the country prohibited any disrespect to the monarchy, so the corporation found itself in the midst of a crisis that pitted it in the middle of an explosive activist movement. The final chapter highlights the repercussions faced by a Japanese corporation that chose to remind its South Korean customers about their colonial past under Japanese rule. Expectedly, this led to an outcry and consumer boycotts, leading to the closure of some of the stores of the Japanese corporation. Yet, this is another case of a lack of cultural sensitivity in advertising and communication.

This case study book continues my effort to link culture with crisis communication more deeply and broadly than it has been in extant literature. It is my hope that this collection of nine crisis cases from Asia will affirm the status of culture as a key variable to make crisis communication more holistic and relevant. It is my hope that this book will serve as the harbinger of many more attempts to link socio-cultural variables with crisis communication. As this nexus is just being explored, I would suggest using the case study method at this point, which I hope will be a long journey of making crisis communication scholarship holistic and globally relevant. After a sufficient number of cases have been collected, the next stage would be to extrapolate from all the information to provide a crisis communication culture matrix. Such a matrix should be very helpful to both scholars and practitioners.

References

Dhanesh, G., & Sriramesh, K. (2018). Culture and crisis communication: Nestle India's Noodle Case. *Journal of International Management*, *24*(3), 204–214.

Sriramesh, K., & Dhanesh, G., (in press). Risk and crisis communication research in India. In Schwarz, A., Seeger, M., & Kim, S. (Eds.), *The handbook of international risk and crisis communication research*. Wiley-Blackwell.

1

EXTENDING THE HORIZONS OF CRISIS COMMUNICATION SCHOLARSHIP AND PRACTICE

A Socio-cultural Perspective

Krishnamurthy Sriramesh

Crises are ubiquitous in modern times, and their impact is becoming ever more serious and global for a variety of reasons, including the increased interdependency of the global population and the emergence of digital and social media. Crisis communication, then, is of vital importance to cope with the challenges posed by crises. Given the significance of crisis communication to global societies, it is disheartening that crisis communication scholarship has been lacking because of its ethnocentricity. Ethnocentricity in crisis communication research is evident in several key dimensions. Scholars have almost exclusively taken an organization-centric perspective focused on the financial and reputational damage caused to organizations – particularly for-profit corporations. Definitions of crises are also organization-centric and rarely, if ever, take a social perspective. After all, societies also face crises as seen in the current conflict between Russia and Ukraine, and Hamas and Israel, which have displaced tens of millions while also affecting global trade, travel, food distribution, etc. Further, crisis communication scholarship has also been based on organizational experiences in developed Western countries. Perhaps because of this, scholarship has almost entirely neglected the critical role that socio-cultural variables play in crisis communication. This multidimensional ethnocentricity has severely restricted the usefulness of crisis communication literature to advance effective practice. This is particularly exaggerated in non-Western socio-cultural environments whose experiences are marginally included in current crisis communication scholarship. If scholars want their work to inform practitioners around the world and help increase effective crisis communication, making crisis communication literature holistic would be paramount.

DOI: 10.4324/9781003411802-2

Concerted scholarship in crisis communication is about three decades old. Image restoration theory (image repair theory) was proposed by William Benoit (1995, 1997) as a way for individuals and organizations to restore their reputation/image in the event it is damaged from a crisis. The focus was almost exclusively on brands (corporations) or individuals. After reviewing the existing literature on crisis communication in the first edition of his book, Coombs (1999) began developing what he termed the situational crisis communication theory (SCCT) (Coombs, 2004, 2007). The title of his 2007 article was: "Protecting Organizational Reputations During a Crisis: The Development and Application of Situational Crisis Communication Theory." A clear indication of the focus of SCCT. Coombs kept refining the theory in six successive editions of his book starting in 2007 (Coombs, 2022). Both Benoit and Coombs deserve credit for building a solid foundation of crisis communication scholarship given that their theories have dominated literature over the past three decades.

Given the critical role that crisis communication has been called upon to play in societies around the world, it behooves scholars to build on that foundation by making crisis communication scholarship more holistic and less ethnocentric. Only then will this scholarship become more relevant and useful to diverse societies and cultures. With that goal in mind, it is cogent to note that both the image restoration theory and the SCCT have few, if any, references to the role that culture plays in crisis communication, let alone making culture a key variable in analysis. Perhaps because crisis communication scholarship has been so dominated by these two perspectives, ethnocentricity pervades the rest of the literature on the topic as well. A review of 15 scholarly books on crisis communication revealed only three that made a few references to culture as a variable that influences crisis communication. However, they did not accord this key variable the central focus it so richly deserves. Of the other books, only a few made occasional references to culture. Frandsen and Johansen (2017) were the exception because they devoted one chapter to discussing culture's role in crisis communication. However, in none of these books do we find culture being given the primacy it deserves because of its significant impact on crisis communication.

Of the 15 reviewed books, three did claim to address culture/international perspectives. Of these, one (George & Pratt, 2012) did not rely on a common conceptual framework to analyze crisis cases. The second (Bernhardsdottir, 2015) used grid group cultural theory (GGCT) to analyze crisis communication. GGCT focuses on four dimensions of societal culture: Hierarchy, egalitarianism, individualism, and fatalism. Although any analysis that gives credence to culture is a step forward, there are many more dimensions to societal culture than the ones used by Bernhardsdottir, which is a limiting factor. Further, societal culture is but *one* environmental variable of relevance to this field as contended in this book. The third book (George & Kwansah-Aidoo, 2017) offered case studies from several non-Western countries. As heartening as their approach is, once again, the focus was only on societal culture and in a "transboundary context," and other socio-political variables were not at all addressed.

Based on this review, it is reasonable to contend that a comprehensive cultural perspective of crisis communication is long overdue. Further, one can also posit that by ignoring the importance of socio-cultural variables, crisis communication scholarship is poorer and less relevant to communication practice. This chapter provides an overview of how socio-cultural perspective can be integrated into crisis communication scholarship. At the outset, it adopts a more expansive definition of the term *culture* going beyond the anthropological orientation to the term. The proposed interdisciplinary definition includes political, economic/developmental, media, and activist cultures in addition to the anthropological notion of societal culture as expounded in Sriramesh and Vercic (2020). The next sections provide a brief review of the literature for each of these five variables and linking each conceptually to crisis communication. Taking the Covid-19 global pandemic as the case example, each section addresses the link between the five variables (cultures) and crisis communication. Each variable is being addressed separately for clarity in analysis. However, it is important to note that the five socio-cultural variables do influence each other in every society. Therefore, the analysis will explicate how these five socio-cultural variables can be linked to all dimensions of crisis communication such as the definition of a crisis, crisis origin, crisis diffusion, damage caused, and crisis resolution. It is hoped that such an analysis will provide ample justification for a more in-depth inclusion of socio-cultural perspectives in crisis communication scholarship in the future.

Political System

Every modern society is governed by a political system. As individuals, we have ceded our independence to political rulers, whether by choice, force, or a combination. O'Neil et al. (2006) defined political regimes as "the norms and rules regarding individual freedoms and collective equality, the locus of power, and the use of that power" in a society. The most obvious dichotomy in political systems is that of democracy versus authoritarianism, indicating the level of freedom or control each system seems to accord to those under its rule. Of course, there are variations within democratic and authoritarian systems vis-à-vis freedom and control. Young and McCann (2020) pointed out that information transparency creates trust in democracies (Linz & Stepan, 1997; Rockman, 1997), while the control of information is vital to authoritarian governments (Byman & Lind, 2010; Taubman, 2007). Young and McCann concluded: "These differences create very different policy outcomes and, as a result, marked differences with regard to the overall way in which society, the economy, and the policymaking process function."

As discussed in Sriramesh and Vercic (2020), there are other types of political systems. In **theocratic systems**, religion dominates governance and public policy. **Military dictatorships**, while authoritarian in nature, have different motives and modes of operation than a civilian autocrat. **Corporatism** as a political system involves a society being organized into major interest groups that negotiate between these groups and the State. Corporativism can be seen in both democratic and authoritarian systems. For example, Singapore is a corporatist political system where the government seems to have coopted trade unions by providing the head of the umbrella trade union National Trades Union Congress (NTUC) a seat in the cabinet – as part of the Tripartism system adopted by the country. The NTUC has been closely associated with the People's Action Party (PAP), which has ruled Singapore since its inception as a Republic. **Monarchies** are still quite prevalent in many countries – wielding varying degrees of power between constitutional monarch and absolute monarchs.

Our task as communicators is to analyze how different political environments influence what we do. We can go back almost 50 years to the work by Jay Blumler and Michael Gurevitch (1975, 1990) to guide us in the process of linking different political systems with variances in communication. We (Sriramesh & Vercic, 2003, 2009, 2020) extended those conceptualizations to public relations as part of the framework for global public relations analyzing how different political systems impacted public relations practice.

Covid-19 and Political Ideology

We can use the same logic to also analyze how political systems affect crisis communication by taking the Covid-19 global pandemic as a case example. By all accounts, the SARS-Cov2 that caused the Covid-19 pandemic originated in China (Ye et al., 2020) in late 2019. Yet, the world only heard about it months later in early March 2020 because Chinese authorities chose not to disclose it to the public for several months. The political system of the People's Republic of China is undoubtedly the primary reason for this delay. As a country ruled by a single party, China was already quite strictly authoritarian in nature even after the economic liberalization that began under former premier Deng Xiaoping through successive presidents. But under the presidency of Xi Jinping, government control seems to have increased many fold by accounts of keen observers. China imposed among the strictest curbs on its residents while also closing its border completely far longer than the rest of the world. Such draconian restrictions were possible because of its totalitarian political system, unfettered by any challenge from the media as the Fourth Estate, resulting in minimum activism from civil society. Citizens rarely question dictatorship in such authoritarian political systems. It is pertinent to note that after three years of stifling lockdown measures – perhaps unparalleled by any other nation on the earth, the government was forced to relax the lockdown owing to protests (often violent) by the otherwise deferential Chinese citizens.

On the other hand, in a more liberal system such as South Korea, we see a different response to the same pandemic. When news of this deadly virus hit South Korea in early March 2020, the government was open and transparent about the risks involved and used public communication to alert citizens on risk and crisis mitigation measures. Transparency, public trust in government measures, and effective use of information and communication technologies (ICTs) are often cited as the reasons for South Korea's success in the early days of the pandemic.

However, it would be too simplistic for us to put political systems only along the freedom-control continuum while linking it to crisis communication. The United States, also a democracy like South Korea, responded to the pandemic in a totally different way than South Korea did. Public divisions and acrimony on all matters relating to the pandemic were evident from the very outset of the pandemic – a sharp contrast to South Korea. There was a clear demarcation between the liberal (democratic) and conservative (republican) party faithful. More conservative state administrations such as Florida, resisted any restrictions on individuals proposed by governmental agencies such as the Centers for Disease Control (CDC). Therefore, risk mitigation measures such as masking, social distancing, lockdowns, vaccinations, etc., were fiercely opposed by a sizeable section of the populace – almost exclusively republican in ideology.

Ironically, the Chief Executive of the country, then-president Donald Trump, himself led the charge against federal agencies of his own administration by questioning the science behind these curbs and refusing to wear a mask. In addition, he offered anecdotal and untested (some would even say dangerous) solutions that directly contradicted the informed and measured recommendations of public health officials. It was a disturbing spectacle to see conservative members of the Congress of the United States, for example, challenging the wisdom of health directives from the National Institute of Allergy and Infectious Diseases going after its then head Dr. Anthony Fauci in public hearings. To this day, staunch conservatives continue to criticize Fauci, who had an impeccable record as a public health specialist. Being home to a more pluralistic media system, the United States saw polarization in the media – between a liberal approach to the pandemic versus a more conservative one. Government and media communication about the pandemic seemed to further divide an already divided citizenry along liberal and conservative ideologies vis-a-vis public policy.

Countries of the European Union had their own diverse approaches to the pandemic that highlighted differences in political ideology as well as the debate between individual freedom and responsibility versus protecting the public good. Intergovernmental organizations (IGOs) such as NATO and WHO were also affected by stark differences in the political ideologies of member-states. This brief analysis confirms the critical role that political culture plays in risk and crisis communication.

Economic System/Political Economy

The political system of a society directly affects its economic ideology – hence the term Political Economy. Although political economy began in the 18th century as a holistic, multi-disciplinary view of the economy, the dawning of the classical school of economics in the 19th century brought the beginning of an emphasis of economic over political and/or social considerations (Duhé & Sriramesh, 2009; Lawniczak, 2009). Economic and political phenomena are explicably intertwined in societal life. The study of political economy discusses the inherent tensions, unintended consequences, and inevitable influences economic and political activities have on society, as opposed to the study of economics, political science, or sociology, which examines these respective dimensions unilaterally. As previously mentioned, this is truly a multi-disciplinary approach to crisis communication. Kollontai (2002) eloquently captured this idea:

> Political economies attempt to understand the functioning of an economy in a broader societal context. This is a task of growing complexity, given the constantly increasing division of labour, interdependencies, changing technologies, regulatory mechanisms, and evolving economic, organisational, management and other structures. As distinct from pure economics – which concentrates on the internal logic of economic systems – political economies in varying degrees acknowledge the impact of economic developments of political and (to a lesser extent) ideological, cultural and other societal factors and make it a part of their analysis.
>
> (p. 218)

We (Duhé & Sriramesh, 2009, Duhe, et. al. 2020) had proposed that a political economy perspective provides an ideal basis for an integrated understanding of multiple variables relevant to public relations in general and global public relations in particular. Because communication with various stakeholders is the foundation that crisis communication shares with public relations, I assert that political economy has a similar relationship with crisis communication as well. In political economy theories, the economic perspective tends to dominate the political. That is, the market tends to be the primary unit of analysis, with political and other social activities as either emanating from, or at least adjacent to, the market. One could make a parallel claim that marketing (consumer-driven) and economic repercussions dominate discussions about crisis communication as well. In fact, crisis communication scholarship is very heavily skewed toward the financial impact from crises – predominantly for corporations but also for governments and non-profits. Political economies influence the saliency of issues and how organizations choose to respond (if at all) to change pressures related to those issues.

For instance, environmental initiatives have political (public policy), social (quality of life), and economic (cost/benefit) implications. These parallel the three broad types of organizations – government, civil society, and corporations. Whereas firms within a political economy that values individual wealth creation (e.g. enhancing returns to shareholders) may actively resist NGO pressures to adopt environmental care standards beyond those mandated by law, firms operating in political economies that place comparatively greater value on the collective good of society (Hofstede, 2001, referred to this as *collectivism*) may proactively seek working partnerships with environmental NGOs as a normal course of business. Political economies dictate the proper role of firms, special interests, and governments in powerful and lasting ways. Activism, to be discussed in the following pages, is often rooted in a passionate resistance against the long-standing tenets of political economies as social values and thoughts about the proper role of institutions change, albeit slowly, over time.

Covid-19 and Economic System

The economic state of a society – heavily influenced by political ideology – plays a significant role in spawning crises, defining what is a crisis, crisis response, and finally post-crisis resumption. The Covid-19 pandemic is an excellent example to illustrate this. Governments around the world, regardless of their political ideology, were forced to reckon with the economic impact from extended lockdowns resulting in business closures and loss of jobs. The global supply chain ground to a halt resulting in cessation of manufacturing. China, dubbed the workshop of the world, faced severe post-pandemic economic downturn including the real estate sector to this day. Economic incentives to deal with the loss of income – especially to the lower economic strata of every society – resulted in inflation some of which has still not abated in many leading economies. When India was forced to mandate a nationwide lockdown, it led to a massive migration of laborers who had to return to their rural homes hundreds of miles away. Tens of millions of them were stranded with nowhere to go and little to eat. So, in addition to dealing with the health issues from the pandemic, the federal government also had to find solutions to the economic repercussions including mass human migration. In many democratic countries, big corporate interests lobbied their respective governments to quickly ease lockdowns or even eliminate them. Further, corporations also pressured governments to release vast sums of corporate subsidies to tide over the losses from lockdowns.

In many instances, especially big corporations (e.g. airlines) threatened to cut thousands of workers if government subsidies were not sanctioned. Therefore, although it began as a public health crisis, this pandemic spawned several layers of economic crises that touched every stratum of societies of all political types. The ripple effect continues to the present time, and policymakers are still grappling with the economic effects from the pandemic.

Level of Economic Development

Corollary to a society's political economy/economic system is the level of economic development itself. The United Nations Department of Economic and Social Affairs, the United Nations Conference on Trade and Development, and the five United Nations regional commissions publish an annual report titled World Economic Situation and Prospects (WESP). Within the report, the UN places every country into one of three economic categories: Developed economies, economies in transition, and developing economies. Although the criteria for categorizing countries is based primarily on per capita gross national income (GNI), the analysis makes further distinctions between fuel exporters and fuel importers, thereby adding additional nuance to the description of economies in transition and developing economies. The general purpose of the WESP report is to paint a picture of economic conditions in a given country, as well as to highlight global economic trends and potential risks. In its latest report (UN, 2024), the august UN body poignantly observed: "Growth prospects for many developing countries, especially vulnerable and low-income countries, have remained weak, making a full recovery of pandemic losses ever more elusive." It forecasts "headwinds" and weak economic outlooks for Africa, East Asia, Latin America, and the Caribbean. It noted that South Asia, is the one region with growth "driven by a robust expansion in India." The same report noted that although the developed economies of the world (e.g. the United States, Japan, and the EU) showed resilience from pandemic disruptions, they continue to face the risk of economic slowdowns.

In communication terms, risk and crisis communication dominated the early weeks and months of the Covid-19 global pandemic. But, as the economic impact of the crisis began to spread and go deeper in every society around the globe, the nature of crisis communication also changed and continues to evolve presently. The three major types of organizations – governments, non-profits, and corporations – have had to devise their crisis communication strategies and tactics on the go. Unfortunately, crisis communication scholarship has not measured up to offer empirically tested frameworks to deal with the range of economic implications of such a global pandemic. Similarly, the level of economic development has rarely been directly addressed as a key variable affecting risk and crisis communication. The body of knowledge of crisis communication will become more holistic and relevant to hitherto neglected societies around the world if we scholarship were to empirically address the link between political economy and the level of economic development and risk and crisis communication.

Societal Culture

Culture – central to all human interactions – is arguably the most neglected concept in communication scholarship and certainly in crisis communication research. That is the reason for the famous anthropologist Edward T. Hall (1973, 1990) to call culture as the *silent* language stating: "*There is no experience independent of culture against which culture can be measured*" (p. 187). He also succinctly described the interrelationship between culture and communication observing that communication is culture and culture is communication. I had offered three dimensions of the relationship between culture and public relations (Sriramesh, 2012). As public relations is fundamentally a communication activity, we can use the term communication and thereby broaden the relevance of these dimensions to crisis communication.

First, culture can be viewed as an antecedent variable influencing the nature of public relations/communication in a society. Hofstede (1980, 1984, 2001) would, of course, be among the most popular scholars in this genre of research with his dimensions of culture: Power distance, uncertainty avoidance, individualism/collectivism, masculinity/femininity, long-term orientation, and Confucian dynamism. Despite several lacunae (some of which Hofstede himself pointed out), these dimensions of culture have been used by generations of scholars studying the impact of culture on organizations and their communication patterns. Cross-cultural consultant Richard Lewis (Hammerich & Lewis, 2013) used his extensive experience to plot countries on three continua (set as the three sides of an isosceles triangle) based on three cultural dimensions: Multi-Active, Linear-Active, or Reactive. Several other dimensions of culture also fall into this category such as time orientation and high and low context (Hall, 1973; 1990); universalism versus particularism, specific versus diffuse, and achievement versus ascription (Trompenaars & Hampden-Turner, 2000); mastery-harmony-subjugation to nature; past-present-future orientation; and belief of human nature as being good versus bad (Triandis, 1982). This first relationship between culture and communication is probably the one that has been studied most in this genre.

A second relationship we can discern between the two is the influence that public relations has on culture. An organization's public relations/communication department often acts as an agent for acculturation in a society creating wants and needs through communication campaigns. Advertising and marketing campaigns are also frequently used around the world to "expand" markets for goods and services. This kind of communication has often been criticized by critical scholars for its "hegemonic" role. Scholarship on mass media effects on society and the agenda-setting function of the media typify this kind of relationship. Developmental campaigns are another example as they typically import information and experiences from one part of the world to influence behavior in another. Social marketing is another good example. Wiebe (1951) pioneered social marketing with the question: "Why can't you sell brotherhood and rational thinking like you sell soap?" (p. 679). After discussing four case studies of radio and television campaigns, the author concluded that mass media can "produce forceful motivation" among audience members aimed at social good.

The third dimension of the relationship views public relations itself as *a culture.* Taking such a perspective distinguishes public relations practitioners from practitioners of allied communication disciplines such as advertising, marketing, and even journalism. The activities, rites, rituals, and standing of public relations are distinct from these other communicative disciplines. For most people, within and outside the field, public relations is a "business" function that should help improve "the bottom line" of corporations. This erroneous perspective is not informed by empirical evidence but is mostly a result of conjecture and anecdotal evidence. I had commented that such erroneous beliefs continue to get perpetuated because public relations scholarship has not at all focused on this third dimension of the culture – public relations nexus. It would be interesting for to extend this to crisis communication and address to what extent crisis communication professionals have a distinct culture that sets them apart from other communication professionals.

Another way of analyzing the culture – crisis communication nexus is to view culture at the *macro, meso,* and *micro* levels of analysis (Sriramesh, 2020). At the macro level, we can address the culture of a collective – society – and see how it influences how crises spawn, spread, and are addressed in a societal context. At the meso level, we can address the impact of *organizational culture* on the way crisis communication is strategized, perceived, and implemented by the three major organization types. At the micro level, we can analyze how the personality of individual stakeholders such as senior managers and decision makers or communication strategists result in specific crisis communication strategies.

Covid-19 and Culture

When we extrapolate the above conceptual links between culture and communication to the Covid-19 case, we see multiple dimensions. Most Asian cultures (including all the nine countries studied in this book) are communitarian in nature – what Hofstede termed as collectivistic cultures. Collectivism was quite evident in how the populace in Asia perceived this pandemic and reacted to the mitigation steps by their respective governments with, of course, regional differences. For example, China received unconditional obedience to its very draconian lockdown measures that, in addition to being the most stringent, were also the longest (almost three years). No other country has witnessed that extent of acceptance by citizens influenced by factors such as collectivism and power distance, which spawns implicit deference to authority. At the other end of the spectrum, we can observe high levels of individualism displayed in the United States vis-à-vis pandemic restrictions and mandates. A significantly large section of the population (mostly Republicans) saw public health mandates as an infringement of their individual freedoms. From the president down to several state governors and other political leaders, one saw a concerted pushback to public health mandates. This opposition even took on ugly turns of accusation in public and even personal threats.

Taking the *micro*-level analysis described above to account, we observe that the cantankerous and combative personality of the then-president against science and scientists functioned as the catalyst for the naysayers in the country. In India, power distance – as depicted in social stratification – contributed significantly to how the lockdown and resulting migration of tens of thousands of migrant rural workers were perceived by the citizenry. The matter was exacerbated by the fact that a large number of these are illegal Bangladeshi migrants.

Societal culture cannot be discussed devoid of religion. Unfortunately, religion has spawned crises for societies for millennia. However, crisis communication scholars have paid scant attention to this key cause of crises perhaps because most of these scholars are in the United States and Western developed democracies where a separation of Church and State is professed (even if not fully practiced). Religion not only spawns' crises but also determines crisis response and, eventually whether crises are even resolved. Especially in the current millennium, terrorism has been an outcome of religious fervor. The ongoing societal crisis in the Holy Land is a prime example of this while also reminding us that religion may be the most complex crisis cause because of which a complete resolution of crises spawned by it is most elusive. Individual personality is also innately influenced by religious beliefs and faith and may make compromise most difficult to achieve.

Media Culture

Media can not only spawn, and exacerbate, crises but they are also needed for effective crisis communication management. The world became a "global village" during the 20th century (McLuhan & Fiore, 1967) because of the emergence, and growth, of print and broadcast media. As we (Vercic & Sriramesh, 2020) noted: "The dawn of the 21st century saw new, digital media (primarily enabled by the Internet, social networks and mobile smartphones) that turned the global village into a global living room." As a result we now not only live *with* media that are connecting us instantaneously across the world, but we live *in* them (Deuze, 2012).

However, despite their universal presence and use, media take on multiple forms and manifestations depending on a variety of factors including political and economic systems. The annual freedom report from the Freedom House paints us a reliable picture of freedoms in the 195 countries of the world that should be a beacon for how crisis communication can harness media in each. Presenting its 2024 report, it remarked that global freedom had declined in 2023 for the 18th consecutive year. It found "widespread problems" with elections including violence and manipulation that resulted in "deterioration in rights and freedoms." Further, the report noted that a total of 52 countries saw declines in individual freedoms while only 21 improved on that score. In its analysis of 195 countries scoring them on *Freedom in the World* indicators, Freedom House noted that 35 countries had "the worst possible scores on the indicators for free and fair executive and legislative elections." The report also noted that 80% of the world's population lives in countries that are labeled as "partly free" (42%) or "not free" (38%). This rather damning, if accurate, depiction is the background in which we need to address the efficacy of crisis communication efforts.

The normative theories of the mass media, first proposed by Siebert et al. (1956), and subsequently expanded by others (e.g. Hachten, 1981, 1993; Martin & Chaudhary, 1983; Merrill, 1974; Merrill & Lowenstein, 1971), helped shed light on media cultures around the world. Much of that theorizing was based on the extent of editorial freedom (or lack thereof) owing to the political system of a country – democratic or authoritarian. The nature of media was also influenced by the economic system, as depicted by the infrastructure of a country for mass media activity – developed versus developing. The normative theories of mass media systems and their relevance to international public relations was previously reviewed by Sriramesh and Verčič (2009). Those normative theories were based on the Cold War ideological divisions and toward the latter part of their conceptualization, ended up dividing the media around the world into autonomous, i.e. "free" (Western and Social Responsibility media systems), and ancillary, i.e. not "free" (Authoritarian, Communist, and Developmental media systems).

With the fall of the "Soviet bloc," many" developing" (i.e. non-Western) countries catching-up with the" developed" (i.e. Western) world, and the onset of ICTs and social media, the relevance of the normative theories of the media discussed between the 1950s and late 1980s vastly diminished even if some parts that conceptualization continue to resonate. China's communist party, for example, continues to exercise absolute control over the mass media. Russia, under the iron fist of Putin has reverted to Soviet-era media tactics. North Korea is another example of the authoritarian theory. Western liberal media ideology is still prevalent as is the social responsibility theory (albeit to a lesser extent, sadly). Media in developing countries also continue in many of the ways previously discussed. The environment of the 21st century demands that we use new lenses to describe, and analyze, media systems around the world. Dietrich (2014) offered the PESO model for displaying four distinct types of media that can be seen around the world: Paid (e.g. advertising), earned (through media relations by public relations practitioners), shared (e.g. social media), and owned (e.g. organizational web sites). Finally, one can also discern media systems by using the three factors I had proposed (Sriramesh et al., 1999) consisting of *media control* (not always aligned with media ownership), *media outreach* (the nature of media diffusion/saturation in a society) and *media access* (the extent to which individuals and groups in a society can influence media content. The "democratization" of digital and social media has circumvented the role of media gatekeepers to a great extent, thus creating varied challenges and opportunities.

Covid-19 and Mass Media

The diversity of media environments around the world became starkly evident in the way this pandemic was addressed. Leaders from countries along the authoritarian–democratic continuum were challenged by the scale of disruption that was not seen in modern times. It was easier to exercise *media control* in authoritarian political systems. China's authoritarian political culture ensures that its media system is entirely subjugated to the dictates of the ruling party. The mass media certainly does not operate as the Fourth Estate in China, as was evident throughout the three years of severe lockdowns in the country. The control over the media also contributed to suppressing news about the virus within China and, of course, from the rest of the world clearly leading to global diffusion of the virus. It is worth asking how the course of this global pandemic might have changed had the virus originated in a more pluralistic political system with a more liberal media environment. In other words, socio-political systems can also spawn crises, as happened during this pandemic, because of the lack of transparency. It is fair to assume that the public and the rest of the world would have heard of the potential public health crisis almost immediately, thus perhaps setting in motion steps to mitigate its impact much sooner with different global consequences. Democratic political systems had their own challenges in dealing with risk and crisis communication surrounding the pandemic. In the United States, for example, there was a clear division between the far right and mainstream media. Conspiracy theories from the likes of Qanon (Morelock & Narita, 2022) became a serious competition to the efforts of public health officials to keep the citizens well-informed and safe. In democratic India, for instance, "40% of media coverage of treatments options provided misleading information, such as suggesting plasma therapy or chloroquine, were effective" (Gupta et al., 2021). Crisis communication literature would benefit from a deeper understanding of different media environments.

Activism

Activism has been prevalent in societies for millennia. Social movements and uprisings have brought revolutionary changes to the way of life of societies around the globe. Yet, crisis communication has taken a rather narrow view of activism, often limiting its role to that of organizational adversary. A more functionalist perspective would see activist pressure as threats external to the organization that has to be managed (Brooks et al., 2018; Mules, 2018). After reviewing various definitions, we (Kim & Sriramesh, 2009) had defined activism as:

> The coordinated effort of a group that organizes voluntarily in an effort to solve problems that threaten the common interest of members of the group. In the process of problem solving, core members of the group attract other social constituents or publics, create and maintain a shared collective identity among members for the time being, and mobilize resources and power to influence the problem-causing entity's decision or action through communicative action such as education, negotiation, persuasion, pressure tactics, or force.
>
> (p. 82)

We had also identified two dimensions of activism: Confrontational intensity and breadth of issue spectrum. Confrontational intensity refers to the depth or *fierceness* of activism and can be measured using indicators such as the use and frequency of violent action, and the number of mobilized participants. The breadth of activism is the variety of issues that activists seek to pursue. We had posited that political, economic, cultural, media, and organizational environments influence both these dimensions and had offered a conceptual model that mapped the effects of socio-cultural variables on the nature and extent of activism (Figure 1.1). Thus, we had reaffirmed the interactive relationship between the five socio-cultural variables also because each of the other variables can similarly be linked to the other four. After a thorough review of the literature on activism and public relations published between 2009 and 2019, we (Dhanesh & Sriramesh, 2020) summarized the literature into three categories: (a) Theoretical frameworks, (b) activist strategies, and (c) digital activism. We concluded that although progress had been made in theorizing on the relationship between activism and societal culture, "much more research is needed on other socio-cultural environmental variables such as the level of economic development, the media environment, and political factors that could foster activism in a country."

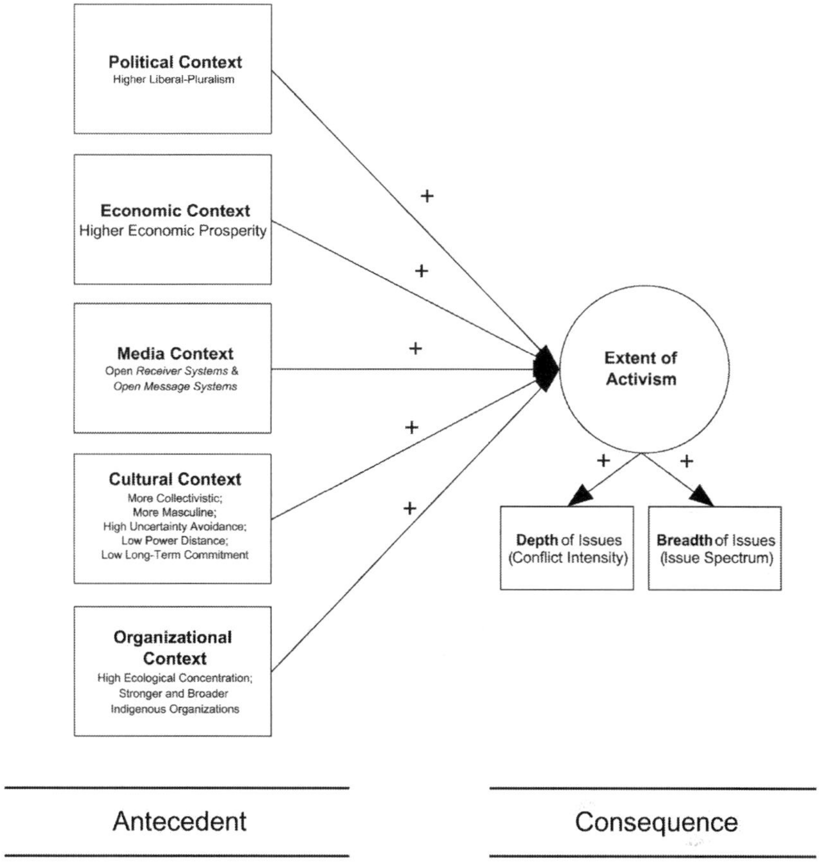

FIGURE 1.1 A conceptual model: The effects of socio-cultural environmental variables on the extent of activism. Source: Kim & Sriramesh. "Activism and Public Relations," in Sriramesh, K., & Vercic, D. (Eds.). (2009). *The Global Public Relations Handbook, Revised and Expanded Edition: Theory, Research, and Practice* (2nd ed.). Routledge. https://doi.org/10.4324/9780203889374. Reprinted by permission of the publisher (Taylor & Francis Ltd, http://www.tandfonline.com).

To address the lacuna in integrating socio-cultural variables to activism, we (Dhanesh & Sriramesh, 2018) conducted a case study of the crisis faced by the Nestle corporation vis-à-vis its very popular instant noodles brand (Maggie noodles) in India. A regional government alleged that the instant noodles contained seven times the permissible levels of lead. Nestle, confident in its product and tests conducted in its laboratories in Switzerland, initially ignored this allegation. Within weeks, however, the allegation went national, spurred by a variety of activist groups (some of whom were always opposed to foreign brands) and farmer activists leading to a total ban of the product in the country. Although there was no truth to the allegations, Nestle took a pounding in the court of public opinion and recalled and incinerated about US$70 million worth of product. By the time it had weathered the crisis and regained its dominant market share, it had lost an estimated half a billion dollars. Activism had played a role in the damage. However, we concluded that Nestle's lack of attention to the socio-political climate of India had played a crucial role as well in exacerbating the crisis. We further discussed the relevance of socio-cultural variables to crisis communication in (Sriramesh & Dhanesh, *in press*).

Covid-19 and Activism

This pandemic brought out different types of activism in different socio-political systems. While some of the activism was the result of economic hardships from lost jobs during lockdowns, others were directed at the limits placed on people's movements perceived as limiting individual freedoms. Misinformation and conspiracy theories were also drivers of some of this activism even in developed countries. The most glaring example is from China, where the populace experienced some of the most stringent lockdown measures. In addition to their stringency, the Chinese lockdown was also the longest in the world. It began as a local lockdown in Wuhan on January 23, 2020 and gradually extended to neighboring cities and ultimately the entire nation until a series of protests in different parts of the country led to the government rescinding the measures on December 7, 2022. Known as *White Paper Protests* (*Bái zhǐ kàngyì* in Chinese), the protests began with some anonymous posters in Beijing in October 2022 and gradually spread to other cities and regions. The protests also took on a pro-democracy tone and the government quickly took note and conceded to the demands of lifting the lockdowns – quite a victory in an authoritarian environment.

India saw massive protests by migrant workers who were stranded in railway stations when attempting to return home. Israel, Indonesia, Iraq, Hong Kong, and Malaysia were among the many Asian countries where Covid-spawned activism prevailed. Similar protests occurred in Africa, Latin America, and Oceania. As already mentioned in earlier sections, the United States saw plenty of activism against lockdown measures – led by the president himself and his ardent followers. Misinformation and conspiracy theories also were propagated by the same actors including President Trump publicly advocating injecting bathroom disinfectants as a cure against lung infection from the virus! Further, the governor of Washington state accused the president of fomenting domestic rebellion owing to the incendiary rhetoric from the first citizen against lockdown measures. The nexus between activism and this pandemic was much broader than anything that current crisis communication scholarship has chronicled.

Concluding Thoughts Looking to the Future

After nearly three decades of concerted scholarship, research in crisis communication is ripe for the next phase of its development – a phase that will involve increasing both its depth and breadth. The need of the hour is to make crisis communication scholarship more holistic, thereby increasing its meaningful application to efficacious practice in diverse regions of the world. To that end, this chapter proposes a socio-cultural framework of five variables that play an innate role in the various stages of crisis communication – from spawning crises to crisis resolution. It contends that the seeds of crises are often embedded in far deeper socio-cultural factors than current research seems to even acknowledge, let alone address. For example, lately "terrorism" has been listed as a crisis type in crisis communication literature. The focus is mostly on how communication takes place after terrorism has occurred as a crisis. This is akin to treating the symptoms of an illness rather than delving into the cause of the illness to address it permanently. A deeper analysis of the causes of modern terrorism leads us invariably to the socio-cultural factors discussed in this chapter. For example, religion – a manifestation of societal culture – has spawned many a societal crisis over millennia and continues to do so in the 21st century as evidenced in the current conflict in the Middle-East that has every potential to spread in the region.

Crisis communication literature also offers various crisis response strategies that organizations can use when confronted with a crisis. The Situational Crisis Communication Theory (Coombs, 2006) for example, offers a continuum of 10 crisis response strategies ranging from completely denying responsibility to full apology. There is scant discussion in the literature of the fact that cultural idiosyncrasies are the underlying foundation on which these choices are made. For example, Japanese culture is widely known to extoll public apology as a virtue. It is not uncommon for organizational leaders to publicly apologize without mincing words and be lauded for it. Contrast that with another democratic political system – the United States – which views organizational apology from a legal culpability perspective. Communication is built around the reality that apology implies accepting culpability, which invariably attracts expensive lawsuits. Looking only at the overt action without deeply analyzing the world views that drive these actions is often counterproductive.

Further, organizational culture plays a critical role in the choices made vis-a-vis crisis response strategies. The purpose and values of the three major types of organizations – for-profit corporations, not-for-profits, and government agencies are quite different, thus driving different organizational cultures. Beyond the missions of these three major organizational types, organizational culture is also deeply influenced by societal culture as seen in the individual personalities of organizational leaders who often determine/dictate communication choices. In a globalizing (globalized?) world, organizational employees hail from multiple ethnicities and cultures – most of them first-generation migrants and thus acculturated to their home cultures more than host cultures. Employee communication and organizational strategies are thus influenced by this "melting pot" of culturally diverse members. Currently, literature seems to assume "employees" almost as a homogenous block with predictable thoughts and actions. Thus, the culture–crisis communication nexus is dynamic and complex, and therefore worthy of deeper empirical analysis. Crisis communication is culture-specific and not culture-free. Crisis communication literature would immensely benefit from such studies about these neglected drivers of crisis communication, thus making it less ethnocentric and more globally relevant.

To that end, conceptual links have been offered in this chapter between crisis communication and the political system, economic system, media culture, and activism while recognizing the interconnectedness of these five variables as a prelude to the crisis cases from nine countries that follow. There is a dire need for effective crisis communication in a conflict-ridden world, and so it behooves scholars to strive to make the body of knowledge more holistic. Working toward that laudable goal, the next phase in the development of the body of knowledge of crisis communication should involve incorporating socio-cultural variables into the literature. Building on a few of our essays proposing this framework (Dhanesh & Sriramesh, 2018; Sriramesh & Dhanesh, *in* press), this book is an earnest effort in that direction. The case study approach seems ideal for the current stage of this process of integration. Future studies would expand the linking of this framework to crisis communication by addressing crisis cases from different regions of the world representing different socio-cultural environments. When a core set of such cases has been established, further empirical research can lead to creating a matrix of cultural types (culture broadly defined) and crisis communication strategies and tactics. The elements of that matrix can be tested through quantitative and qualitative studies in the years to come. In essence, this chapter and this book are the harbingers of several years – perhaps even a decade or more – of concerted efforts to make crisis communication scholarship more culture-specific and, thereby, more holistic and global.

References

Benoit, W. (1995). *Accounts, excuses, and apologies: A theory of image restoration strategies*. State University of New York Press.

Benoit, W. L. (1997). Hugh Grant's image restoration discourse: An actor apologizes. *Communication Quarterly*, *45*(3), 251–267.

Bernhardsdottir, A. E. (2015). *Crisis-related decision-making and the influence of culture on the behavior of decision makers*. Springer International Publishing AG.

Blumler, J. G., & Gurevitch, M. (1975). Towards a comparative framework for political communication research. In S. H. Chaffee (Ed.), *Political communication* (pp. 165–193). Sage.

Blumler, J. G., & Gurevitch, M. (1990). Political communication systems and democratic values. In J. Lichtenberg (Ed.), *Democracy and the mass media*. Cambridge University Press.

Brooks, K. J., Wakefield, R. I., & Plowman, K. D. (2018). Activism, prosocial public relations and negotiation: The case of St Vincent de Paul. *Corporate Communications: An International Journal*, *23*(1), 139–150.

Byman, D., & Lind, J. (2010). Pyongyang's survival strategy: Tools of authoritarian control in North Korea. *International Security*, *35*(1), 44–74.

Coombs, W. T. (1999). *Ongoing crisis communication: Planning, managing, and responding*. Sage.

Coombs, W. T. (2004). Impact of past crises on current crisis communication: Insights from situational crisis communication theory. *Journal of Business Communication*, *41*(3), 265–289.

Coombs, W. T. (2006). The protective powers of crisis response strategies. *Journal of Promotion Management*, *12*(3-4), 241–260.

Coombs, W. T. (2007). Protecting organization reputations during a crisis: The development and application of situational crisis communication theory. *Corporate Reputation Review*, *10*(3), 163–176.

Coombs, W. T. (2022). *Ongoing crisis communication: Planning, managing, and responding*. Sage.

Deuze, M. (2012). *Media life*. Polity Press.

Dhanesh, G. S., & Sriramesh, K. (2018). Culture and crisis communication: Nestle India's Maggi noodles case. *Journal of International Management*, *24*(3), 204–214.

Dhanesh, G., & Sriramesh, K. (2020). The nexus between activism and public relations. In K. Sriramesh, & D. Vercic (Eds.), *The global public relations handbook: Theory, research, and practice* (3rd ed.). Routledge.

Dietrich, G. (2014). *Spin sucks: Communication and reputation management in the digital age*. Pearson.

Duhe, S., Fisher, J., & Sriramesh, K. (2020). The intersection of political and economic systems in global public relations. In K. Sriramesh, & D. Vercic (Eds.), *The global public relations handbook: Theory, research, and pract, NYice* (3rd ed.). Routledge.

Duhé, S. C., & Sriramesh, K. (2009). Political economy and public relations. In K. Sriramesh, & D. Verčič (Eds.), *The global public relations handbook: Theory, research, and Donepractice (expanded and revised edition)* (pp. 22–46). Routledge.

Frandsen, F., & Johansen, W. (2017). *Organizational crisis communication: A multivocal approach*. Sage.

George, A. M., & Kwansah-Aidoo, K. (2017). *Culture and crisis communication: Transboundary cases from nonwestern perspectives*. John Wiley & Sons.

George, A. M., & Pratt, C. B. (2012). *Case studies in crisis communication: International perspectives on hits and misses*. Routledge.

Gupta, M., Keshri, V. R., Konwar, P., Cox, K. L., & Jagnoor, A. J. (2021). Media coverage of COVID-19 health information in India: A content analysis. *Health Promotion International*. *37*(2), 1–11.

Hachten, W. (1981). *The world news prism: Changing media, clashing ideologies*. Iowa State University Press.

Hachten, W. A. (1993). *The growth of media in the third world: African Failures, Asian successes*. Iowa State University Press.
Hall, E. (1973). *The silent language*. Anchor Press/Doubleday.
Hall, E. (1990). *The hidden dimension*. Anchor Books.
Hammerich, K., & Lewis, R. D. (2013). *Fish can't see water: How national culture can make or break your corporate strategy*. John Wiley & Sons.
Hofstede, G. (1980). Culture and organizations. *International Studies of Management & Organization, 10*(4), 15–41.
Hofstede, G. (1984). *Culture's consequences: International differences in work-related values*. Sage.
Hofstede, G. (2001). *Culture's consequences: Comparing values, behaviors, institutions, and organizations across nations* (2nd ed.). Sage Publications.
Kim, J., & Sriramesh, K. (2009). Activism and public relations. In K. Sriramesh, & D. Vercic (Eds.), *A theoretical framework for global public relations research and practice* (pp. 79–100). Routledge.
Kollontai, V. (2002). The new political economies: A view from Russia. *American Journal of Economics and Sociology, 61*(1), 217–232.
Lawniczak, R. (2009). Re-examining the economic roots of public relations. *Public Relations Review, 35*, 346–352.
Linz, J., & Stepan, A. (1997). Toward consolidated democracies. In L. Diamond, M. Plattner, Y. Chu, & H. Tien (Eds.), *Consolidating the third wave democracies*. Johns Hopkins University Press.
Martin, L. J., & Chaudhary, A. G. (1983). *Comparative mass media systems*. Longman.
McLuhan, M., & Fiore, Q. (1967). *War and peace in the global village*. Bantam.
Merrill, J. C. (1974). *The dialectic in journalism: Toward a responsible use of press freedom*. Louisiana State University Press.
Merrill, J. C., & Lowenstein, R. L. (1971). *Media, messages, and men*. Longman.
Morelock, J., & Narita, F. Z. (2022). The nexus of QAnon and COVID-19: Legitimation crisis and epistemic crisis. *Critical Sociology, 48*(6), 1005–1024. https://doi.org/10.1177/08969205211069614
Mules, P. (2018). Changing representations of activists and activism in public relations textbooks. *Journal of Communication Management, 23*(1), 18–30.
O'Neil, P. H., Fields, K., & Share, D. (2006). *Cases in comparative politics*. W. W. Norton & Company.
Rockman, B. (1997). Institutions, Democratic stability, and performance. *Institutions and Democratic Statecraft*. ed. M. Heper, A. Kazancigil, B. Rockman. Boulder, CO: Westview.
Siebert, F. S., Peterson, T., & Schramm, W. (1956). *Four theories of the press*. University of Illinois Press.
Sriramesh, K. (2012). Culture and public relations: The missing link. In K. Sriramesh, & D. Vercic (Eds.), *Culture and public relations*. Routledge.
Sriramesh, K. (2020). The *silent language* is also the *forgotten* language. In K. Sriramesh, & D. Vercic (Eds.), *The global public relations handbook: Theory, research, and practice* (3rd ed.). Routledge.
Sriramesh, K., & Dhanesh, G. (in press). Risk and crisis communication research in India. In A. Schwarz, M. Seeger, & S. Kim (Eds.), *The handbook of international risk and crisis communication research*. Wiley-Blackwell.
Sriramesh, K., & Duhé, S. C. (2009). Extending cultural horizons: Political economy and public relations. *Public Relations Review, 35*(4), 368–375.
Sriramesh, K., Kim, Y., & Takasaki, M. (1999). Public relations in three Asian cultures: An analysis. *Journal of Public Relations Research, 11*(4), 271–292.
Sriramesh, K., & Vercic, D. (2003). *The global public relations handbook: Theory, research, and practice*. Lawrence Erlbaum Assoc. Inc.

Sriramesh, K., & Vercic, D. (2009). The global public relations handbook: Theory, research and practice. Routledge.
Sriramesh, K., & Vercic, D. (2020). *The global public relations handbook: Theory, research, and practice* (3rd ed.). Routledge.
Taubman, G. (2007). A not-so world wide web: The internet, China, and the challenges to nondemocratic rule. *Political Communication*, *15*(2), 255–272.
Triandis, H. C. (1982). Dimensions of cultural variation as parameters of organizational theories. *International Studies of Management & Organization*, *12*(4), 139–169.
Trompenaars, A., & Hampden-Turner, C. (2000). *Riding the waves of culture: Understanding cultural diversity in business* (2nd ed.). Nicholas Brealey Pub.
UN. (2024) https://www.un.org/development/desa/dpad/wp-content/uploads/sites/45/WESP2024_ES_EN.pdf (Retrieved on February 28, 2024).
Vercic, D., & Sriramesh, K. (2020). The media and international, transnational and global public relations. In K. Sriramesh, & D. Vercic (Eds.), *The global public relations handbook: Theory, research, and practice* (3rd ed.). Routledge.
Wiebe, G. D. (1951). Merchandising commodities and citizenship on television. *Public Opinion Quarterly*, *15*(4), 679.
Ye, Z. W., Yuan, S., Yuen, K. S., Fung, S. Y., Chan, C. P., & Jin, D. Y. (2020). Zoonotic origins of human coronaviruses. *International Journal of Biological Sciences*, *16*(10), 1686–1697. https://doi.org/10.7150/ijbs.45472.
Young, L., & McCann, J. (2020). Comparative political systems and public relations: An overview. In K. Sriramesh & D. Vercic (Eds.), *The global public relations handbook: Theory, research, and practice*. Routledge.

2

VIETNAM

Lost in Translation: Coca-Cola's Advertisement Sparks Crisis

Mae Nguyen, Pui Fong Loh, Emmeline Jie Yi Tan, and Angeline Onasis

Introduction

It was a campaign meant to cheer on the Vietnamese national football (also known as "soccer") team in their quest. However, Coca-Cola's good intention was foiled when its campaign slogan "Mở Lon Việt Nam," loosely translated as "opening Vietnam's can," opened a proverbial can of worms for the beverage giant – the tagline ran afoul of the largely conservative nation.

Vietnam, the world's 15th most populous nation, occupies the eastern side of Southeast Asia. As a developing country with a rapidly expanding market economy (Buttinger, n.d.), Vietnam has worked to raise the quality of life of its people. It joined the Human Capital Project in 2019 – an international initiative by the World Bank aimed at improving well-being and nutrition, grant access to quality education, and enhance workforce development (The World Bank, 2022).

The 1986 free-market reform "Đổi Mới" transformed Vietnam from a centrally planned economy to a market-oriented economy. This, coupled with beneficial global trends, accelerated Vietnam's growth (The World Bank, 2022). When Vietnam became a member of the World Trade Organization (WTO) in January 2007, it became more integrated with the global economy (PWC Worldwide Tax Summaries, 2022). To date, Vietnam has a few key industries including infrastructure, manufacturing, retail, food, and agriculture (Eye on Asia, n.d.). Vietnam has plans to become an upper-middle-income country with modern industry by 2030, and a high-income, developed country by 2045 (PWC Worldwide Tax Summaries, 2022). To achieve this, the economy would have to grow at about 5% per capita on average annually for the next 25 years (The World Bank, 2022). Economically, Vietnam has performed well in its expansion

DOI: 10.4324/9781003411802-3

into the global market. While globalization efforts have introduced "liberal" values and different moral standards to society, culturally, Vietnam remains a conservative nation.

Coca-Cola Advertising Controversy

In June 2019, Coca-Cola launched an advertising campaign with the slogan "Mở Lon Việt Nam" – loosely translated as "Opening Vietnam's Can" – printed prominently on billboards (Nien, n.d.) and Coca-Cola cans – to cheer along with the Vietnamese people for Vietnam's national football team at the ASEAN AFF Championship as football is loved by the locals (VOV.VN, 2023). The image of "golden boys" representing Vietnam's footballers was integrated into the advertisement (Binh, 2019). While some Vietnamese did not find the slogan problematic, others did.

Based on Vietnamese phonology, the word "Lon" without diacritic could be understood as "a can." If diacritics were added, "Lon" refers to female genitals, and the phrase "Lon Việt Nam" was inappropriate, especially when placed beside "Vietnam." Many felt that the word "Vietnam" should not be placed next to "Lon" as it was disrespectful, lacked culture and aesthetics, and was grammatically incorrect (EloQ Communications, 2021). Critics also suggested missing a preposition between "Lon" and "Việt Nam" made the slogan meaningless (Saigoneer, 2019). The content violated provisions of Clause 3, Article 8 and Clause 1, Article 19 of the country's advertising law on the conformity of fine customs and traditions. It also showed signs of deceitful advertising and was unsuitable for Vietnam's conservative customs and traditions (Nguyen, 2019).

Coca-Cola in Crisis

The popularity of the slogan "Mở Lon Việt Nam" in Coca-Cola's advertising campaign came to the attention of government authorities in Vietnam. On June 22, 2019, the Ministry of Culture, Sports and Tourism ordered that Coca-Cola stop all campaign-related activities (Nga, 2019). By then, the campaign slogan had become a mockery and was eventually banned (Dieu, 2019) on June 29, 2019 (Hạnh, 2020). The ban was reported on mainstream media, and Coca-Cola's past controversial advertisements in other countries also surfaced and was scrutinized by the public (Hung, 2019). Additionally, Coca-Cola's vendor, Probina Advertising Company, was fined VN$25 million (US$1,065) for displaying the campaign billboards without a permit (Nguyên, 2019a). Media coverage highlighted that the advertising campaign received community-wide criticism because of the slogan "Mở Lon Việt Nam" (Anh, 2019a). It also sparked a fierce debate on social media platforms, with comments that the slogan was crude and disrespectful to Vietnamese culture (Hung & Anh, 2019). As a result, Coca-Cola's image and reputation were negatively affected to a certain extent with members of the public speculating if they intentionally tried to market their products through unconventional means, which further placed Coca-Cola in a bad light.

"Coca-Cola" and "Mở Lon Việt Nam" rapidly became the most searched phrases on Google (Đức, 2019) after the government released official statements that Coca-Cola had infringed the law on advertising (Nga, 2019). Following this, Coca-Cola acknowledged publicly that it did not consider the philological elements and had failed to review the semantics of the phrase. Campaign banners were changed to "Cơ hội trúng vàng mỗi ngày," which translated as "There are chances of winning gold every day" (Saigoneer, 2019). Coca-Cola also subsequently pledged to strictly adhere to production, business and legal regulations in future, and reported its efforts to comply with the demands of the Department of Culture (Economy, 2019).

Coca-Cola and Its Stakeholders

When a crisis happens, different parties are often drawn into the case and are affected differently. The Coca-Cola fiasco was no exception with the Vietnamese government, the academia, and disparate members of public expressing their opposition toward the campaign.

Political Party

The Ministry of Culture, Sports, and Tourism is in charge of state administration in Vietnam for culture, family, sports, and tourism, as well as public services in these areas (Bộ Văn hóa Thể thao và Du lịch, 2023). They set the crisis in motion by saying that the phrase did not adhere to traditional conventions. In addition to demanding that Coca-Cola Vietnam change the slogan, they reiterated that it was necessary to protect the integrity of the Vietnamese language. The ministry also expressed sympathy and understanding for a foreign business that unintentionally created an advertising slogan without proper consultation on the suitability of chosen words and cultural norms of the country (Đức, 2019).

Academia

The Vietnamese language embodies centuries of rich cultural identities, and if a clause, word, or phrase is removed from its original context and placed in a new one, it could result in an entirely different meaning. In the aftermath of the crisis, some linguists agreed with the Ministry of Culture, Sports and Tourism's decision. Aside from the fact that the word "lon" on its own has an obscene meaning, there was also the question as to whether Coca-Cola was qualified to represent all of Vietnam's beverages. This concern arose due to the inclusion of the name "Vietnam" giving the impression that the brand was officially recognized as

Vietnam's national beverage despite the fact that Coca-Cola, a foreign brand, does not account for the majority of drinks sold in Vietnam (Thanh, 2019).

A Divided Public

The crisis sparked debate among different sections of the public with two opposing viewpoints – those who were neutral and those who were fiercely against the advertising campaign slogan. Many social media users identified as neutrals voiced their perplexity as to why the slogan "Mở Lon Việt Nam" was prohibited. They did not think the phrase had any meaning that could be interpreted as disrespectful and that it was wholly subject to an individual's interpretation. The group also believed that many would not have noticed it if the authorities had not called attention to it, as suggested in this social media comment:

> There is nothing vulgar about opening a can of Vietnam; it is only vulgar when people have vulgar thoughts!
>
> (Dieu, 2019)

The opposing camp, which agreed with the Ministry of Culture, Sports and Tourism, reasoned that since the word "lon" is highly sensitive, anyone who reads it will easily relate to its different meaning. Additionally, Coca-Cola should not have used the name Vietnam arbitrarily because it was irreverent and insensitive to Vietnamese culture (Dieu, 2019).

Given that Coca-Cola is a multinational corporation (MNC) that has run numerous successful advertising and communication campaigns with its extensive network of partners, the message in its campaigns should have been culturally sensitive. However, this was not the case in this incident. In 2014, Coca-Cola Vietnam had launched a controversial marketing campaign called "In Tên Lên Lon," which broadly translated as "printing names on cans" with the intention of personalizing Coca-Cola drinks and allowing customers to print their names directly on the beverage packaging. This campaign also sparked a furor with many divergent opinions over the phrase "In Tên Lên Lon" since it included the word "lon" which could be misinterpreted negatively without a diacritic mark. However, the authorities did not take action against the company, possibly because the name "Vietnam" was not in it. Given this experience, some believed that Coca-Cola had intentionally gone ahead with the 2019 advertising campaign (Đức, 2019).

Analysis of the Crisis Using the Global Public Relations (PR) Framework

The Global PR framework (Sriramesh & Verčič, 2020) suggests that organizations develop and sustain a symbiotic relationship with relevant publics who are culturally diverse. In the case of Coca-Cola and its advertising campaign, we use this framework, which has been described in Chapter 1 to better understand where the beverage giant went wrong.

Political System

Vietnam is a communist country. With globalization and modernization, the Vietnamese have become more exposed to the world. Still, they are deeply influenced by Confucianism (Truong et al., 2017), which places patriarchal family as the central unit of society with an inherent hierarchy, and this is also reflected in Vietnam's political structure.

Vietnam is a communist state governed by collective leadership, where power is split among key positions and organized into numerous parallel yet interwoven hierarchies with vertical networks stretching down to the local level, guided by "democratic centralism" (Datta & Mendizabal, 2018). Freedom of expression, religious freedom, and civil society activism are restricted in Vietnam. The government has also increasingly tightened citizens' social media usage and the Internet. In 2016, it threatened to shut down Facebook if they did not censor anti-state and political posts on their platform (Pearson, 2020). This appeared to be implemented in response to public outrage over an environmental crisis brought on by toxic discharges from a steel complex built by Taiwan's Formosa Plastics (TechCrunch, 2016). The government holds central leadership views and perspectives on the information disseminated to the Vietnamese. From a political perspective, the government deemed Coca-Cola's advertising campaign derogatory and saw the need to defend Vietnam's cultural identity; and thus ordered Coca-Cola to take down its advertisements, and Coca-Cola promptly complied.

Tax and Legal System

In 1987, Vietnam passed a new Foreign Investment Law to attract more Foreign Direct Investment (FDIs) into the country. As much as Vietnam wanted to globalize, the government also wanted to maintain control over foreign investors to safeguard its political and legal interests (Lam, 2014). It also enacted stringent taxation laws following an increase in tax-related evasions (Vietnam Law & Legal Forum 2012). Like many other big foreign enterprises, Coca-Cola has had brushes with the government and was accused of evading tax, conducting transfer pricing, and taking undue advantage of Vietnam's laissez-faire taxation policies (Trương, 2020).

In the 2019 advertisement saga, Vietnam's Ministry of Culture, Sports and Tourism issued a document instructing Coca-Cola to rectify its advertising activities as it had violated the advertising law (Xuân, 2019). Coca-Cola acknowledged its mistake (Pv, 2019), edited the slogan, and updated its outdoor advertisements, mainstream and social media to comply with Vietnam's regulations (Nguyên, 2019a).

Coca-Cola's venture into Vietnam highlighted a few issues. First, it was overconfident that it would not encounter issues with the government. However, Coca-Cola's previous brushes with Vietnam's taxation law meant there was greater scrutiny of its business and operations in Vietnam. Secondly, Coca-Cola was not sufficiently sensitive to Vietnamese political and legal systems. Although it adopted quick remedial actions, preventive strategies were lacking. An MNC like Coca-Cola should establish closer partnership and consultations with the government to maintain good rapport and relationship.

Economic System

Since the adoption of free-market economic reforms called "Đổi Mới" in 1986, Vietnam has achieved significant economic progress. From 1991 to 2000, its economy increased annually by 7.5% on average. In 1995, Vietnam became part of the Association of Southeast Asian Nations (ASEAN), and a member of the WTO in 2007. These memberships allowed Vietnam to obtain a record-high FDI of US$71.7 billion in 2008 (Vuong, 2014).

From being one of the poorest countries three decades ago, Vietnam has emerged as one of the fastest growing economies in the world (Bairagi et al., 2020). From 1981 to 2012, poverty in Vietnam fell steeply. However, inequality remains high in the country, with much literature and data revealing a concentration of poverty in Vietnam (Malesky & London, 2014).

Economic Impact on the Non-alcoholic Carbonated Soft Drinks (NCSD) Market

As Vietnam's economy progresses, so too the consumption of NCSD. The total NCSD consumption in Vietnam in 2013 alone was 2,083 million liters (Ha et al., 2017). A 2017 market research on the Vietnamese soft drinks market saw all categories of soft drinks obtaining positive sales (Vietnam Investment Review, 2018), as well as growth of the local NCSD market. Vietnam's significant economic development has led to a change in the eating and spending habits of Vietnamese. Educated Vietnamese, particularly those in the urban areas, were observed to be spending more, including on NCSD (Bairagi et al., 2020; Figuié & Moustier, 2009). With changing consumer trends and a booming NCSD market, demand for Coca-Cola's products has increased. Such a demand is advantageous for Coca-Cola – a powerhouse within the industry – as it could cushion crises and regain possible market loss.

Higher Advertising Volume in Vietnam

Traditionally, due to limited access to media and high illiteracy rate, the Vietnamese government tends to utilize billboard advertising to roll out social messages (Ciochetto, 2013). Private advertising was prohibited in Vietnam before 1991, and when it was finally allowed, many foreign companies who had invested in the country were able to enter the market (Figuié & Moustier, 2009). As the demand for products grew significantly among more affluent consumers, advertising volume also soared in Vietnam (Ciochetto, 2013).

Advertisements on Fast-Moving Consumer Goods (FMCG) by foreign companies are more widespread as disposable income levels are low (Ciochetto, 2013). FMCG companies like Coca-Cola and Suntory PepsiCo are among the primary advertisers in Vietnam (Le & Jolibert, 2001). As a key advertiser, Coca-Cola needs to be extra sensitive to advertising content. While some did not view the slogan as problematic (Saigoneer, 2019), the controversy created tension between Coca-Cola and the government, who had deemed the slogan distasteful.

Intense Market Competition

The NCSD industry is dominated by Suntory PepsiCo, followed by Coca-Cola Vietnam, and local rival – Tan Hiep Phat (Son, 2020). Suntory PepsiCo may be the market leader, but Coca-Cola's advertisements have been more prevalent than other foreign soft drinks (Ciochetto, 2013), likely owing to its higher advertising budget than its competitors (The Investopedia Team, 2023). With higher advertising frequency, all the more Coca-Cola needs to conduct due diligence to ensure that its advertising content is not perceived negatively by stakeholders. Undeniably, Coca-Cola incurred significant reputational loss from its ill-conceived advertising campaign (Saigoneer, 2019). Moreover, Coca-Cola's breach of law meant that it would be under closer scrutiny, thereby creating tension between the company and the government.

Media System

Vietnam's print and broadcast media include newspapers, magazines, books, radio, television, and online websites, all of which are state-owned (BBC, 2018). Among the broadcast media, television, online and outdoor advertising are the more popular mediums in the country in 2019, the year in which the crisis occurred (Nguyen, 2021). The national networks are run by Vietnam Television (VTV), and subscription television owned by VTV carry some foreign channels (BBC, 2018). Vietnam's official newspaper, the Nhan Dan (People), serves as the voice of Communist Party of Vietnam and is the main medium for disseminating information to the public. The Ministry of Information and Communications has control over all print and broadcast media, and

Vietnamese law requires online content by print and broadcast media outlets to follow their offline versions strictly. However, due to the proliferation of online content, the government has found it hard to contain the Internet. The government has depended on rules and regulations, which allows it to regulate online content including Decree 72, to forbid the use of online services or content that goes against the government, harms social peace, and confutes the country's custom, among many other deeds (Abuza, 2017).

As of January 2019, Vietnam has 64 million Internet users and 62 million active social media users, representing approximately 66% and 64% of the population respectively. Social media provides Vietnamese an outlet for online discussion, with YouTube and Facebook (Kemp, 2019) being the most popular platforms. Blogging, which started in 2005, continues to be popular, while a meme culture has been active here since 2013. This creative form of self-expression is often used on social media, blogs, and discussion boards (Sharbaugh, 2013). With the advent of digital media, an increasing number of people have endangered themselves opposing the Vietnamese government by uncovering news they deemed insufficiently reported in the media (Abuza, 2017). Bloggers and citizen journalists who are caught doing so could face legal actions (Abuza, 2017; BBC, 2018).

Media Responses to Coca-Cola's Advertising Slogan in Vietnam

When Coca-Cola's crisis began, the Department of Grassroots Culture in Vietnam spoke to the press about Coca-Cola's choice of words. Newspapers published related articles on the incident (Binh, 2019; VNS, 2019), and Coca-Cola's history of banned or controversial advertisements in other countries like Australia were also brought up (Hung, 2019).

In his article in Nhan Dan, Dr Nguyen Si Dung commented that Coca-Cola's advertising slogan was not only obscene but also lacked humility and was unrepresentative of Vietnam. The author also noted the history of tax disputes between Coca-Cola Vietnam and the government. As Coca-Cola's image deteriorated, Dr Nguyen reaffirmed that Vietnamese consumers had every reason to boycott it (Nguyen, 2019).

Whether it was on digital media or print media, different stakeholders including marketing experts (Vinalink Media, n.d.), linguistic experts (Saigoneer, 2019), and the public (Anh, 2019b) had their say on the matter. These negative sentiments tarnished the Coca-Cola brand image and reputation. There were numerous memes, such as a meme with cartoons depicting tone marks and an angry can telling one another that there will be trouble if they stick together (Taichinhvietnam, 2019). And videos with the hashtag #MoLonVietnam went viral on Facebook and YouTube. Hashtags that organize discussions around the subject or occurrences (Small, 2011) evolved into an indicator of where potentially problematic content may be discovered (Gerrard, 2018). The hashtag #MoLonVietnam dominated most Internet conversation, with not only members of the general public but also public relations professionals, journalists, and lawyers weighing in on the subject. Additionally, there were others who rode the wave for their own financial gain, promoting their products or services using the hashtag or mentioning the case.

Coca-Cola's Use of Traditional (Offline) and Digital (Online) Media

Coca-Cola owns a Vietnam-specific website (The Coca-Cola Company, 2021) and its Facebook page with 25,000 followers (Coca-Cola Beverages Vietnam Facebook Page, n.d.). It also has a global YouTube account with 3.64 million subscribers (Coca-Cola YouTube, n.d.). The campaign video with the amended slogan has to date garnered a total of 5.5 million views (Coca-Cola, 2019). Coca-Cola utilized both offline and online means, including television, outdoor banners, and digital media for its advertising campaigns. After it was warned about the inappropriate use of words in the advertising slogan, Coca-Cola revised and updated the advertisements across all its media (Nhung, 2019).

The media served a dual function in this incident. While they highlighted the wrong choice of words in the advertising campaign, they also amplified Coca-Cola's quick response, which included acceding to the government's order and amending its slogan. Its representative also updated the media on its crisis response strategies thereafter. As most media in Vietnam are state-owned, and Internet content is regulated by the government, Coca-Cola was treading on thin ice when it breached the law with its controversial advertising slogan. Any attempt to defend itself could have caused further media backlash, and its decision to adhere to the authority promptly was observed as a prudent approach.

Societal Culture

Impact of Confucianism Culture on Vietnamese Society, Values, and Attitudes Towards Sex

Confucian culture forms the foundation for social behavior in Vietnam (Borton, 2000; Goldin, 2011; McHale, 2002). Confucianism emphasizes individuals as part and parcel of human relationships (Yao, 2000) and that fulfilling one's responsibilities forms the fundamentals in harmonious living and societal stability (Truong et al., 2017). Men are superior to women, and sons are valued more than daughters. A virtuous woman is subordinate to her father before marriage, to her husband after marriage and to her son in widowhood (Gao et al., 2012). Sexuality is viewed as a taboo and discussions about sex are forbidden. Premarital sex and sex outside of marriage is not condoned. In particular, women are supposed to be chaste, and are virgins before marriage and remain faithful to their husbands, whether alive or dead (Gao et al., 2012). Vietnamese believe there are upsides to such conservative attitudes towards sex. Banning sex before marriage would prevent unwanted pregnancy and sexually transmitted diseases. Retaining a woman's virginity would lead to true love and a healthy, happy marriage (AsiaLife, 2013).

Yet, traditional Confucian values have been eroded in pockets of its society. Premarital sex is increasingly prevalent among young people. Studies have suggested that migration, globalization, industrialization, modernization, and higher education have resulted in challenges to traditional and Confucian values (Gao et al., 2012). Mixed conservative and liberal attitudes towards relationships and sex have impacted how Vietnamese society reacts to marketing and publicity campaigns in the country. Additionally, Hofstede's cultural dimensions of power distance, collectivism, masculinity, uncertainty avoidance, and long-term orientation add greater insights to Coca-Cola's campaign. According to Hofstede, Vietnam has high power distance (70), low individualistic orientation (20), low masculinity (40), low uncertainty avoidance (30), and a moderate long-term orientation (57) (Hofstede, n.d.).

Power Distance

Having a high-power distance score suggests that Vietnamese society operates with a top-down structure. This differs from Coca-Cola's corporate culture, as its Asian subsidiaries are empowered with autonomy in organizational processes (Rothacher, 2004). The organization attempted to explain that its campaign slogan was intended to guide consumers to the coupon codes hidden beneath can tabs, and acknowledged that it had failed to consider linguistic aspects in the phrase (Tuân, 2019). As a foreign operator, Coca-Cola should have conducted a thorough evaluation of its commercials, especially getting help from locals to align its communication with the cultural norms of the country. Given the corporation's history of success and its team of experienced marketing personnel, it is difficult to conclude whether the incident was merely negligence or a calculated publicity stunt.

Collectivism

Vietnam is a collectivist culture that emphasizes relationship building (Hofstede, n.d.). Families generally have close ties with a strong sense of belonging and commitment (IES, 2021). The popularity of Coca-Cola in Vietnam is matched by the company's commitment to the Vietnamese people: "The Coca-Cola Company has tried in its own small way to contribute to Vietnam's community and social development, with activities targeting the well-being and improvement of rural and urban communities (McKinney, 2006). Coca-Cola's previous campaigns in Vietnam have always emphasized the importance of family unity and the prominence of sharing happiness. The brand associates happiness with distinct social and cultural circumstances in each region, allowing the message to spread more easily and gaining success in its marketing initiatives. During the 2015 Lunar New Year celebrations, a short Coca-Cola movie titled Tet Gift accompanied by a cultural campaign, gained widespread support from the Vietnamese community (Phương Mai, 2015).

Unfortunately, Coca-Cola's message was not thoroughly thought out with regard to this crisis. Coca-Cola tried to expound on collectivism in its campaign during the AFF Cup 2018 to celebrate the victory of Vietnam's national football club. Since Vietnamese people took great pride in their national soccer team, the corporation's objective with this campaign was to share their happiness. From the locals' perspective, Coca-Cola was not merely a beverage, but a symbol of optimism, inspiring and bringing happiness to millions of people. The organization also worked with the national football team to conquer the "golden" dream (BinhDinh Online, 2018). A brilliant advertising idea without the tagline was developed to mark the occasion – the classic color of Coke products with the players in red representing the color of the team and country.

Masculinity

People are motivated to be the best (masculinity) and desire to enjoy what they do (feminism). In this respect, Vietnam has a score of 40 on masculinity, suggesting that the country leans toward a feminine society. The core societal values include caring for others and striving toward enhanced quality of life (Hofstede, n.d.). Despite rapid urbanization, traditional gender standards prevail. Masculinity is still associated with a man's ability to participate in economic activities. Feminine norms revolve around women's primary job of caring for the family. Although Vietnamese men are raised with conventional masculine values, it was reported that they are likely to embrace globalization and urbanization that alter gender norms. This suggests that young males, especially in urban areas, are beginning to favor gender equality (ISDS, 2020).

Coca-Cola Vietnam's General Director, Sanket Ray, emphasized that "by developing sustainable sources and making constant efforts to contribute to the Government's priorities, Coca-Cola not only builds a solid foundation for our success, but it also brings practical values and a better life to the community and the country of Vietnam" (Tung, 2018). Coca-Cola has four significant priorities in its sustainable development strategy, based on the principle of "global brand, local knowledge": "Water — Women — Packaging waste management — Quality of life" (Tung, 2018). Furthermore, by focusing on women as its second mission, Coca-Cola Vietnam strives to empower women and provide them with more opportunities to express themselves and achieve a better life. Ironically, Coca-Cola was insensitive in the campaign messaging given that many claimed that the unclear message had opened the door to interpretations or inferences, some of which were obscene in nature.

Uncertainty Avoidance

Vietnam scored 30 on this Hofstede dimension, indicating its low inclination to avoid uncertainty. Low uncertainty avoidance cultures have a more relaxed attitude in which practice trumps principles, and deviance from the norm is more easily tolerated. Most individuals in such societies believe that unnecessary, complicated and unproductive rules should be abandoned or altered (Hofstede, n.d.). Many Vietnamese believed that the authorities should not appear forceful by issuing administrative orders and implementing bans simply because Coca-Cola's slogan contained "Lon." The government may be perceived as viewing the incident subjectively rather than from a legal standpoint (Van Huy, 2019). However, in hindsight, the authorities were also in a difficult position as a lack of intervention would not sit well with groups who deemed the slogan as inappropriate.

Long-term Orientation

This dimension illustrates how every society must maintain ties to its past while dealing with present and future concerns, and how societies prioritize these two existential aims differ. Vietnam has a score of 57, indicating that it is a pragmatic culture. People in pragmatic societies believe that truth is highly dependent on situation, context and time. Thus, they demonstrate an ability to easily adapt traditions to changing circumstances, as well as a solid proclivity to save and invest (Hofstede, n.d.). Even though Vietnam is increasingly globalized, it continues to maintain its roots and customs. Coca-Cola's advertising strategy in Vietnam faced several challenges primarily due to culture, lifestyle, customs, and habits that differ between the country's North and South. The Vietnamese language is also complicated and requires the use of standard phrases and appropriate circumstances in order to avoid unintended problems during communication and interaction. Nguyen Van Dung of the Institute of Information and Communication Technology Applications said: "It is unacceptable to use the Vietnamese name alongside the word "lon" to convey confusing messages in a variety of ways, including inference, gossip, and even obscene directions" (Nguyên, 2019b).

For many Vietnamese, their language's rich history is a source of great pride, and its tonal character offers many options for wordplay. The semantics of a sentence, word, or phrase could have a plethora of completely distinct meanings depending on the context in which it is used. In other words, there are innumerable synonyms for the same act of eating, with dozens of distinct phrases. The campaign slogan would have been appropriate if used correctly, but it highlighted an offensive connotation when interpreted differently (Every Culture, 2008), and as such, it was deemed inappropriate by the Vietnamese. Under cultural dimensions, Coca-Cola's misalignment impacted its operations in Vietnam.

Activist Culture

Although Coca-Cola's campaign did not result in street protests or activism of any violent nature, digital activism was active, facilitated by Vietnamese's collectivist and patriotic culture. Digital activism has gained momentum with the advent of social media in Vietnam; its potential user anonymity, and lack of gatekeepers to regulate content on the online space allow Vietnamese to engage in dialogic communication about issues concerning them, and it indirectly evokes emotions of significant regard and patriotism for the country. Because the campaign slogan was viewed as insensitive and impinged on Vietnam's sense of purity, stakeholders such as political representatives and the academia, who were respected and influential in their respective fields, actively highlighted their concerns on media platforms. The views of the general public were also aligned with the political representatives and those in academia. Reader Xuyen Quynh, for example, remarked:

> We are a nation, an independent sovereign nation. Vietnam is not a can for Coca-Cola to open when it wanted to and in a way it desired.
>
> (Pv, 2019)

Crisis Communication Analysis

Political and Media Dynamism During a Crisis

Paternalistic in nature, the Vietnamese government strives to safeguard conservative traditions, values, and interests of the country. Coca-Cola's publicity saw the government proactively denouncing the phrase and derogatory remarks and protecting its sovereignty and purity. Overall, the political system acts as a powerful overarching defense against malicious indirect attack on the country. It is beneficial for Coca-Cola to maintain a two-way dialogic and symmetric relationship with the government and have a good understanding of existing and new legislations, as well as corporate governance processes.

The media in Vietnam is intertwined with the political system, as the former is largely controlled by the government. Various media channels echoed the government's position and amplified their message across offline and online media platforms. While most members of the public were influenced by the government's position and approach, Vietnamese who were more liberal toward cultural identities and attitudes did not perceive Coca-Cola's campaign as an infringement on their rights and values. They were receptive to unconventional advertising phrases. This suggests that although the Vietnamese government's stance was strong, and media outlets sought to align their position and content with that of the government, both the government and the media could still potentially find it challenging to fully control the mindsets and attitudes of citizens, given the erosion of values in a globalized economy and the influence of alternative online media channels.

Alternative Views Due to Economic Advancements

From an economic perspective, the influx of foreign investments and companies into Vietnam, as well as a more educated populace influenced by liberal ideas has shifted Vietnamese's perceptions and expectations of Coca-Cola's campaign objectives and messaging from a conservative to a more liberal one. The locals, while retaining their cultural roots, may no longer place too much emphasis on traditions, values, and heritage. With growing wealth, material consumption takes precedence, and Vietnamese may not pay much attention to how publicity messages undermined their cultural values. Rather, they may view Coca-Cola products purely as a commodity and lifestyle drink. The process of Coca-Cola gaining popularity in Vietnam is an insignificant by-product of Vietnamese's love for carbonated drinks.

Significance of Cultural Variables

Given that Vietnam is collectivistic and harmonious relationships are highly prized, the Coca-Cola crisis did not result in violent protests. Instead, digital activism was more prevalent and keyboard warriors from two camps – one neutral and the other negative – emerged. Online sentiments resulted in an escalation of the crisis. For companies to operate seamlessly in a different market, the cultural variables discussed in Chapter 1 are critical considerations for communication and public relations to succeed. In this case study, the extent of power distance amongst government authorities, foreign companies and the public was a key factor. As for the political culture of the country, it was evident that the Vietnamese government is the central command and control to both legislative and administrative decisions in the country. The media and the people generally take directions from the Vietnamese government. It would be worthwhile for any foreign firm to consult relevant government authorities before embarking on any publicity campaigns, especially since the advertising campaign with the slogan "Mở Lon Việt Nam" was pegged at the national level to cheer for Vietnam's national football team. Even though Coca-Cola had been in Vietnam since 1960 (CNBC, 2012), this case study proves that the corporation had not yet established a sufficiently strong two-way symmetrical communication and good rapport with the government, resulting in the crisis.

As collectivism and harmony is greatly valued, Vietnamese prioritize the sharing of joy and happiness. While Coca-Cola attempted to celebrate the victory of Vietnam's national football team, it neglected the nuancing of its messaging, resulting in friction with the government and the conservative segments of society. Being mindful of the cultural environment would have helped the firm to avoid the backlash. As Vietnam is feminine culturally, MNCs operating in the country need to respect women's rights and avoid making condescending remarks about them.

Importance of Social Monitoring to Respond to Crises

Corporations operating in a foreign country should embark on social monitoring and listening to develop crisis response strategies to navigate successfully on social media platforms. Coca-Cola's case underscores the need to address negative online comments promptly to appease affected stakeholders. The concept of "Golden Hour" timeliness of response is critical in crisis management in order to avoid information vacuums and reputational risks (Coombs, 2020).

Conclusion

Coca-Cola's advertisement saga highlighted the importance of understanding the confluence of a country's political, economic, cultural, media, and activist systems. It is necessary for companies operating in Vietnam to be cognizant of the potential difference in the level of uncertainty avoidance between the government authorities and society in general. While society generally adopts a more relaxed attitude and are more accepting toward deviance from the norm, the Vietnamese authorities defended the country against derogatory remarks in a bid to protect its sovereignty and urged Coca-Cola to review its publicity slogan. This case study illustrated the need for foreign firms to work with and manage the expectations of various stakeholders such as government regulators, the academia, community, and customers, to be able to interpret ambiguity and unknowns; and the country's long-term orientation that values standing interests and partnerships as opposed to short-term monetary gains.

References

Abuza, Z. (2017, July). Stifling the Public Sphere. Media and Civil Society in Vietnam. National Endowment for Democracy. In International Forum for Democratic Studies. http://www.ned.org/wp-content/uploads/2015/10/Stifling-the-Public-Sphere-Media-Civil-Society-Vietnam-Forum-NED.pdf. (Vol. 29).

Anh, L. (2019a, June 29). Coca-Cola adjusts ads 'not suitable for Vietnamese customs and traditions'. *Zing News*. https://zingnews.vn/coca-cola-dieu-chinh-quang-cao-khong-phu-hop-thuan-phong-my-tuc-vn-post961595.html

Anh, L. (2019b, June 29). "Opening a can in Vietnam": What is it if you don't open a can? https://vov.vn/van-hoa-giai-tri/mo-lon-viet-nam-khong-mo-lon-thi-la-gi-926633.vov

AsiaLife. (2013, March 3). Sex Before Marriage in Vietnam. https://www.asialifemagazine.com/vietnam/sex-before-marriage-in-vietnam/

Bairagi, S., Mohanty, S., Baruah, S., & Thi, H. T. (2020). Changing food consumption patterns in rural and urban Vietnam: Implications for a future food supply system. *Australian Journal of Agricultural and Resource Economics*, *64*(3), 750–775.

BBC. (2018, November 20). Vietnam Profile — Media. https://www.bbc.com/news/world-asia-pacific-16567840

Binh, N. (2019, June 29). Coca-Cola decided: Remove the 'can' from the advertising slogan. TuoiTre Online. https://tuoitre.vn/coca-cola-quyet-dinh-bo-lon-khoi-slogan-quang-cao-20190629224701566.htm

BinhDinh Online. (2018, April 12). Coca-Cola Vietnam officially becomes a partner of VFF. http://baobinhdinh.vn/viewer.aspx?macm=12&macmp=12&mabb=99778

Borton, L. (2000). Working in a Vietnamese voice. *Academic of Management Executive*, *14*(4), 20–19.

Bộ Văn hóa Thể thao và Du lịch. (2023, January 16). Chức Năng Nhiệm Vụ Của Bộ. https://bvhttdl.gov.vn/gioi-thieu-ve-bo/chuc-nang-nhiem-vu-cua-bo.htm

Buttinger, J. (n.d.). Vietnam. *Britannica*. https://www.britannica.com/place/Vietnam/Climate

Ciochetto, L. (2013). Advertising Vietnam, Cambodia and Laos in the first decade of the 21st century: Promise of things to come? *Media Asia*, *40*(3), 274–282.

CNBC. (2012, November 11). Coca-Cola Steps Up Investment in Vietnam. https://www.cnbc.com/id/100052077

Coca-Cola. (2019, June 29). Cơ hội trúng vàng mỗi ngày với Coca-Cola. YouTube. https://youtu.be/hWkJbY2rmnM

Coca-Cola Beverages Vietnam Facebook. (n.d.). Coca-Cola Beverages Vietnam. https://www.facebook.com/ccbvl?mibextid=ZbWKwL

Coca-Cola YouTube (n.d.). Coca-Cola. YouTube. https://youtube.com/c/TheCoca-ColaCompany

Coombs, W. T. (2020). Conceptualizing crisis communication. In *Handbook of risk and crisis communication* (pp. 99–118). Routledge.

Datta, A., & Mendizabal, E. (2018, January 16). Political and economic transition in Vietnam and its impact on think tank traditions. *Medium*. https://medium.com/@info_92670/political-and-economic-transition-in-vietnam-and-its-impact-on-think-tank-traditions-381ffd8ef303

Dieu, M. (2019, June 29). 'Opening a can of Vietnam' is considered offensive: Netizens don't understand why it's offensive. https://thanhnien.vn/mo-lon-viet-nam-bi-cho-la-phan-cam-dan-mang-khong-hieu-vi-sao-phan-cam-post862799.html

Đức, V.. (2019, June 30). "Mở lon Việt Nam" của Coca-Cola: Tai nạn hay chiêu trò?. ZingNews.Vn. https://zingnews.vn/mo-lon-viet-nam-cua-coca-cola-tai-nan-hay-chieu-tro-post961849.html

Economy. (2019, June 29). Coca-Cola stopped advertising the words "Open a can in Vietnam. https://nld.com.vn/kinh-te/coca-cola-dung-quang-cao-dong-chu-mo-lon-viet-nam-20190629142203035.htm

EloQ Communications. (2021, July 13). Understanding the Vietnamese market and its people. https://www.pr-network.biz/understanding-the-vietnamese-market-and-its-people/

Every Culture. (2008, January 9). Culture Of Vietnam — History, People, Clothing, Traditions, Women, Beliefs, Food, Customs, Family. https://www.everyculture.com/To-Z/Vietnam.html#ixzz79R52Om1m

Eye on Asia. (n.d.). Vietnam — A Country Profile. https://www.eyeonasia.gov.sg/asean-countries/know/overview-of-asean-countries/vietnam-a-country-profile/

Figuié, M., & Moustier, P. (2009). Market appeal in an emerging economy: Supermarkets and poor consumers in Vietnam. *Food Policy*, *34*(2), 210–217.

Gao, E., Zuo, X., Wang, L., Lou, C., Cheng, Y., & Zabin, L. S. (2012). How does traditional Confucian culture influence Adolescents' sexual behavior in three Asian cities? *Journal of Adolescent Health*, *50*(3), S12–S17. https://doi.org/10.1016/j.jadohealth.2011.12.002

Gerrard, Y. (2018). Beyond the hashtag: Circumventing content moderation on social media. *New Media & Society*, *20*(12), 4492–4511. https://doi.org/10.1177/1461444818776611

Gócnhìn Marketing. (2019). MỞ LON VIỆT NAM' của Coca-Cola: TAI NẠN HAY CHIÊU TRÒ? [Status update]. Facebook. https://www.facebook.com/GocnhinMarketingEDM

Goldin, P. R. (2011). *Confucianism*. University of California Press.

Ha, N. T., Le, T. T. H., & Luu, Q. T. (2017). Knowledge, attitude, frequency and level of consumption regarding non-alcoholic carbonated soft drinks among students from two high schools in Hanoi, Vietnam in 2015. *AIMS Public Health*, *4*(1), 62. https://pubmed.ncbi.nlm.nih.gov/29922703/

Hạnh, L. (2020, August 03). Coca-Cola's "Can Open Vietnam" campaign: So what do you open if you don't open the can? Giai Phap Digital Marketing. https://marketingai.admicro.vn/chien-dich-khui-lon-viet-nam-cua-coca-cola-the-khong-khui-lon-thi-khui-cai-gi/

Hofstede (n.d.). Vietnam — Hofstede Insights. Hofstede Insights. https://www.hofstede-insights.com/country/vietnam/

Hung, V. (2019, June 29). Soft drinks instead of filtered water and the controversial ads of Coca-Cola. *Zing News*. https://zingnews.vn/nuoc-ngot-thay-nuoc-loc-va-nhung-quang-cao-gay-tranh-cai-cua-coca-cola-post961636.html

Hung, V., & Anh, L. (2019, June 29). Coca-Cola corrects advertising slogan 'Open a can of Vietnam'. *Zing News*. https://zingnews.vn/coca-cola-sua-slogan-quang-cao-mo-lon-viet-nam-post961677.html

IES (2021). Vietnamese Culture — Business Culture. Cultural Atlas. https://culturalatlas.sbs.com.au/vietnamese-culture/vietnamese-culture-business-culture#vietnamese-culture-business-culture

ISDS (2020). Men and masculinities in a globalising Vietnam — ISDS. Institute for Social Development Studies. http://isds.org.vn/en/an-pham/men-and-masculinities-in-a-globalising-viet-nam/

Kemp, S. (2019, January 31). Digital 2019 — Vietnam. Datareportal. https://datareportal.com/reports/digital-2019-vietnam

Lam, T. D. (2014). *Foreign direct investment in Vietnam. Center for Vietnamese and southeast Asian studies*. University of Social Sciences and Humanities, Vietnam National University.

Le, T. M., & Jolibert, A. (2001). Advertising practice in a transitional economy: An examination of advertising industry in Vietnam. *International Journal of Advertising*, *20*(3), 369–391.

Malesky, E., & London, J. (2014). The political economy of development in China and Vietnam. *Annual Review of Political Science*, *17*, 395–419.

McHale, S. (2002). Mapping a Vietnamese Confucian past and its transition to modernity. In B. A. Elman, J. B. Duncan, & H. Ooms (Eds.), *Rethinking Confucianism: Past and present in China, Japan, Korea and Vietnam* (pp. 397–430). University of California.

McKinney, B. C. (2006). Public relations in Vietnam: A six-year perspective. *Public Relations Quarterly*, *51*(2), 18.

Nga, T. (2019, July 1). 'Mở Lon Việt Nam' Coca-Cola: Phong Phú đến Hiểu NHẦM Của Tiếng Việt! Trithuccuocsong.vn. Retrieved from https://kienthuc.net.vn/xa-hoi/mo-lon-viet-nam-coca-cola-phong-phu-den-hieu-nham-cua-tieng-viet-1246883.html

Nguyen, T. (2019, June 29). "Why is Coca Cola's 'open can of Vietnam' banned?" Thanh Nien. https://thanhnien-vn.translate.goog/mo-lon-viet-nam-cua-coca-cola-vi-sao-bi-cam-post862769.html?_x_tr_sl=vi&_x_tr_tl=en&_x_tr_hl=en-GB&_x_tr_pto=nui,sc

Nguyen, M.-N. (2021, April 15). Advertising reach of main media types in Vietnam 2014-2019. Vietnam: reach of advertising media by type 2019. *Statista*. https://www.statista.com/statistics/1109553/vietnam-reach-of-advertising-media-by-type/

Nguyên, K. (2019a, July 1). Hanoi fines Coca-Cola 25 million dong for 'Opening a can of Vietnam'. *Tienphong*. https://tienphong.vn/ha-noi-phat-coca-cola-25-trieu-dong-vi-mo-lon-viet-nam-post1121498.tpo

Nguyên, K. (2019b, July 2). Controversy of 'Opening a can of Vietnam': Poor coherence, lack of clarity. *Tienphong*. https://tienphong.vn/tranh-cai-quang-cao-mo-lon-viet-nam-kem-mach-lac-thieu-trong-sang-post1121574.tpo

Nhung, P. (2019, June 29). Coca-Cola stopped advertising the words "Open a can in Vietnam". *Nguoi Lao Dong*. https://nld.com.vn/kinh-te/coca-cola-dung-quang-cao-dong-chu-mo-lon-viet-nam-20190629142203035.htm

Nien, T. (n.d.). How is "opening a can of Vietnam" contrary to traditional customs? https://thanhnien.vn/mo-lon-viet-nam.html

Pearson, J. (2020, November 20). Exclusive: Vietnam threatens to shut down Facebook over censorship requests — source. *Reuters*. https://www.reuters.com/article/vietnam-facebook-shutdown-idUSKBN28007K

Phương Mai, Đ. (2015, February 14). Coca-Cola and the "Cultural Navigation" Strategy. NĐH. https://ndh.vn/doanh-nghiep/coca-cola-va-chien-luoc-ieu-huong-van-hoa-1119513.html

Pv. (2019, June 30). Coca-Cola corrects advertising slogan 'Open a can of Vietnam'. *VietnamFinance*. https://vietnamfinance.vn/coca-cola-sua-slogan-quang-cao-mo-lon-viet-nam-20180504224225553.htm

PWC Worldwide Tax Summaries. (2022, February 8). Vietnam — Overview. https://taxsummaries.pwc.com/vietnam

Rothacher, A. (Ed.). (2004). *For God, America and the real thing: The Coke story. Corporate cultures and global brands*. Palgrave Macmillan.

Saigoneer. (2019, July 2). Coca-Cola Removes Slogan Deemed 'Vulgar' by Culture Department. https://saigoneer.com/society/16856-coca-cola-removes-slogan-deemed-vulgar-by-culture-department

Sharbaugh, P. (2013, November 25). Make Lulz, Not War: Will meme culture help transform Asia's authoritarian states on human rights from within? I.M.H.O. https://medium.com/i-m-h-o/make-lulz-not-war-5268ecb6978e

Small (2011). What the hashtag?: A content analysis of Canadian politics on Twitter. *Information, Communication & Society*, *14*(6), 872–895. https://doi.org/10.1080/1369118X.2011.554572

Son, M. (2020, September 21). Non-alcoholic drinks fetch higher revenues. *VnExpress International*. https://e.vnexpress.net/news/business/data-speaks/non-alcoholic-drinks-fetch-higher-revenues-4163992.html

Sriramesh, K., & Verčič, D. (2020). *The global public relations handbook: Theory, research, and practice* (Expanded and rev. ed.). Routledge.

Truong T. D., Hallinger, P., & Sanga, K. (2017). Confucian values and school leadership in Vietnam: Exploring the influence of culture on principal decision making. *Educational Management, Administration & Leadership*, *45*(1), 77–100. https://doi.org/10.1177/1741143215607877

Taichinhvietnam (2019, June 30). Caricature of the Can. taichinhvietnam.net.vn. http://taichinhvietnam.net.vn/biem-hoa-ve-cai-lon-d6791.html

TechCrunch. (2016, May 18). Facebook blocked in Vietnam over the weekend due to citizen protests. Retrieved from https://techcrunch.com/2016/05/17/facebook-blocked-in-vietnam-over-the-weekend-due-to-citizen-protests/

Thanh, D. L. (2019, June 30). Doctor of linguistics dissects Coca-Cola's controversial slogan "Open a can of Vietnam". *Nguoi Dua Tin*. https://www.nguoiduatin.vn/tien-si-ngon-ngu-hoc-mo-xe-slogan-mo-lon-viet-nam-gay-tranh-cai-cua-coca-cola-a439930.html

The Coca-Cola Company. (2021). Coca-Cola. https://en.cocacolavietnam.com/

The Investopedia Team. (2023, February 3). A look at Coca-Cola's advertising expenses. Investopedia. Retrieved from https://www.investopedia.com/articles/markets/081315/look-cocacolas-advertising-expenses.asp

The World Bank. (2022, November 7). The World Bank in Vietnam. https://www.worldbank.org/en/country/vietnam/overview#1

Trương, B. (2020, January 13). Before the arrears of 821 billion, how did Coca-Cola evade taxes? *Techz.vn*. https://www.techz.vn/182-120-5-truoc-khi-bi-truy-thu-821-ty-coca-cola-tron-thue-nhu-the-nao-ylt503830.html

Tuân, V. (2019, June 29). Department of Grassroots Culture: 'Vietnamese name cannot be used arbitrarily in advertising'. *VnExpress*. https://vnexpress.net/cuc-van-hoa-co-so-ten-goi-viet-nam-khong-the-dung-tuy-tien-trong-quang-cao-3945431.html

Tung, T. (2018, October 12). Coca-Cola accompanies sustainable development with Vietnam. *Vietnam Business Forum*. https://vccinews.vn/news/20835/coca-cola-dong-hanh-phat-trien-ben-vung-cung-viet-nam.html

Van Huy, N. (2019, June 30). Prohibition of Advertising "Opening Cans in Vietnam": When the word can is guilty! Tuoi Tre Phap Luat. https://phapluat.tuoitrethudo.com.vn/cam-quang-cao-mo-lon-viet-nam-khi-chu-lon-mang-toi-25780.html

Vietnam Investment Review. (2018, November 7). Soft drinks see hard competition. *Vietnam Investment Review* (7). https://vir.com.vn/soft-drinks-see-hard-competition-63611.html

Vietnam Law & Legal Forum. (2012, December 28). Transfer pricing costs Vietnam trillions dong each year. *Vietnam Law and Legal Forum*. https://vietnamlawmagazine.vn/transfer-pricing-costs-vietnam-trillions-dong-each-year-4622.html

Vinalink Media. (N.d.). Slogan Open cans of Vietnam Coca Cola. *Vinalink Media*. https://copywrite.vn/tin-tuc/slogan-mo-lon-viet-nam-cocacola.html

VNS. (2019, July 3). Coca Cola fined over advertisement. *Viet Nam News*. https://vietnamnews.vn/society/522158/coca-cola-fined-over-advertisement.html

VOV.VN. (2023, August 15). Prime Minister Pham Minh Chinh meets with Vietnam women's national football team. *VOV*. https://vov.vn/chinh-tri/thu-tuong-pham-minh-chinh-gap-mat-doi-tuyen-bong-da-nu-quoc-gia-viet-nam-post1039527.vov:

Vuong, Q. H. (2014). Vietnam's political economy: A discussion on the 1986–2016 period. CEB-ULB WP, (14/010). Retrieved from https://dial.uclouvain.be/pr/boreal/object/boreal%3A143486/datastream/PDF_01/view

Xuân, H. (2019, July 1). [VNF perspective] State management and market ethics from the case of 'Opening a can of Vietnam'. *VietnamFinance*. https://vietnamfinance.vn/goc-nhin-vnf-quan-ly-nha-nuoc-va-dao-duc-thi-truong-nhin-tu-truong-hop-mo-lon-viet-nam-20180504224225585.htm

Yao, X. (2000). *An introduction to Confucianism*. Cambridge University Press.

3

INDIA

McDonald's Faces Boycott Over Halal Meat

Shabbir Akhtar and Hannah Luz Awitan

Introduction

Not everyone in India was saying "I'm lovin' it" in August 2019, when a tweet from McDonald's India landed the company in trouble resulting in #BoycottMcDonalds trending on Twitter. A popular fast-food chain in the country, McDonald's India staff were simply carrying out good customer service by promptly addressing a patron's inquiry regarding the halal certification of the meat they offer. Little did McDonald's India know that an answer in the affirmative would push them into the center of an online furor. In a country with rich religious diversity, companies must ensure they treat all groups equally. Unfortunately, due to the tweet, McDonald's India appeared to favor one religious group over another, thus sparking the #BoycottMcDonalds crisis of 2019. This chapter explores the company's response to the crisis in a densely populated and culturally very diverse nation where 99 percent of the population identify with a religion (Boyon, 2023).

The Corporation and the Crisis

McDonald's entered the Indian market in 1996 using a "think global and act local" strategy (Mishra & Dwivedi, 2013) to cater to the dense and diverse population of the country, where an estimated quarter of the population is vegetarian (Kannan, 2014). KFC, another popular international fast-food chain, tried to enter India in 1995, but its efforts proved to be less successful because nearly a decade after its entry, it could only manage five outlets in the country (Friend, 2013). That does not mean McDonald's entry into India was without

DOI: 10.4324/9781003411802-4

any challenges. The fast-food chain's most popular burger, globally, is the Big Mac with two slabs of beef patties. However, beef consumption is limited in India due largely to religious reasons since the majority of Indians are Hindus who do not consume beef. This has resulted in chicken, potato, and other vegetarian ingredients to form the core of McDonald's menu in India. Rice or *rotis* (wheat flat bread) with several other accompaniments are staple meals for the masses in India. So, it was not surprising that only a small portion of the population acknowledged burgers as a proper meal. Hence, while Indians were keen to try American food, they needed to see the flavors and ingredients they were already familiar with or enjoyed in these foods (Wells, 2020). Moreover, in the 1990s, eating at home was the norm, and dining out was reserved for special occasions such as birthdays, anniversaries, or other celebrations. Until the early 2000s, the frequency of eating out averaged three meals out of 100 (Goyal, 2021). Another key element was the affordability of eating out. Enjoying inexpensive street food, was, and remains, an important facet of daily life in India. Hence, street food stalls are seen as direct competitors to McDonald's in India (Wells, 2020).

While McDonald's has become India's common man's *Happy Meal* over the past 25 years, the path has not been one of linear growth, more a turbulent one. Since 1996, McDonald's India has accumulated a loss of INR4.21 billion (The Economic Times, 2018). In 2019, it faced legal and contractual problems with its joint venture partner, Connaught Plaza Restaurants Limited, for the North and East India outlets (ET Online, 2019), which affected its operations during this period.

To manage the logistics of catering to such a massive and culturally diverse country, McDonald's tried to develop its entire supply chain within India (Wells, 2020), which it continues to this day (Goyal, 2021). By modifying its offerings to suit the local palate and implementing marketing and advertising tactics alongside pricing strategies such that some individual products are available at as low as US$0.50 (Wells, 2020), McDonald's India has been successful in breaking down the various cultural barriers to make its fast-food meals a household name in the country (Mishra & Dwivedi, 2013).

However, in August 2019, a tweet (which has since been deleted) asking whether McDonald's India is "Halal certified" (Kuchay, 2019) drew a response from the corporation that sparked a crisis:

> Thank you for taking the time to contact McDonald's India. We truly appreciate this opportunity to respond to your comments. The meat that we use, across our restaurants, is of the highest quality and is sourced from government-approved suppliers who are HACCP certified. All our restaurants have HALAL certificates. You can ask the respective restaurant Managers to show you the certificate for your satisfaction and confirmation.
>
> (McDonald's India, 2019a)

Halal translates to "permissible" in Arabic, and animals slaughtered following Islamic rites are considered halal (Eardley, 2014). There is a popular belief that halal meat is forbidden for Hindus and Sikhs who follow the jhatka slaughter method – killed with a single blow – so the tweet from McDonald's India caused an outcry among those from other religions; it led to the hashtag #BoycottMcDonalds to trend on Twitter (Kuchay, 2019; The Indian Express, 2020). Responses on Twitter included claims that by trying to please the Muslims, McDonald's had offended the rest of the other religions, including Jainism, Sikhism, and Buddhism. Other Twitter users urged Hindus to unite and boycott restaurants such as McDonald's for only giving regard to Muslim sensibilities while ignoring theirs.

Before this public outcry, McDonald's India had been actively engaging with stakeholders on Twitter, starting conversations and answering their complaints. However, when the crisis ignited, McDonald's India did not react in a timely manner. Media outlets were quick to cover the incident and release articles such as those by the *Economic Times* and *India Today*. Nevertheless, updates as to what the company did and to what extent the boycotts worked were scarce. As per Google Trends, #BoycottMcDonalds was only trending in India between August 25 and 31, 2019. In October 2019, two legal notices were sent to McDonald's India by Harish Sharma, a social worker, through Ishkaran Singh Bhandari, a political analyst, supreme court advocate, and legal expert from New Delhi, on the grounds that the company had discriminated against non-Muslims of India (OpIndia, 2019a; OpIndia, 2019b). Despite being present in the country since 1996, no one has asked the fast-food chain publicly about its meat preparation practices. With the instantaneous and viral nature of Twitter, the company's response gained significant attention among the netizens in the country.

Even then, McDonald's India stayed strategically silent, which is "a deliberate lack of organizational communication and if there is any, the information is intentionally scant or ambiguous" (Le et al., 2019, p. 163). In the next section, we outline the legal and financial ramifications McDonald's India faced following the controversial tweet.

Impact on McDonald's India

Legal Ramifications

Ishkaran Singh Bhandari challenged McDonald's India on its stance on serving only halal meat in its menu and served the fast-food giant a legal notice referencing its social media tweets. He claimed that the company had indulged in racial, social, economic, and religious discrimination. He further pointed out that McDonald's India adopts contradictory policies when compared to its counterparts in other countries such as Canada and the United States. He wanted the

American fast-food company to publicly clarify its position on its policies and to stop any discriminatory practices by serving all types of meat – meat prepared following the jhatka method for Hindus and Sikhs and halal meat to satisfy Muslims. He also started an online petition on Change.org to rally supporters to get McDonald's India to serve both jhatka and halal meats (TFIPOST, 2019). With the involvement of prominent, vocal personalities like Ishkaran Singh Bhandari and right-wing group Hindu Sena national president Vishnu Gupta (Kuchay, 2019), the impact on McDonald's India – both reputational and legal – became more severe.

Financial Ramifications

There appears to be no conclusive evidence of a significant impact on McDonald's India's financials aside from a relatively small year-on-year increase in financial year (FY) 2019/2020's Gross Revenue at 11.5%, as compared to the previous two years – 23.7% in FY 2018/2019, and 22.2% in FY 2017/2018 (Westlife Development Limited, 2020). Even then, there are many factors that can affect a company's gross revenue, and hence causation cannot be established here. However, it was found that McDonald's India's legal and professional fees went up by 29% from INR106.2 million to NR137 million during FY2020 (Westlife Development Limited, 2020). This could be attributed to the several suits filed by activists such as Ishkaran Singh Bhandari (OpIndia, 2019b). Another possible form of financial impact from the 2019 crisis could be the drop in McDonald's India's market share in 2020, even as it ranked second in market shares. In contrast, the market shares of its competitors such as Domino's Pizza, KFC, Subway, and Pizza Hut, saw increases (Euromonitor International, 2021).

The #BoycottMcDonalds crisis in India is one of the several examples of a reputational crisis faced by a multinational brand as it failed to take into consideration the cultural intricacies of the host country in the context of a rapidly changing digital landscape. McDonald's India's silence during the crisis can possibly be attributed to the interaction of the five systems of the Global Public Relation Framework at play (Sriramesh & Vercic, 2020) in India.

Case Analysis

The crisis McDonald's India faced in 2019 came about because of its response to a tweet from an Indian consumer and the subsequent silence from the multinational brand. We will analyze McDonald's crisis through the lens of India's socio-cultural environment using the convergence and the complexity of the Global Public Relation Framework's five systems – political, economic, media, societal and organizational culture, and activist culture discussed in Chapter 1 (Sriramesh & Verčič, 2020).

Political System

Known as a land of extraordinary diversity, India is a place where many different beliefs and traditions come together. India has overtaken China as the most populous country, with its populace living in 29 states that are largely segmented by linguistic lines. This heterogeneity creates its own set of complexities. While the constitution recognizes 22 different languages (Profile – National Portal of India, 2021), as many as 780 different languages and dialects are spoken in India (Hindustan Times, 2013). There are six main religions: Hinduism, Islam, Christianity, Sikhism, Buddhism, and Jainism with a very small population of Jewish and Zoroastrians. Hindus account for 79.8% of the population; Muslims make up 14.2%; Christians, Sikhs, Buddhists, and Jains make up the majority of the remaining 6%, along with several other religions (Kramer, 2021). Before becoming the largest democracy in the world in 1947, India was under British rule from 1858. India's present-day government is based on the Westminster system with three branches – the executive with the president as head of state and the prime minister as head of the government; the legislature composed of a parliament, and the judiciary led by the Supreme Court (Profile – National Portal of India, 2021).

In 2014 and again in 2019, the Bhartiya Janta Party (BJP) won two consecutive terms in the general elections, ousting the incumbent Congress in 2014 with a sweeping majority. BJP's extensive use of social media in both the 2014 and 2019 elections has made Prime Minister Narendra Modi one of the most followed politicians on Twitter (The Wire Analysis, 2020; Social Blade, n.d.). Modi has succeeded in garnering a huge fan following on Twitter, which has worked hugely in his favor in terms of gathering supporters. Possessing such extensive and committed followers has emboldened the BJP to continue in its pro-nationalist ideologies. The Indian constitution gives considerable authority to both the state and the central government, ensuring a balance of power in a federal political system. With coalition parties being formed and state elections being conducted almost every year, the power shift is constant. Furthermore, the Supreme Court can exercise judicial prudence and override the central government on important issues, thus keeping a strong check on any overly authoritarian rule.

In this crisis affecting McDonald's India, the trolling highlighted the company's bias towards serving food preferred by people from a single religion, which gained fervor amongst netizens as they rallied for a boycott of the fast-food giant. As mentioned earlier, McDonald's India chose to remain silent on the issue when #BoycottMcDonalds started trending in August 2019. With such a diverse religious landscape of India, the fast-food giant probably thought that it is best for the company to avoid confrontations when they cross paths with religious beliefs (Pew Research Center, 2017). While social media allowed issues to escalate faster than ever before, it is common industry practice for companies in such instances to "lie low until the dust settles" so that online rage and unhappiness do not transcend offline to mass protests and vandalism (Tewari & Nair, 2021). In addition, responses to McDonald's India tweets had religious connotations, and members of the ruling government were tagged. Any response from McDonald's India would mean having to craft messages that may stir religious or political sentiments, which could further anger other segments of society or the opposition in the government, leading to a renewed or fresh crisis (McDonald's India, 2019b).

McDonald's India could have performed better by observing the mistakes of others. Public uproars against brands – both international and local – are not foreign to India. Also in 2019, food delivery service Zomato was called out for taking the moral high ground by tweeting publicly about food not having a religion when a customer specifically demanded a Hindu food delivery agent, while at the same time refusing to cancel a non-halal delivery order for a Muslim delivery agent. In 2020, Tata-owned jewelry brand Tanishq came under fire for featuring an interfaith baby shower ceremony as part of its Ekatvam campaign, resulting in Tanishq having to withdraw the campaign's film. Most recent was the backlash on Bharat Matrimony, an online matrimonial platform, for its Holi 2023 ad, which doubled as its International Women's Day campaign featuring a woman with bruises on her face underneath the Holi colors. The ad tried to call for a safe Holi celebration for women but instead garnered criticism for associating the festival of Holi with sexual harassment (The Quint, 2023). It is thus imperative that multinational corporations such as McDonald's pre-empt the consequences of public policy and political ramifications of their statement in a foreign country, more so in a culturally sensitive and religiously diverse nation like India.

Economic System

Even before the pandemic, India's gross domestic product (GDP) had taken a dip because of the demonetization of two large denomination currencies and the introduction of goods and services tax (GST) by the central government (India Today, 2018). The COVID-19 pandemic further impacted the economy of India, by adversely affecting all sectors (Upadhyay, 2021). But, with the pandemic seeing a gradual end, India's fast-food sector is expected to grow rapidly until 2025 as McDonald's India and other brands resume their growth in the smaller cities of the country (Bansal, 2021).

The growth of McDonald's India and other fast-food restaurants in the nation happened during the 1990s and 2000s, when the growing GDP in the latter part of the 1990s and early part of the 2000s gave buying power and optimism to the growing middle class (Statista, 2002; Roy, 2018). In the early 2000s, Indian consumers spent 6.8% of their income on eating out, which was much higher than the 1.4% spent on entertainment (India Today, 2005).

The above reasons, coupled with factors such as rapid urbanization in India, dual-income families and changing lifestyles, growing familiarity with international cuisine, increase in living standards and the introduction of food courts and online ordering have aided in the growth of fast-food companies such as McDonald's (AIMS Institutes, n.d.).

Nation-wide McDonald's India had 527 stores and as of March 2023 (Chaturvedi, 2023; Sharma, 2023), it accounted for over 10% of the fast-food sector revenues in India (The Economic Times, 2018). Over the next decade, McDonald's India aims to open another 1,000 outlets, and the joint venture heads in India are adapting and working with the Indian regulatory requirements to achieve this goal (Goyal, 2021). This increase in exposure, alongside a visible upward trend among Indians to eat out more often, meant possibilities of greater market penetration for McDonald's India and other fast-food chains in the future (Singh, 2020).

As for telecommunications expansion, Reliance Jio – India's largest telecom network, launched the 4G data plan in 2016 and made it available to millions of Indians for free for the first six months, bringing with it around 400 million consumers online, and changing the face of the telecom industry (Ghosh, 2019; Business Standard, 2020). This launch accelerated the growth of the Indian online market even more. Currently, India is home to 700 million active Internet users, making it the world's second largest online (Farooqui, 2023). Such widespread accessibility to the Internet has helped propagate the nationalist ideology across the country.

In the case of McDonald's India, despite being placed on a pedestal for being one of the pioneers to crack the localization model in India with its vegetarian offerings, affordable food, and mindset change of a burger being a meal, the company had evidently underestimated the power of social media and its far-reaching consequences. Its tweet, while factual in nature and reiterated a business-driven decision, exhibited a lack of cultural and religious sensitivity toward the country it is operating in, failing to consider that majority of the population are not consumers of halal meat. While McDonald's started off on a good note when it began operations in India with efforts to localize, its adherence to one method of slaughter – in this case, halal – did not adapt to the evolving political and cultural landscape of the country (Kannan, 2014; Kuchay, 2019).

Media System

The number of Internet users in India, including rural regions, has grown exponentially over the two decades (Kantar & Internet and Mobile Association of India, 2021). Many users cite entertainment, communication, and social media as reasons for their Internet use with mobile phones as the most predominant way of accessing the Internet. In 2019, India had the cheapest Internet rates in the world (Roy, 2019) but lost the title in early 2021 to Israel. Even then, its average rate (US$0.68 per gigabyte) is still significantly below that of the global average (US$4.21 per gigabyte) (Bhalla, 2021). India had the largest number of Facebook users in the world, with 314.6 million users in early 2022 (Kemp, 2023). Twitter currently has 27.25 million Indian users, and many use social media primarily to stay connected with family and friends, read news stories and updates, and to watch videos (Kemp, 2023).

While rapid urbanization and Internet penetration have brought with them greater opportunities, it has also made businesses and even the government more susceptible to online public scrutiny. Social media has lent a voice to anyone and everyone with a smartphone and an Internet connection. Twitter, for example, is now used as a medium by many – from politicians to the common man – to share and influence opinions. Although content provided by social media is highly accessible, misinformation and disinformation are rampant and hard to combat, and such a phenomenon has a tremendous influence on individuals' perceptions, which can easily enhance or destroy corporate reputation. Because of this, the government has released new rules for big technology companies to follow the constitution and laws of India and effectively regulate social media content in the country (Choudhury, 2021a; PIB Delhi, 2021). These regulations were implemented after India asked Twitter to suspend more than 1,000 accounts that were allegedly spreading misinformation about farmers protesting, to which Twitter only partially fulfilled (Choudhury, 2021b).

Despite the growing ubiquity of the Internet and social media platforms, television still holds the largest audience segment in India, accounting for 40% of the Indian media market (India Brand Equity Foundation, 2021). Among the available channels, 43% are those providing news (Ernst & Young & FICCI, 2021), and the viewership share of such channels increased in 2020.

A key consideration for news outlets in India is how the news cycle now largely depends on where the interest of the audience lies (Gloviczki, 2015). Gone are the days of news outlets dictating the headlines as the Internet passed the power baton over to consumers – now, audiences are "talking forward" to news providers as they decide what they want to talk about and how they want to talk about it (Gloviczki, 2015). Therefore, to attract readers to their channels, India's mainstream media outlets are largely focused on sensational and eye-catching news that are trending on social media (Dhanesh & Sriramesh, 2018; Madan, 2022).

Given this current media landscape where netizens are used to instant responses from peers and even businesses, McDonald's attempt to do good customer service through replying quickly to a question must be commended. The tweet, which appeared to be a direct reply to a simple question, unfortunately triggered a religious firestorm leading to the #BoycottMcDonalds crisis. Instead of being proactive in its response, McDonald's India decided to be passive about the allegations. The company also remained evasive in terms of responding to the legal notices received (OpIndia, 2019b). This is a very different approach compared to what other companies have done in response to calls for boycotts – issue statements and communicate with their online audiences immediately to limit and repair the damage to their reputation. We surmise that McDonald's India's silence might have been an attempt to contain the crisis on Twitter, where the number of users is significantly smaller than that of Facebook, which is the most popular among Indians. In addition, silence meant limited coverage of the crisis in traditional media outlets forcing news agencies to move on to the next sensational and trending story.

On the surface, McDonald's India appeared to have benefited from using silence as a strategy since the incident did not escalate further, limiting the lifespan of the crisis. Had McDonald's India responded and defended itself online immediately, the crisis could have been more extensive and possibly sensationalized by both mainstream and online media. In the US, in 2020, a McDonald's franchisee was sued by a Muslim woman for religious discrimination including denying her permission to take prayer breaks and for sexual harassment (Kunzelman, 2020). In 2022, a settlement has been reached but details of which were not disclosed (Dorrian, 2022). The same year, a discrimination complaint had been filed against McDonald's in the US because employees knowingly served bacon to a Muslim family who ordered a fish sandwich (Pratt, 2022). Details of which are not yet available as of the writing of this chapter. In an earlier case, McDonald's was sued for hundreds of thousands of dollars related to serving halal-certified food (Hall, 2013). McDonald's has been involved in several religious discrimination complaints involving its food offerings and treatment of employees. In addition to financial ramifications, McDonald's reputation is repeatedly damaged, and thus, it could not afford another incident especially in a culturally and religiously diverse country like India.

While such a response strategy may look like the company was wise to "contain" damages in the short term, it is too early to determine the ramifications and losses that McDonald's India will face in the longer term since the negative perceptions generated by the crisis have not been nullified or addressed in the minds of millions of Indians. In the digitally driven environment that we live in today, stakeholders expect companies and brands to update them on important matters in real time. Further, with online spaces populated with unaddressed negative comments, such adverse news reports about the company will remain permanently in cyberspace and never be forgotten. Thus, it is imperative for companies to understand the media landscape in the country they wish to do business in and to train their employees on the proper communication techniques to not offend any group – majority or minority.

Societal Culture

In the context of societal culture, Hofstede's (2017) workplaces in India on a high score for Power Distance (77), an intermediate score for Individualism (48) and Long-term Orientation (51), a moderately high score for Masculinity (56), and a low score for Uncertainty Avoidance (40) and Indulgence (26). In the #BoycottMcDonalds crisis, India's high-Power Distance, moderately high Masculinity, and intermediate Individualism and Uncertainty Avoidance are particularly relevant.

High Power Distance denotes the acceptance of unequal distribution of power among the different segments of society (Hofstede, 2017). With India having diverse religions, the groups calling for the boycott of McDonald's India did so on the grounds that showing preference to halal-certified meat, which favored only one religious group, was not appropriate while neglecting the religious and cultural sentiments of the majority (India Today, 2019; Kramer, 2021). A moderately high Masculinity score denotes a visual display of success and power (Hofstede, 2017). The ruling government in India, and its pro-nationalist stance, has increased a sense of nationalism across the country (Frayer & Khan, 2019). This sense of nationalism is being exercised in a display of power against practices that are not aligned to the beliefs of the majority in the country and are deemed detrimental to their position – thus justifying the call for a boycott of McDonald's India for procuring halal-certified meat for its products (Khan, 2021; Kuchay, 2019; Vaishnav, 2019).

An intermediate Individualism score indicates a society with both collectivistic and individualistic traits – collectivism being displayed through high preference for the greater good of one's defined in-groups (Hofstede, 2017). The emergence of nationalism has given rise to a sense of in-groups among a section of the majority of the populace who consider preference toward halal-certified meat being discriminatory – the fact that a practice from a different faith is being unknowingly forced on others fueled the call for a boycott of McDonald's India (Khan, 2021; Paranjape, 2020; Vaishnav, 2019).

While a low Uncertainty Avoidance score indicates tolerance for the unexpected, incidents in India over the last few years have shown that there is a divide among Indians, who demonstrated a range of intolerant behavior not witnessed in the past (Hofstede, 2017; Krishnan, 2018; The Economist, 2020). While the halal method of slaughter has been practiced in India for years, with "halal certification" gaining popularity in the early part of the previous decade, it is only in recent years that a call for the boycott of halal products gained popularity in the country with the cases of food delivery service Zomato and McDonald's India (Chibber, 2013; Kader, 2021; The Week, 2019).

Given that Indian society is also collectivistic, this means that individuals take on their respective religious identities fervently as faith-based groups are usually very united and tightly knitted. Such strong group identities also breed polarization in the country. Hence, this polarity amplified the McDonald's India crisis as the tweet highlighted the practices of one group (a minority) being followed by the company in a country with diverse religions. The division was further driven by the instantaneous nature of social media, especially Twitter, where people are trigger-happy and are easily able to respond to those who do not share their own sentiments.

Activist Culture

Activism in India has had an enduring and well-established history; its roots can be traced to the nation's successful fight for independence from British rule (Sriramesh, 2018). In the 21st century, with greater economic development and the advent of social media, India has seen the ascent of new forms of protest, namely citizen activism (Sriramesh, 2018). Such activism involves individual citizens who emerge in the public spaces – whether physical or digital – in protest, but who do not view themselves as aligned with any political ideology (Singh, 2014 as cited in Sriramesh, 2018). While online and offline activism can manifest itself differently, it is often an extension of each other – what happens in the digital space can have an influence on real life (Bhatia, 2021). Both forms of activism are influenced by social identities, especially gender and religion (Bhatia, 2021). Even online activism, where activists are often assumed to be nameless and faceless "keyboard warriors," has not been spared from the power structures of gender, class, and religion, which can make it challenging to speak up and voice opinions (Bhatia, 2021).

Besides economic and technological developments, activism is shaped as much, if not more, by the political power in dominance, as well as social and cultural norms and expectations. Recent events – the Supreme Court taking control over the government's handling of the jobless migrant laborers' crisis during the COVID-19 lockdown, and the reversal in stance of the government over the contentious anti-Muslim National Register of Citizens and the Citizenship Amendment Act – lend proof to the growing power and impact of activism in India and the change it can bring about in the future (Khan, 2020). In the case of the McDonald's India crisis, citizen activism was largely contained online and carried out predominantly on Twitter. And in true social media fashion, McDonald's India received – almost instantly – major backlash from Twitter users for not only serving halal meat in its restaurants but openly declaring it through its tweets. The debates that raged online took on a distinctly religious slant, with people calling out McDonald's India for serving halal meat in a country of diverse religions and cultures. The devil was indeed in the (religious) details – comments online extended to the differences between and respective benefits of slaughtering animals the halal way, in accordance with

Islamic laws, or the jhatka way, as followed in Hinduism and Sikhism. Twitter responses and even threats from the public included messages such as the halal way of animal slaughter was more inhumane than that of the Hindus or Sikhs; they would urge others not to eat at the joints, and the fast-food chain would lose customers from these two groups and face financial ruin.

As mentioned earlier, offline, social worker Harish Sharma (OpIndia, 2019a) filed a legal notice against McDonald's India, seeking clarification on the fast-food chain's halal-only meat policy, asserting that the Islamic method of slaughter, which cannot be conducted by non-Muslims, demonstrates discrimination by McDonald's India against other religious groups who are involved in the business, thus denying them equal earning opportunities. Serving only halal meat, and not jhatka or kosher meat, he opined, also amounts to social, racial, and religious discrimination and violates basic rights listed in the country's constitution. Vishnu Gupta, National President of Hindu Sena, added that McDonald's India was ignoring the sensitivities of other religious groups and that it was not right for McDonald's India to "force halal meat" on those who eat jhatka meat (Kuchay, 2019).

However, there was also the other side of the camp, which took to Twitter and the media to air their thoughts, seemingly speaking on behalf of McDonald's India and saying that whether it is a halal way of killing the animal or not, it would still suffer, and that customers should not be irrational over such issues #BoycottMcDonalds.

Sushmita, a researcher based in New Delhi, announced that she did not care where her meat came from, preferring to focus on the processing of food and the amount of nutrients it contains (Kuchay, 2019). Sushmita described the Twitter war as a case of "everyday pitting of one community against another" and instilling hatred in Indian society. Activist Shabnam Hashmi from New Delhi saw the incident as yet another opportunity for one group to attack another. (Kuchay, 2019). Nishita Sood from Delhi asserted netizens were "making an issue out of a non-issue," and this stemmed from prejudice and bigotry against the another community (Kuchay, 2019).

India's economic development has allowed rapid urbanization and Internet penetration. The growing Internet-exposed population of India is being bombarded with religious hate and identity politics on both mainstream and social media (Mohsina, 2020). With most of the populace lacking digital media literacy, there has been a steep rise in religious intolerance in the country (Arya, 2020; Mohsina, 2020; The Financial Express, 2018).

This is not the first time that religious differences have caused conflicts in India. In August 2023, seven died in violent clashes between Hindus and Muslims in Gurugram, near the capital New Delhi, where a Hindu procession was attacked, and a mosque was burned in retaliation (Jain, 2023). A quick Internet search showed that the conflicts have been present as early as the

19th century when Muslims were given a different electorate than Hindus by the British (Pillalamarri, 2019). Regardless of the origin, the existence of these disputes cannot be denied. Having to fight for a particular side or in this case, religious belief, implies that activism has been around for a while, especially in a collectivist society with high power distance.

Particularly in India where there is high Power Distance and moderately high Masculinity, an organization must establish that they are aligned – or at least not in contradiction – with the religious beliefs and cultural sentiments of the various religions. MNCs must then be quick to review their sentiments and be cautious when taking stances. Given this context, it appears best for corporations in India to communicate with their stakeholders in a neutral tone such that no religion is favored over another while remaining personal and empathetic with their diverse audiences.

Conclusion

In 2019, McDonald's India found itself in the middle of a crisis stemming from its response to a tweet confirming that the meat they use is halal – as required by the Islamic faith. In a country with a religiously diverse population, the company drew negative sentiments from other religious groups that prefer its meat to be slaughtered differently as compared to halal meat. McDonald's India remained silent as the crisis played out online. While the use of silence in crisis communication has been criticized by scholars for not engaging proactively with key stakeholders and hence, not taking advantage of the opportunity to "steal the thunder," the case of McDonald's India suggests that keeping silent limits damages (financial, legal, and reputation) inflicted by the crisis on the global fast-food giant. However, we argue that silence is, at best, helping to ease the backlash temporarily. In the longer term, businesses may suffer greater losses as stakeholders' negative emotions and unhappiness are left to linger, hence possibly leading to greater aggravations should another issue about McDonald's India erupts.

This chapter analyzed the crisis in light of the socio-cultural factors in the country as discussed in Sriramesh and Vercic (2020). The company chose to remain silent given the current interactions of these factors. With the Internet being readily available to more Indians and the rise of online activism, individuals are given the confidence to share their sentiments online, show support for those who share their beliefs, and oppose those who do not. Moreover, as the mainstream media covers sensational and trending stories, it appeared that it was beneficial for McDonald's India to let the crisis run its course and "die" naturally on Twitter.

Ultimately, the #BoycottMcDonalds crisis shows how a single seemingly harmless response, if not well-thought-out, could lead to lasting damage to an organization. To reduce the prevalence of such incidents in the future, multinational corporations in India must be sensitive and aware of the different religious beliefs and traditions in the country. MNCs should ensure employees, especially those who face stakeholders online and offline, are knowledgeable on how to spot statements that are potentially insensitive or offensive to other religions and how to respond such that no crisis ensues. Furthermore, a crisis communication plan should be created so employees, in the absence of a crisis communication team, will know what to do if an issue erupts into a crisis. This is to ensure that the organization will be communicative during the crisis period and not remain silent as remaining silent is not always ideal. Silence could allow stakeholders online to fill the information vacuum with sentiments that might not necessarily reflect the stand of the organization. When this happens, it would make it difficult for the organization to communicate effectively to both its internal and external stakeholders and to successfully repair its corporate reputation.

References

AIMS Institutes (n.d.). Rise of the restaurant industry in India. AIMS Institutes. https://theaims.ac.in/resources/rise-of-the-restaurant-industry-in-india.html

Arya, S. (2020, December 26). RSS lookalike social media pages spew militant Hindutva. *The Times of India*. https://timesofindia.indiatimes.com/city/nagpur/rss-lookalike-social-media-pages-spew-militant-hindutva/articleshow/79958414.cms

Bansal, S. (2021, February 22). Indians still hungry for fast food: Report. *Mint*. https://www.livemint.com/news/india/indians-still-hungry-for-fast-food-report-11613997244459.html

Bhalla, K. (2021, April 14). As telcos push for higher ARPU, India no longer has the world's cheapest mobile data plans. *Inc42*. https://inc42.com/buzz/as-telcos-push-for-higher-arpu-india-no-longer-has-the-worlds-cheapest-mobile-data-plans/

Bhatia, K. V. (2021). The revolution will wear burqas: Feminist body politics and online activism in India. *Social Movement Studies*, *21*(5), 1–17. https://doi.org/10.1080/14742837.2021.1944850

Boyon, N. (2023, May 11). Two global religious divides: Geographic and generational. *Ipsos*. https://www.ipsos.com/en/two-global-religious-divides-geographic-and-generational

Business Standard. (2020). Jio becomes first telco to cross 400 million subscribers mark: Trai. https://www.business-standard.com/article/companies/jio-becomes-first-telco-to-cross-400-million-subscribers-mark-trai-120101201306_1.html

Chaturvedi, A. (2023, March 15). McDonald's north and east to invest up to ₹600 cr. *The Economic Times*. https://economictimes.indiatimes.com/industry/services/hotels-/-restaurants/mcdonalds-north-and-east-to-invest-up-to-600-cr/articleshow/98640917.cms?from=mdr

Chibber, A. (2013, June 13). India's halal story is one of missed opportunities. *Foodnavigator-Asia.Com*. https://www.foodnavigator-asia.com/Article/2013/06/14/India-s-halal-story-is-one-of-missed-opportunities

Choudhury, S. R. (2021a, February 11). India rebukes Twitter for not fully complying with government order to ban certain accounts. *CNBC*. https://www.cnbc.com/2021/02/11/india-rebukes-twitter-for-not-fully-complying-with-government-order.html

Choudhury, S. R. (2021b, April 20). India wants to cut big tech down to size. Critics say the new rules may give the state too much power. *CNBC*. https://www.cnbc.

com/2021/04/20/indias-social-media-law-puts-big-techs-power-into-states-hands-critics-say.html

Dhanesh, G. S., & Sriramesh, K. (2018). Culture and crisis communication: Nestle India's Maggi noodles case. *Journal of International Management*, *24*(3), 204–214. https://doi.org/10.1016/j.intman.2017.12.004

Dorrian, P. (2022, September 14). Muslim McDonald's worker settles suit over prayer breaks, hijab. *Bloomberg Law*. https://news.bloomberglaw.com/litigation/muslim-mcdonalds-worker-settles-suit-over-prayer-breaks-hijab

Eardley, N. (2014, May 12). What is halal meat? *BBC News*. https://www.bbc.com/news/uk-27324224

Ernst & Young & FICCI. (2021, March). *Playing by new rules: India's media & entertainment sector reboots in 2020. Ernst & Young Associates LLP.*

ET Online (2019, May 14). Vikram Bakshi is finally out and McDonald's India is lovin' it. *The Economic Times*. https://economictimes.indiatimes.com/industry/services/hotels-/-restaurants/vikram-bakshi-is-finally-out-and-mcdonalds-india-is-lovin-it/articleshow/69309704.cms?from=mdr

Euromonitor International. (2021). *Consumer Foodservice in India*. https://www.euromonitor.com/consumer-foodservice-in-india/report

Farooqui, J. (2023, March 16). Report says over 700 million active internet users in India as of December 2022. *The Economic Times*. https://economictimes.indiatimes.com/tech/technology/report-says-over-700-million-active-internet-users-in-india-as-of-december-2022/articleshow/98673654.cms

Frayer, L., & Khan, F. L. (2019, May 3). The powerful group shaping the rise of Hindu nationalism in India. *NPR*. https://www.npr.org/2019/05/03/706808616/the-powerful-group-shaping-the-rise-of-hindu-nationalism-in-india

Friend, E. (2013, December 24). Third-ranked KFC is winning the fast food battle in India. *Euromonitor International*. https://www.euromonitor.com/article/third-ranked-kfc-is-winning-the-fast-food-battle-in-india-for-now

Ghosh, S. (2019, August 18). How the 'Jio effect' brought millions of Indians online and is reshaping Silicon Valley and the internet. *Business Insider*. https://www.businessinsider.in/how-the-jio-effect-brought-millions-of-indians-online-and-is-reshaping-silicon-valley-and-the-internet/articleshow/70723349.cms

Gloviczki, P. (2015). *Journalism and memorialization in the age of social media* (2015th ed.). Palgrave Macmillan. https://doi.org/10.1057/9781137460875

Goyal, S., (2021, September 7). 25 years on, is McDonald's a success in India? *Campaign India*. https://www.campaignindia.in/article/blog-25-years-on-is-mcdonalds-a-success-in-india/472393

Hall, J. (2013, January 23). McDonald's pays out $700,000 to Muslim community after restaurant "falsely claimed its food was halal." *The Independent*. https://www.independent.co.uk/news/world/americas/mcdonald-s-pays-out-700-000-muslim-community-after-restaurant-falsely-claimed-its-food-was-halal-8463070.html

Hindustan Times. (2013, July 17). 780 languages spoken in India, 250 died out in last 50 years. https://www.hindustantimes.com/books/780-languages-spoken-in-india-250-died-out-in-last-50-years/story-Y3by8ooYbXRA77xP2AEWKN.html

Hofstede Insights. (2017, August). *India*. https://www.hofstede-insights.com/country/india/

India Brand Equity Foundation. (2021, October 12). Media and entertainment industry in India, Indian media industry. https://www.ibef.org/industry/media-entertainment-india.aspx

India Today. (2005, July 11). Urban India picks up taste for eating out. https://www.indiatoday.in/society-&-the-arts/story/20050711-indain-food-industry-growing-as-indians-eating-out-more-than-787348-2005-07-11

India Today. (2018, January 6). Thanks to demonetization and GST, India's GDP growth hit a 4-year low at 6.5 per cent. https://www.indiatoday.in/education-today/gk-&-current-affairs/story/demonetization-gst-slowed-down-gdp-growth-of-india-1123939-2018-01-06

India Today. (2019, August 23). #BoycottMcDonalds trends online after they say they serve halal meat. So food has religion, says internet. https://www.indiatoday.in/trending-news/story/boycott-mcdonalds-trends-halal-food-religion-zomato-1590737-2019-08-23

Jain, R. (2023, August 3). Hindu-Muslim riots expose risk at major Indian business hub. *Reuters*. https://www.reuters.com/world/india/hindu-muslim-riots-expose-risk-major-indian-business-hub-2023-08-03/

Kader, S. A. (2021, January 17). Halal even by no name: India continues to export meat by Islamic requirements despite gov't dropping the h word. *Salaam Gateway*. https://www.salaamgateway.com/story/halal-even-by-no-name-india-continues-to-export-meat-by-islamic-requirements-despite-govt-dropping-t

Kannan, S., (2014, November 19). How McDonald's conquered India. *BBC*. https://www.bbc.com/news/business-30115555

Kantar & Internet and Mobile Association of India. (2021, June). Internet adoption in India. *Kantar*. https://images.assettype.com/afaqs/2021-06/b9a3220f-ae2f-43db-a0b4-36a372b243c4/KANTAR_ICUBE_2020_Report_C1.pdf

Kemp, S., (2023, February 13). Digital 2023: India. *Datareportal*. https://datareportal.com/reports/digital-2023-india

Khan, S. (2021, September 9). Why #SayNoToHalal is trending on Twitter? *The Siasat Daily*. https://www.siasat.com/why-saynotohalal-is-trending-on-twitter-2189577/

Khan, S. U. (2020, May 28). Activism may be a dirty word in Modi's India, but it still works. Here are 3 recent examples. *ThePrint*. https://theprint.in/opinion/pov/activism-still-works-in-india-here-are-3-recent-examples/431123/

Kramer, S. (2021, September). Religious Composition of India. *Pew Research Center*. https://www.pewforum.org/2021/09/21/religious-composition-of-india/

Krishnan, M. (2018, February 2). India's intolerance is hurting the country. *The Lowly Institute*. https://www.lowyinstitute.org/the-interpreter/indias-intolerance-hurting-country

Kuchay, B. (2019, August 26). McDonald's faces boycott threats in India for serving halal meat. *Al Jazeera*. https://www.aljazeera.com/economy/2019/8/26/mcdonalds-faces-boycott-threats-in-india-for-serving-halal-meat

Kunzelman, M. (2020, August 14). Muslim woman accuses McDonald's franchisee of discrimination. *AP NEWS*. https://apnews.com/article/religious-discrimination-religion-discrimination-thurgood-marshall-business-d377475db86fddfd51f0e86eaf158923

Le, P. D., Teo, H. X., Pang, A., Li, Y., & Goh, C. Q. (2019). When is silence golden? The use of strategic silence in crisis communication. *Corporate Communications: An International Journal*, *24*(1), 162–178. https://doi.org/10.1108/ccij-10-2018-0108

Madan, G. D. (2022). Understanding misinformation in India: The case for a meaningful regulatory approach for social media platforms. Cornell University. https://arxiv.org/abs/2207.01508

McDonald's India [@mcdonaldsindia]. (2019a, August 23). Thank you for taking the time to contact McDonald's India. We truly appreciate this opportunity to respond to your comments. The meat that we use, across our restaurants, is of the highest quality and is sourced from government-approved suppliers who are HACCP certified. (1/2) [Tweet]. *Twitter*. https://twitter.com/mcdonaldsindia/status/1164583979883753472

McDonald's India [@mcdonaldsindia]. (2019b, August 23). All our restaurants have HALAL certificates. You can ask the respective restaurant managers to show you the certificate for your satisfaction and confirmation. (2/2) [Tweet]. *Twitter*. https://twitter.com/mcdonaldsindia/status/1164584030647377920

Mishra, B., & Dwivedi, S. (2013). Success story of mc. d in India: Story of its struggle in Indian market. *Asian Journal of Science and Technology*, *4*(07), 066–070.

Mohsina, N. (2020, October 22). Hindutva vigilantism: Online hate, offline harms. *Global Network on Extremism & Technology*. https://gnet-research.org/2020/10/22/hindutva-vigilantism-online-hate-offline-harms/

OpIndia (2019a, 1 October) Buying only halal meat and not jhatka, kosher is discriminatory: McDonald's India gets legal notice. *OpIndia*. https://www.opindia.com/2019/10/buying-only-halal-meat-and-not-jhatka-kosher-is-discriminatory-mcdonalds-india-gets-legal-notice/

OpIndia. (2019b, October 3). McDonald's India gets second legal notice for evasive reply regarding their 'Only halal meat' policy in their restaurants. *OpIndia*. https://www.opindia.com/2019/10/mcdonalds-india-halal-meat-second-notice/

Paranjape, M. R. (2020, June 13). Hindus, halal and political correctness. *The Indian Express*. https://www.newindianexpress.com/opinions/2020/jun/13/hindus-halal-and-political-correctness-2155982.html

Pew Research Center. (2017, April). Global restrictions on religion rise modestly in 2015, reversing downward trend. https://www.pewforum.org/2017/04/11/global-restrictions-on-religion-rise-modestly-in-2015-reversing-downward-trend/

PIB Delhi. (2021, February 21). Government notifies Information Technology (IntermediaryGuidelines and Digital Media Ethics Code) Rules 2021. https://pib.gov.in/PressReleseDetailm.aspx?PRID=1700749

Pillalamarri, A. (2019, March 16). The origins of Hindu-Muslim conflict in South Asia. *The Diplomat*. https://thediplomat.com/2019/03/the-origins-of-hindu-muslim-conflict-in-south-asia/

Pratt, M. (2022, June 1). Complaint: McDonald's intentionally sold Muslim family bacon. *AP NEWS*. https://apnews.com/article/health-religion-massachusetts-islam-c6148debbd2615017029c3ee1526c577

Profile – National Portal of India. (2021). National Portal of India. https://www.india.gov.in/india-glance/profile

Roy, A, (2018). The middle class in India: From 1947 to the present and beyond. *Association for Asian Studies*, *23*(1), 32–37. Asian Politics.

Roy, P. K. (2019, March 18). Mobile data: Why India has the world's cheapest. *BBC News*. https://www.bbc.com/news/world-asia-india-47537201

Sharma, A. (2023, May 9). McDonald's India franchisee Westlife Foodworld to add 580-630 new restaurants by 2027. *ETRetail.com*. https://retail.economictimes.indiatimes.com/news/food-entertainment/food-services/mcdonalds-india-franchisee-westlife-foodworld-to-add-580-630-new-restaurants-by-2027/100101334

Singh, R. (2014). New citizens' activism in India: Moments, movements, and mobilisation. *Center for Democracy and Social Action*. https://www.boell.de/sites/default/files/study-new-citizens-activism-in-india.pdf

Singh, S. S., (2020, August 11). How American fast food gets desifide in India. *The Teal Mango*. https://www.thetealmango.com/latest/desified-american-fast-food-india/

Social Blade. (n.d.). Top 25 Twitter Users by Followers. https://socialblade.com/twitter/

Sriramesh, K., & Vercic, D. (2020). *The global public relations handbook: Theory, research, and practice (third edition)*. Routledge.

Statista. (2002, May 18). India: Gross domestic product (GDP) in current prices from 1987 to 2027. https://www.statista.com/statistics/263771/gross-domestic-product-gdp-in-india/

Tewari, S., & Nair, P. (2021, October 22). How brands can control narratives and fight cancel culture. *CNBC*. https://www.cnbctv18.com/advertising/storyboard-how-brands-can-control-narratives-and-fight-cancel-culture-11177832.htm

TFIPOST. (2019, August 27). Legal notice against McDonald's for shoving halal meat down the throats of customers. https://tfipost.com/2019/08/mcdonalds-legal-notice-halal-ishkaran-singh-bhandari-01/

The Economic Times (2018, December 26). After 22 years, McDonald's makes its 1st India profit. *The Economic Times*. https://economictimes.indiatimes.com/industry/services/hotels-/-restaurants/after-22-years-mcdonalds-makes-its-1st-india-profit/profit-after-two-decades/slideshow/67256485.cms

The Economist. (2020, January 27). Narendra Modi stokes divisions in the world's biggest democracy. https://www.economist.com/leaders/2020/01/23/narendra-modi-stokes-divisions-in-the-worlds-biggest-democracy

The Financial Express. (2018, September 24). A look at India's deep digital literacy divide and why it needs to be bridged. https://www.financialexpress.com/education-2/a-look-at-indias-deep-digital-literacy-divide-and-why-it-needs-to-be-bridged/1323822/

The Indian Express. (2020, December 26). 'Halal' meat against Hinduism, Sikhism, restaurants must specify: South Delhi Body. https://indianexpress.com/article/cities/delhi/halal-meat-against-hinduism-sikhism-restaurants-must-specify-south-delhi-body-7120423/

The Quint. (2023, March 10). Bharat matrimony's holi ad draws flak: Why are there calls for boycott? https://www.thequint.com/gender/bharat-matrimony-holi-festival-advertisement-violence-against-women-backlash

The Week. (2019, August 23). Now, McDonald's faces boycott call for serving halal meat. https://www.theweek.in/news/india/2019/08/23/after-zomato-mcdonalds-faces-the-heat-for-serving-halal-meat.html

The Wire Analysis. (2020, March 3). "Thinking of giving up": How Narendra Modi has used social media to fuel his politics. *The Wire*. https://thewire.in/politics/narendra-modi-social-media-account

Upadhyay, A. (2021, July 24). Impact of Covid-19 on Indian economy. *Times of India*. https://timesofindia.indiatimes.com/readersblog/mymusiclife/impact-of-covid-19-on-indian-economy-4-35585/

Vaishnav, M. (2019, April 4). Religious nationalism and India's future. *Carnegie Endowment for International Peace*. https://carnegieendowment.org/2019/04/04/religious-nationalism-and-india-s-future-pub-78703

Wells, T. (2020, September 2). What's so good about the pricing strategy of McDonald's India? *Taylor Wells*. https://taylorwells.com.au/pricing-strategy-of-mcdonalds-in-india/

Westlife Development Limited. (2020). Annual Report 2019–2020. https://www.bseindia.com/bseplus/AnnualReport/505533/65160505533.pdf

4

MALAYSIA

Environmentalists Rally Against MNC Over Radioactive Waste

Ryan Lim and Nikole Wong

Introduction

Malaysia, well known as a resource- and culture-rich country, has undergone rapid development to meet the global needs of the 21st century. Intertwining its cultural traditions with modern developments such as a revitalized economic system and a diverse media landscape, its progress has been met with several high-profile crises. One of the more notable crises is the 1Malaysia Development Board Berhad (1MDB) scandal involving former Malaysian Prime Minister Najib Razak, who was found guilty of laundering RM$42 million (US$9.5 million) (Bedi, 2022). Malaysia has also gone through several changes in political administration following the 2018 election, where the ruling political party Barisan Nasional (BN) lost to the opposition, Pakatan Harapan (PH) (New Straits Times, 2018). However, from February 2020 to 2022, in a political maneuvering dubbed the "Sheraton Move," several members of the PH government defected from their parliamentary positions to form a new coalition, Perikatan Nasional (PN). As a result, PH and former Prime Minister Dr Mahathir Mohamad lost the parliamentary majority to run the country. Mahathir's resignation led to the appointment of PN's leader, Muhyiddin Yassin, as Prime Minister (Reuters, 2020). Political instability, exacerbated by the COVID-19 pandemic, saw Muhyiddin Yassin ousted from power after only 17 months, and Ismail Sabri Yaakob took his place. In 2022, Malaysia's 15th General Election resulted in a hung parliament with no clear winner, and after days of negotiation, Anwar Ibrahim was appointed to lead a unity government (Teoh, 2022).

These high-profile crises overshadowed an economic, environmental, and health crisis that had been brewing since 2011 – Lynas Corporation Ltd's

DOI: 10.4324/9781003411802-5

operation of the Lynas Advanced Materials Plant and its unsafe disposal of radioactive waste. Under normal circumstances, a crisis of such scale and severity would warrant global attention and a comprehensive crisis management response strategy. This chapter highlights how the significance of Lynas Corporation Ltd's role in Malaysia's political and economic systems mitigated the impact of other socio-cultural variables and left the company relatively unscathed in a crisis that was brought to the fore by activists including environmentalists.

The Lynas Crisis

The reputation of companies is increasingly measured by the perceived ability to strike a balance between being effective profit-makers and pillars of the country's economy while also practicing corporate responsibility. Prior to 2012, China dominated the rare earth processing industry with no other viable alternative outside of the country (Fujita, 2022). As countries and multinational companies are increasingly conscious of the geopolitical tensions between the United States and China, the development of the Lynas Advanced Materials Plant in Malaysia is a political and economic success for the Malaysian government as they offer the only comparable alternative for rare earth elements processing outside of China (Stratfor Worldview, 2019, para. 2). The intertwining of Lynas' significant contribution to the Malaysian economy and the country's regional positioning became an effective bulwark against the subpar management of radioactive waste (Lynas Corporation Ltd, 2018e). This chapter examines how Malaysia's political and economic systems were favorable to Lynas' ability to overcome the crisis despite a lackluster crisis management response.

Brief Overview of Lynas

Lynas is an Australian rare earth elements (REE) mining company listed on the Australian Securities Exchange. The company has two major operations – a mining and concentration plant in Mount Weld, Western Australia, and a refining facility in Kuantan (Malaysia) called the Lynas Advanced Materials Plant (LAMP) (Lynas Corporation Ltd, 2021b). The development and operations of the refining facility in Malaysia remain contentious due to its impact on the local community, evidenced by a previous incident. In 1982, Asia Rare Earth Sendirian Berhad (ARE Sdn Bhd), an REE extraction company located in the state of Perak, extracted yttrium, an REE from monazite, which resulted in radioactive waste that caused eight people living in the community to develop leukemia, seven of whom died (Bradsher, 2011). This led to a protracted lawsuit before Mitsubishi Chemical, a majority shareholder of the firm, reached an out-of-court settlement with victims, donated US$164,000 to community schools, and spent an additional US$100 million to clean up the area. Reeling from the environmental pollution and health issues arising from ARE Sdn Bhd's pollution in Perak, Malaysians opposed the use of 250 acres of reclaimed swampland in the state of Pahang for the construction of LAMP, which is the world's biggest REE refinery outside of China (Raghu & Koswanage, 2012). Despite persistent protests by locals, the Malaysian government led by former Prime Minister Najib Razak, with the support of the BN, dismissed their appeals and approved LAMP's operations. LAMP began operations in 2012, and the management of radioactive waste as a result of REE processing evolved into an electoral issue that was discussed in the lead-up to the 2018 Malaysian General Election.

The Lynas crisis was a result of a political transition that led to greater scrutiny of LAMP's operations. Following the loss by the BN in the 2018 Malaysian General Election and the ouster of former Prime Minister Najib, the new government led by PH initiated a review of LAMP's operations (Looi, 2018) with intentions of ceasing its operations. The crisis of Lynas and LAMP in Malaysia demonstrated how deeply entrenched political factors were in every dimension of daily life, highlighting the theme of this book, which is that socio-political variables play a significant role in crisis communication. This also affected Lynas's crisis response strategy as the precedence set by the Malaysian government resulted in the lack of localized responses. It highlighted a gap in Lynas's crisis preparedness to account for first, local sensitivity, and second, the need to address a long-term issue of LAMP's operations, which evolved into a political football.

In September 2018, Lynas faced closure of operations at LAMP when media reports speculated that the PH-led government would appoint an anti-Lynas advocate to review its operations (Ong, 2018). The company released a statement in September 2018 saying that it was aware that a government review may occur, that the government had its full cooperation, and that it was "committed to Zero Harm for our people, environment and communities and have evidence that supports the safety of our operations on all 3 criteria" (Lynas Corporation Ltd, 2018a, para. 7). Following that, Lynas's chief executive and managing director, Amanda Lacaze, penned an open letter seeking clarification on the speculations and fair treatment from the Malaysian government (Jamasmie, 2018; Lacaze, 2018a). Soon after, the government confirmed that the review would be led by Fuziah Salleh, a long-time advocate against LAMP (Reuters, 2018). Scheduled to last three months, the review dealt a blow to already-delayed operations at the plant and also caused the company's share prices to dip by 27% on the Australian Securities Exchange (Sanderson & Palma, 2018, para. 10). Amidst concerns that the executive review committee would be led by an anti-Lynas advocate, a new independent six-member committee was formed by the PH-led government after "attempts by Lynas to spin the issue" (Alagesh, 2018, para. 2), which had claimed that the review process was biased against them.

A public hearing was held in November 2018 in Kuantan, before the review committee submitted the report of its findings (Stutt, 2018).

Crisis Response Strategies and Stakeholders

To mitigate the crisis, Lynas tapped into their in-market presence and utilized three crisis response strategies to reach the following stakeholder groups: (1) Lynas Corporation Ltd's (hereby called Lynas) employees, whose jobs and livelihoods were affected by the potential closure of LAMP; (2) Activists such as the Save Malaysia Stop Lynas group, seen as the main antagonists of LAMP's operations since 2011 and have strong public support over the years; (3) the Executive Review Committee, and by direct relation, the then-ruling PH government, who formed the committee to represent their interests in the review process; and (4) local and international English media outlets, whom Lynas directed their press releases and executive statements at to reach English-speaking communities and company shareholders.

The first strategy was an English media campaign to spotlight Malaysian employees. English, instead of Malay, was used as Lynas is an Australian firm, where English is the predominant language, and this was demonstrated by the sole presence of a global English webpage (Lynas Corporation Ltd, 2021a). Two advertorials featured employee testimonials that highlighted how Lynas had improved their livelihoods, promoted an inclusive working environment, of how it ensured safety, environmental and training standards, and how Lynas had positively impacted the lives of residents living in the vicinity of LAMP (Lynas Corporation Ltd, 2018c; Lynas Corporation Ltd, 2018d). Additionally, the company published a fact sheet on Lynas Malaysia's operations, featuring the vice-president of Lynas Malaysia, academics, and scientists (Lynas Corporation Ltd, 2018b).

The second strategy showcased the economic impact that Lynas had in Malaysia as a foreign direct investor. In November 2018, Lynas published an Economic Impact report detailing several important economic benefits, including a cumulative RM$2.6 billion contribution to Malaysia's Gross Domestic Product (GDP), Malaysia's position as the only REE processor outside of China, the creation of skilled jobs in the state and the increase in local investment around Gebeng (Lynas Corporation Ltd, 2018e). Lacaze also allayed the concerns of shareholders at the company's annual general meeting by relating with their frustration, saying that "we [Lynas] will work diligently to move our way through this" (Kruger, 2018, para. 11).

The third strategy was an attempt to shift attention from the issue of radioactive waste to other topics such as the livelihood of Malaysian employees and misinformation. This took place on Twitter, which was Lacaze's go-to channel. On October 11, 2018, Lacaze tweeted that the attempt to shut down the

REE processing plant may only be a matter of jobs to the government, but it would have a greater impact on the wider community of employees, and thus she was committed to supporting them (Lacaze, 2018b). She addressed the issue of safety when the findings of the Review Committee were released:

> *The health and well being of our staff and surrounding communities is always our first priority. Our people and communities deserve accurate information.*
>
> (Lacaze, 2018c)

This tweet attempted to shift attention away from the Malaysian government, and the disinformation that anti-Lynas protestors had been spreading. In addition, she tweeted her support for the employees who organized a peaceful protest outside of the Malaysian parliament, which highlighted that the company, the livelihoods of its employees and their families, were affected:

> *I'm so proud of the Lynas Malaysia team. They visited parliament today to ask for their voices to be heard: [Link]*
>
> (Lacaze, 2018d)

Domain experts also contributed their views on the crisis and supported the findings of the Review Committee, contrary to the claims made by anti-Lynas protestors. In a letter published in the *New Straits Times*, Professor Datuk Dr Ahmad Ibrahim supported the decision of the government to include non-affiliated experts in the reviewing process and noted that Lynas had adhered to the international standards on safety (Ibrahim, 2018). He also criticized anti-Lynas protestors and their "claims of health-threatening radiation levels" (Ibrahim, 2018, para. 28), shifting the attention to the demonstrators and the misinformation that they had spread regarding Lynas and its operations.

The crisis subsided after the Executive Review committee released findings stating that the operations of the plant had "low risk and highly compliant with applicable laws" (Lynas Corporation Ltd, 2018f, para. 3). The ruling PH-led government backtracked on its earlier intentions to shut Lynas and extended the company's operating license on the condition that it would identify a permanent facility to store its radioactive waste (Reuters, 2019b).

Impact of Socio-cultural Variables on the Crisis

This crisis is unique because even though Lynas failed to contextualize its response strategies and was unprepared in addressing a long-standing issue that had been opposed by various stakeholders since 2011, the influence of the political and economic system mitigated the mistakes the company made, resulting in the crisis blowing over with minimal reputational damage. We next analyze the effect that the Malaysian political and economic systems had on Lynas' crisis communication and mitigated the impact of the media system, societal and organizational culture, and activism, allowing Lynas to avert devastating consequences and retain its license to operate in the country. In doing so, we will be highlighting the tension between Lynas's lack of understanding of Malaysian socio-cultural contexts discussed in Chapter 1 and the significance that the company had for Malaysia in the global economy.

Political System

Malaysia's political system is a federal parliamentary constitutional monarchy, where the Yang di-Pertuan Agong or king as the head of state appoints a prime minister from the House of Representatives (Dewan Rakyat) to preside over the Cabinet (Central Intelligence Agency, 2022; Grote, 2016). The 222 members of the House of Representatives are elected through general elections every five years. During the run-up to the general elections, candidates would announce campaign promises on highly salient issues to garner support. Public outcry over Lynas's mismanagement of its radioactive waste disposal was on the campaign agenda of the opposition coalition Pakatan Harapan (PH) during the 2018 General Elections.

In 2012, despite public opposition, the plan to develop LAMP in Malaysia was approved by then Prime Minister Najib Razak and his party, BN (Phua, 2016). The government strongly defended the project, and Najib assured the public that the government had "studied the project and [they] have come out with scientific evidence endorsed by local and international experts that the Lynas plant and REE residues are safe" (Malaysian Insider, 2012). During the 2013 General Elections, the opposition parties announced commitments to review the LAMP project and potentially close it. This resulted in Lynas's share value dropping more than 13% (Steger & Hoyle, 2013). To calm stakeholders and shareholders, Lynas emphasized that its "real-time independent monitoring of environmental data from the Lynas Advanced Materials Plant (LAMP) in Malaysia verifies no increase in radiological risk and that all emissions and discharges are below permissible limits" (Lynas Corporation Ltd, 2013, p. 5).

The inflection point occurred during the 2018 General Elections when the opposition coalition PH, led by former Prime Minister Dr Mahathir, trumped BN at the polls. During PH's electoral campaign, Mahathir and his party included Promise 39 within their election manifesto – to protect people's welfare and environmental sustainability as well as to not be dictated by large corporations and asserted his commitment to hold Lynas accountable for their mismanagement (The Straits Times, 2019a). The PH government was quick to initiate a review of Lynas's long-standing environmental concerns and the radioactive waste created during processing, with speculation of an imminent closure of LAMP (Looi, 2018; Ong, 2018). Media reports on the issue resulted in a fall in Lynas's shares by 27% (Sanderson & Palma, 2018, para. 10). Lynas plunged into crisis at the risk of operations being ceased, which undermined investor confidence in the company's outlook. The expediency of launching a review of Lynas shortly after taking office bolstered perceptions that former Mahathir and his government were committed to fulfilling their electoral promise during the first year of their term.

However, Lynas's second crisis response strategy of reinforcing the company's economic impact on the Malaysian economy was an effective reminder to the government. In 2019, the government shifted its position and extended Lynas's operating license for six months (Teoh, 2019). This happened in response to the trade war between the United States (US) and China (Reuters, 2019b), and a license extension ensured that Malaysia was the only country outside of China to have rare earths production capabilities, making them a valued trade partner for the US and the rest of the world. Pressure from Japanese-backed lobbyists also contributed to the reversal of position after Lynas signed a ten-year loan extension with Japanese companies and committed to double the supply of REEs (Reuters, 2019a). This elevated Malaysia's position in a highly valued and monopolized sector, enhancing its international economic competitiveness and benefitting the local economy in the long run. Hundreds of anti-Lynas protesters rallied against the government's reversal, with several tearing up Promise 39 of the PH's manifesto, noting the party's significant departure from its original electoral promise (The Straits Times, 2019a). In response, Mahathir publicly stated that "Lynas Corp cannot be treated as an outcast as it is a necessary investment that has created many quality jobs for Malaysia" (The Straits Times, 2019b, para. 1). PH had vowed to govern based on sustainable development, but Mahathir's contradictory remarks indicated a reshuffling of interests – Lynas's significant contribution to the Malaysian economy and Malaysia's international standing as having the largest REE producer outside of China – ahead of the Malaysian people's interest. This shift in position greatly benefited Lynas as it ensured that its license to operate remains and demonstrated the significant influence that the political sphere had – the political will of the incumbent government to elevate Malaysia in the international trade order was largely the deciding factor in mitigating the impact of the crisis on Lynas.

Economic System

The Malaysian economy is organized by the formula of "a variety of private freedom, combined with centralized economic planning and government regulation" (Michigan State University, 2022, para. 1). This section examines the strategic importance that Lynas had in the Malaysian economic system and how it became "too big to fail," which ultimately led to the dissolution of the crisis and Lynas's continued license to operate. Located in the heart of resource-rich Southeast Asia, Malaysia is a major trading hub and is the fourth biggest economy in the 10-member Association of Southeast Asian Nations (ASEAN) (Murugiah, 2021, para. 6). Maritime trading remains a cornerstone of the Malaysian economy with approximately 98% of the country's trade conducted via sea (Malaysian Investment Development Authority, 2021). Its status as an ASEAN member also plays a key role, giving the country access to various free trade agreements that promote the free flow of goods (ASEAN Secretariat, 2022). As a politically neutral association, ASEAN, and therefore Malaysia, is one of the few bridging points outside of the spheres of Chinese and American manufacturing. This includes the trade of vital goods such as REEs, which accorded Lynas its strategic importance in the Malaysian economic system.

Since its independence, the country has relied heavily on trade and the inflow of Foreign Direct Investments (FDIs) for economic growth. According to The World Bank (2022), 40% of the total jobs in Malaysia are related to the export sector. The reliance on FDIs is also demonstrated through economic commitments made by the Malaysian government, such as the rollout of a series of short-term recovery measures known as the Pelan Jana Semula Ekonomi Negara (PENJANA) to attract more FDIs (Onn, 2021).

Despite the progress made over the past decades, Malaysia still lags behind other high-income economies such as Hong Kong, Japan, and Singapore. To compete, the government had to adopt a new development model that prioritizes "the quality of schooling to improve learning outcomes, rethinking nutritional interventions to reduce childhood stunting, and providing adequate social welfare protection for household investments in human capital formation" (The World Bank, 2022, para. 6). However, substantial global and local shocks have affected the economy. The government had since become more cautious with the COVID-19 pandemic, prolonged geopolitical uncertainties, and a looming recession (Tan, 2022).

The Malaysian government identified REE as a niche area that the country could monopolize. REEs are critical components in the development of modern technology such as mobile phones, electric cars, and weapons (Lu, 2021). Capitalizing on this, the Malaysian Investment Development Authority (MIDA) has been promoting REE in the Promotion of Investment Act 1986 (Malaysian Investment Development Authority, 2022). Although REE deposits can be found all over the world, China had dominated the industry by 2010, accounting for 97% of the global REE supply (Fujita, 2022). To incentivize Lynas to build LAMP in Malaysia, the government offered a 12-year tax break to construct the plant (Bradsher, 2013). LAMP is the world's largest processing plant outside of China and is a main driver of economic performance for both Lynas and Malaysia (Cholteeva, 2021). The expected annual output of the plant was equivalent to 1%, or US$1.7 billion, of the total economic output of Malaysia, and the company had plans to contribute 0.05% of the plant's income to the Malaysian Atomic Energy Licensing Board to fund radiation research efforts (Bradsher, 2013).

The investment in midstream industries of the REE ecosystem enabled Malaysia to position itself at the forefront of the REE global trade. The presence of Lynas and LAMP in Malaysia was of great importance as the country became an alternative supplier for countries such as Japan and the US, who were looking to reduce dependency on Chinese supplies. The motivation to reduce dependency on China's supply of REE was exacerbated amid geopolitical tensions as China threatened to embargo its REE exports to the US and Japan in 2010 (Stratfor Worldview, 2019, para. 2). With LAMP, Malaysia became a leading global exporter of REE as the plant has the capacity to meet a third of global demand.

The success of specialized companies, such as Lynas, is highly dependent on the political environment in which they operate. In this case, when a publicly listed company faces scrutiny during a crisis, coupled with the risk of economic loss resulting from public and government opposition (Coombs, 2019, p. 13), the company would respond in a strategic and thoughtful manner. However, Lynas escaped mostly unscathed as there was a strong incentive for the continued support of its operations to advance Malaysia's economic standing and fulfilling the demands of Japanese backers who were determined to secure a long-term supply of REEs from Lynas (Reuters, 2019a). Its economic contribution to Malaysia amid increasing geopolitical tensions meant that LAMP became "too big to fail," as evidenced by the findings of the executive review committee and its continued license to operate in the country.

Media System

Developments in Malaysia's diverse media system have resulted in multiple platforms for Malaysians to readily access the news, voice their opinions, gather support for their cause, and hold government and companies accountable for their wrongdoing. Although there remains a monopoly of ownership of print broadcast and digital media by the government and major political parties, control in the media has diffused across licensed media outlets, independent news organizations, and the Malaysian people.

Following PH's victory in Malaysia's 2018 General Elections, local and international websites that were critical of the government were made accessible, giving Malaysians a greater range of media outlets to access information from (BBC, 2020). In parallel, private and state-owned news outlets that were affiliated with BN started to produce more politically neutral coverage due to reduced political pressure and coercion (Freedom House, 2019). However, media ownership did not diffuse. Political actors attempted to gain control of the digital news environment by buying online news portals (Zain, 2022). This was done through the following major Malaysian media companies – Media Prima, Utusan Melayu, Star Media Group, Astro, and Media Chinese International Limited, a representation of the "politics-media nexus in Malaysia" (Zain, 2022, para. 4). On top of monopolized ownership, media freedom was impacted by the COVID-19 pandemic after the Malaysian government utilized its emergency powers to enact a new law that targeted misinformation about the pandemic or the country's state of emergency, subject to the interpretation of the authorities (Sipalan, 2021).

Malaysia is well connected with infrastructure in place for its people to access the Internet. With 30.25 million active social media users at the start of 2022, social media has an 89.6% penetration rate (Kemp, 2022). The most used social media platform is Facebook, followed by Instagram, TikTok, and Twitter. The growing popularity of social media among Malaysians is parallel to their increasing reliance on online news outlets and social media as main sources of information (Zain, 2022). Social media also serves as a "great leveller and a democratic force that has opened up a new realm for wider public participation on societal issues, especially in countries where traditional media is controlled by the ruling establishment" (Kaur, 2015, p. 311). This allowed social media users to frame narratives that resonated with larger rural Malaysian communities in real-time, and in their native languages such as Malay or Mandarin Chinese, which Lynas avoided using in its communication efforts. Over time, a collective movement that transcended geographical distance was formed, evidenced by the growing anti-Lynas sentiments when plans to construct LAMP were first announced. Tim et al. (2018), in their study on rural Malaysia, found that the use of social media by anti-Lynas protestors increased the level of environmental awareness and active commitment in rural communities to act against Lynas. With various public stakeholders pressuring and calling on Lynas to account for their wrongdoing at LAMP, Lynas attempted to counter the narrative and state their position on the review and the potential outcomes.

The increasing accessibility to social media and online news platforms created a shorter runway for word-of-mouth knowledge to become headline news. However, it also means that real-time information can be gathered quickly and accurately. By having a media monitoring system, communication managers can identify stakeholder sentiments on multiple platforms, including social media (Coombs, 2019). However, prior to this crisis, Lynas was not proactive in addressing the concerns of the anti-Lynas protestors on the issue of radioactive waste. Even though a local communications team was hired after initial anti-Lynas protests (Kaur, 2015), responses were made only when an appeal had been dismissed by the courts, or during this crisis, when Lynas found out that an Executive Review Committee was formed to investigate LAMP's operations.

> *However, Lynas will advocate for a review that is transparent, impartial and scientific, consistent with other recent initiatives of the new government.*
>
> (Lynas Corporation Ltd., 2018a)

Lynas's MD Lacaze, who wrote an open letter, tweeted about the loss of local jobs should the government force LAMP to shut down:

> *For those observing from the West coast of Malaysia it might be "only" jobs. For me it's real people and real families. They are my colleagues, my friends and my Malaysian family. I will fight for them every step of the way.*
>
> (Lacaze, 2018b)

Although this gave Lynas a wider reach, using Twitter to respond to the crisis was not ideal as only 44% of surveyed Internet users in Malaysia used Twitter (Kemp, 2019). Moreover, Lynas and Lacaze responded only in English, whereas the predominant languages in rural Malaysia are Bahasa Malay or Mandarin, which meant that Lynas was communicating only with English-speaking Malaysians. Lynas also failed to address the crux of the crisis – the toxic nature of the radioactive waste and instead shifted attention to the potential adverse impact on the livelihood of Malaysians and the Malaysian economy.

Societal Culture

For our analysis, we relied on the dimensions of power distance and collectivism. Hofstede Insights (2022) views Malaysian culture as one with high power distance and clear boundaries between different segments of society, while a collectivistic society is one where people emphasize the importance of community.

Power Distance

In Malaysian culture, the power distance relationship is demonstrated by an autocratic style of leadership and centralized decision-making in the workplace. The origins of such attitudes are linked to the Malay feudal system as well as British colonialism in the 19th and 20th centuries (Sweetman, 2012). The country has in place a constitutional monarchy that is led by the Sultan of Malaysia. His role dates to pre-colonial Malaysia, where the Sultan and his chiefs of states were responsible solely for governance (Radin, 1960). Under British rule, they were reduced to ceremonial heads of states. A new economic system that introduced the use of money replaced barter trade, which disproportionately benefitted the higher social classes, such as the monarchy, causing greater polarization within Malaysian society (Radin, 1960).

Translating this to workplace culture, decision-making tends to be done among senior executives and leaders, and employees defer to their leadership. For Lynas, the power distance was demonstrated in their response toward anti-Lynas protestors. Prior to the crisis, there were constant dismissals of the appeals of anti-Lynas protestors by the High Court, a manifestation of how the state uses the arms of the government to suppress public opinion. (Yew, 2016). More notable dismissals included those in 2012, which were filed after protestors found out about the construction of the REE processing facility (Duffy, 2012). In 2015, the High Court dismissed an application for a judicial review three years after Lynas was awarded a temporary operating license (Ong, 2015). In their crisis response, Lynas continued to ignore protestors by issuing statements and publishing tweets that targeted the Malaysian government and the Executive Review Committee.

Collectivism

Lynas attempted to tap into the collectivistic nature of Malaysian society, where people are loyal to a "member" group and within the group, look out for one another (Hofstede Insights, 2022). This attribute can be identified from the reaction and reasons for the backlash from anti-Lynas protestors, including a past event that had served as an important proof point. In 1992, Mitsubishi Chemical ceased the operation of an REE refinery in north-central Malaysia after locals claimed that radioactive exposure to waste products there had resulted in birth defects and leukemia (Bradsher, 2011). Informed by this past incident, anti-Lynas protest movements rallied protestors who were involved in this incident, displaying a strong common identity (Yew, 2016). Over time, the movement was supported and even spearheaded by politicians from PH, which led to the formation of the Executive Review Committee.

Tapping the importance of unity, Lynas embarked on a media campaign during the crisis to highlight Malaysian employees whose lives had improved because of LAMP's operations. In so doing, they showed that any unfavorable findings would impact both the company and fellow Malaysians, thus infringing on their collectivistic nature. However, Lynas did not establish dialogic communication with the community, preferring to adopt a one-way model to transmit their messages. Establishing dialogic communication would have allowed an MNC to engage stakeholders more effectively and build a positive post-crisis reputation (Yang et al., 2010). Additionally, MNCs need to be aware that community ties are highly treasured in Malaysian society; thus, any communication efforts will need to address multiple groups of stakeholders at one time to address multiple concerns. Understanding local culture is key to ensuring that MNCs are aware of the appropriate languages to use and the relevant spokespeople to front. In the case of Malaysia, using Bahasa Malay alongside English may be more relevant, as it is the lingua franca. This allows the MNC to build goodwill with the local communities, and this is further enhanced when MNCs are transparent with them.

Activism

Malaysian activism is best described as tenuous, oftentimes its growth and influence have been limited by the Malaysian government. The ruling government adopted a hostile stance on activism during the 1980s and 1990s, even utilizing the Internal Security Act to crack down on activists (Yew & Azmil, 2019). In the late 1990s to early 2000s, the Reformasi movement saw the growth of student activism, but this was met with harsh government action (Karunungan, 2021). To date, the relationship between NGOs and the Malaysian government remains tenuous, and at times, hostile.

To analyze anti-Lynas sentiments, it is key to understand the origins of Malaysian environmentalism, the increasing importance of environmental protection, and the livelihood of locals. Environmentalism began in Malaysia with the establishment of urban-based environmental NGOs (ENGOs) in the late 1960s and early 1970s such as the Environmental Protection Society of Malaysia (EPSM) and the World Wide Fund for Nature Malaysia (WWF Malaysia) which partnered with the government on macro-environmental issues (Yew & Azmil, 2019, p. 289). As Malaysia's economic development came at the cost of the environment during the 1980s and 1990s, smaller ENGOs acted (Yew, 2016). The success of the early environmental movement was due to its effectiveness at "bridging across civil society and connecting with disparate groups concerned with social, political and economic rights" (Cooke & Hezri, 2016, p. 401). Such networks embodied the cultural trait of collectivism, a fundamental component of Malaysian society, as individuals and groups treated one another as "familial" (Cooke & Hezri, 2016). However, despite the progress made by ENGOs in the past decades, the ruling coalition implemented legislation that complicated the registration process for NGOs and restricted media freedom to stamp out NGOs supportive of the policies proposed by the opposition (Khoo, 2013). Consequently, it limited the potential collective impact that ENGOs had, resulting in a stagnant environment where new movements were unable to come to fruition and a lack of imperative on the ruling coalition to act.

Learning from experience, ENGOs soon adopted a coalitional approach to advocacy. To increase traction for their movements, ENGOs sought support from non-environmental NGOs and politicians from the opposition parties (Yew & Azmil, 2019). This multi-pronged mobilization approach created greater pressure on the government through the "normative pressures and solidarity incentives that are encoded within networks" (Tarrow, 2011, p. 30). For example, the Malaysian Environmental NGOs (MENGO) coalition was formed in 2001 to consolidate their efforts and serve as a platform of advocacy for Malaysia's environmental policies (Hati, 2022). The repertoire of ENGOs was further expanded when former Prime Minister Najib repealed the Internal Security Act in 2011, allowing ENGOs to organize mass demonstrations without consequences (Yew & Azmil, 2019). The rise of social media also contributed to the coalition-building efforts that ENGOs and informal movements undertook in Malaysia, utilizing blogs, Facebook, and Twitter in their communication toolkit (Kaur, 2015).

Anti-Lynas activities started in 2011 with mobilized efforts from two ENGOs, Save Malaysia Stop Lynas (SMSL) and the Himpunan Hijau (HH). Yew and Azmil (2019) noted that these organizations depended less on other ENGOs and more on protestors and politicians. Strategies including a social media war, public forums that fronted domain experts, press conferences, and disseminating press releases, were utilized to gather support for their movement (Kaur, 2015). SMSL managed to garner support from Australian environmental activists and politicians, while HH organized rallies in Kuala Lumpur and other cities in West Malaysia to apply political pressure on the government. On the political front, ENGOs supported Wong Tack, a member of the PH coalition, in the state of Pahang to oust the ruling BN in the 2013 General Elections (Nazreen, 2014). With many opposition politicians supporting the anti-Lynas movement, coupled with growing electoral support, the then-ruling BN government set up a project-operations monitoring committee to audit LAMP's operations (Malay Mail, 2013).

Anti-Lynas activism reached new highs during the 2018 General Election, where the issue of radioactive waste gained political salience. To fulfill the campaign promise, PH, the ruling coalition announced a review of Lynas' activities at LAMP (Looi, 2018), led by Fuziah Salleh, a Malaysian member of parliament and an anti-Lynas advocate (Sanderson & Palma, 2018). This created the impetus for political change through the government, leading to an alignment between the ENGOs and the ruling government for anti-Lynas protestors who have attempted to force Lynas to cease operations.

With pressure from both political and ENGO fronts, Lynas embarked on a communication campaign to counter anti-Lynas sentiments through mainstream media and social media. However, their efforts were targeted at the Malaysian government and the Executive Review Committee instead of anti-Lynas protestors. This lack of stakeholder engagement was also observed when Lynas attempted to dispel initial anti-Lynas sentiments as journalists who covered the developments at that time stated that the company "did not strategically engage through social media with concerned residents, NGOs or the general public to allay their fears, leading to the escalation of the issue and public outrage" (Kaur, 2015, p. 314). Lynas also failed to implement a consultative process with the public even after the initial backlash, fueling concerns among Malaysians that the processing of REE is linked to nuclear residues (Ali, 2014). That said, the efforts of protestors were thwarted when the results of the review favored Lynas. Subsequent rulings resulted in the extension of their operating license, further hampering the efforts of ENGOs and activists (Reuters, 2019b).

Conclusion

Political intervention and Lynas' strategic importance to the Malaysian economy helped it to weather the strong public outcry. However, its crisis response strategy of diversion was inadequate as it depended on the refrain of how they had improved the livelihoods of Malaysian employees and their economic contribution to the country. Their crisis response strategy failed to address the key issue of the improper disposal of radioactive waste and was targeted mainly at the government and protestors. The narrow focus meant that concerns from other stakeholders, such as those living in the affected communities, were left unaddressed. This has resulted in continued protests against Lynas till this day. Furthermore, as the response was solely in English, Lynas was unable to engage multiple non-English speaking stakeholder groups effectively, which facilitated the spread of misinformation by anti-Lynas protestors.

The Lynas crisis also demonstrated the importance of the socio-cultural environment in the framing, reframing, or countering of crisis narratives. In a multicultural country such as Malaysia, it is necessary for MNCs to engage with the needs and concerns of local communities within which they operate through knowledge of cultural nuances and societal structures. As a globalized society, while business is primarily conducted in English, there is an increasing need for MNCs to also be conscious of the conversations spoken in their respective native languages. Access to digital platforms, coupled with growing environmentalism and increasing citizen journalism, reinforces the imperative for MNCs to be plugged into the latest conversations to counter misinformation and communicate with different stakeholders at the appropriate times. Additionally, this allows MNCs to grasp the nuances of Malaysian culture, which will inform the building of a localized crisis response strategy, build goodwill with various stakeholders, and protect their reputation.

References

Alagesh, T. N. (2018, October 17). New Lynas review committee to ensure its best to safeguard people's interest. *New Straits Times*. https://www.nst.com.my/news/nation/2018/10/422063/new-lynas-review-committee-ensure-its-best-safeguard-peoples-interest

Ali, S. H. (2014). Social and environmental impact of the rare earth industries. *Resources (Basel)*, *3*(1), 123–134. https://doi.org/10.3390/resources3010123

ASEAN Secretariat. (2022). ASEAN Trade in Goods Agreement. *Invest In ASEAN*. https://investasean.asean.org/index.php/page/view/asean-free-trade-area-agreements/view/757/newsid/872/asean-trade-in-goods-agreement.html

BBC. (2020, February 17). Malaysia profile — Media. *BBC*. https://www.bbc.com/news/world-asia-pacific-15384221

Bedi, R. S. (2022, August 23). Najib to serve 12-year jail sentence after failing in final bid to overturn guilty verdict in 1MDB-linked case. *Channel NewsAsia*. https://www.channelnewsasia.com/asia/najib-1mdb-jail-sentence-fail-appeal-overturn-guilty-verdict-2894851

Bradsher, K. (2013, September 13). Lynas' rare earths project faces protests, opposition. *CNBC*. https://www.cnbc.com/2011/06/29/lynas-rare-earths-project-faces-protests-opposition.html

Bradsher, K. (2011, March 8). Mitsubishi quietly cleans up its former refinery. *The New York Times*. https://www.nytimes.com/2011/03/09/business/energy-environment/09rareside.html

Central Intelligence Agency. (2022). *Malaysia — The World Factbook*. https://www.cia.gov/the-world-factbook/countries/malaysia/#government

Cholteeva, Y. (2021, April 7). Mapping rare earths projects outside China. *Mining Technology*. https://www.mining-technology.com/analysis/mapping-rare-earths-projects-outside-china/

Cooke, F. M., & Hezri, A. A. (2016). Malaysia. In Philip Hirsch (Ed.), *Routledge handbook of the environment in Southeast Asia*. Routledge. https://doi.org/10.4324/9781315474892

Coombs, W. T. (2019). *Ongoing crisis communication: Planning, managing, and responding* (5th ed.). SAGE Publications, Inc.

Duffy, A. (2012, June 18). Malaysian government gives Lynas the thumbs up. *Australian Mining*. https://www.australianmining.com.au/news/malaysian-government-gives-lynas-the-thumbs-up/

Freedom House. (2019). Freedom in the world 2019 — Malaysia. *Freedom House*. https://freedomhouse.org/country/malaysia/freedom-world/2019

Fujita, A. (2022, January 21). Chinese rare earth minerals are 'a national security risk': Sen. Mark Kelly. *Yahoo Finance*. https://finance.yahoo.com/news/chinese-rare-earth-minerals-are-a-national-security-risk-sen-mark-kelly-141923102.html

Grote, R. (2016). *Oxford Constitutional law*. Oxford University Press. https://oxcon.ouplaw.com/view/10.1093/law:mpeccol/law-mpeccol-e408

Hati. (2022). *Malaysian Environmental NGOs (MENGO)*. https://www.hati.my/malaysian-environmental-ngos-mengo/

Hofstede Insights. (2022). *Malaysia*. https://www.hofstede-insights.com/country/malaysia/

Ibrahim, A. (2018, December 12). Lynas' critics proven wrong. *New Straits Times*. https://www.nst.com.my/opinion/letters/2018/12/439738/lynas-critics-proven-wrong

Jamasmie, C. (2018, October 2). Lynas presses Malaysian authorities to explain plant review status. *Mining.com*. https://www.mining.com/lynas-presses-malaysian-authorities-to-explain-plant-review-status/

Karunungan, R. (2021). Reawakening student activism: A case study of Malaysia and Singapore. *Heinrich Böll Stiftung*. https://eu.boell.org/sites/default/files/2021-12/Reawakening%20student%20activism%20FINAL.pdf

Kaur, K. (2015). Social media creating digital environmental publics: Case of Lynas Malaysia. *Public Relations Review*, *41*(2), 311–314. https://doi.org/10.1016/j.pubrev.2014.12.005

Kemp, S. (2019, January 31). *Digital 2019: Malaysia*. Datareportal. https://datareportal.com/reports/digital-2019-malaysia

Kemp, S. (2022, February 15). *Digital 2022: Malaysia*. Datareportal. https://datareportal.com/reports/digital-2022-malaysia

Khoo, Y. H. (2013). The NGO-government relations in Malaysia: Historical context and contemporary discourse, *Malaysian Journal of Democracy and Election Studies*, *1*, 76–85, https://www.researchgate.net/publication/264117714_The_NGO-Government_Relations_in_Malaysia_Historical_Context_and_Contemporary_Discourse

Kruger, C. (2018, November 27). 'It is what it is': Lynas navigate precarious political reality. *The Sydney Morning Herald*. https://www.smh.com.au/business/companies/it-is-what-it-is-lynas-navigates-precarious-political-reality-20181127-p50ioe.html

Lacaze, A. (2018a, October 2). An open letter to the government of Malaysia and the people of Malaysia. *Lynas Rare Earths*. https://lynasrareearths.com/an-open-letter-to-the-government-of-malaysia-and-the-people-of-malaysia/

Lacaze, A. (2018b, October 11). *For those observing from the West coast of Malaysia it might be "only" jobs. For me it's real people and* [Tweet; embedded links to videos]. Twitter [@AmandaLacaze]. https://twitter.com/AmandaLacaze/status/1050283510831800321?cxt=HHwWgoCjibvSrZMdAAAA

Lacaze, A. (2018c, December 7*). The health and well being of our staff and surrounding communities is always our first priority. Our people and communities* [Tweet]. Twitter [@AmandaLacaze]. https://twitter.com/AmandaLacaze/status/1070909795413061632?cxt=HHwWgMCn4Z6y0dwdAAAA

Lacaze, A. (2018d, December 11). *I'm so proud of the Lynas Malaysia team. They visited parliament today to ask for their voice to be heard* [Tweet]. Twitter [@AmandaLacaze]. https://mobile.twitter.com/AmandaLacaze/status/1072352073314897920?cxt=HHwWgMC0we6h4eEdAAAA

Looi, F. (2018, November 26). Controversial rare earths plant in fight for survival in Malaysia. *Al Jazeera*. https://www.aljazeera.com/economy/2018/11/26/controversial-rare-earths-plant-in-fight-for-survival-in-malaysia/

Lu, C. (2021, April 22). Why rare earths are the key to just about everything. *Foreign Policy*. https://foreignpolicy.com/2021/04/22/rare-earths-china-us-greenland-geopolitics/

Lynas Corporation Ltd. (2013). *The path from here: 2013 Annual Report*. https://www.annualreports.com/HostedData/AnnualReportArchive/L/ASX_LYC_2013.pdf

Lynas Corporation Ltd. (2018a, September 24). *Media speculation — potential review of Lynas operations in Malaysia*. https://wcsecure.weblink.com.au/pdf/LYC/02025352.pdf

Lynas Corporation Ltd. (2018b, October 5). *Ask our experts: Frequently asked questions about Lynas Malaysia*. https://lynasrareearths.com/frequently-asked-questions-about-lynas-malaysia/

Lynas Corporation Ltd. (2018c, October 16). *Hear our voices*. https://lynasrareearths.com/hear-our-voices/

Lynas Corporation Ltd. (2018d, October 30). *Hear our voices*. https://lynasrareearths.com/hear-our-voices-2/

Lynas Corporation Ltd. (2018e, November 22) *Estimating Lynas' economic impact on the local and Malaysian economy Final Report*. https://lynasrareearths.com/wp-content/uploads/2019/06/181122-Lynas-Final-Report-full.pdf

Lynas Corporation Ltd. (2018f, December 5). *Review Committee Report Summary*. https://lynasrareearths.com/review-committee-report-summary/

Lynas Corporation Ltd. (2021a). *Lynas Rare Earths*. https://lynasrareearths.com/

Lynas Corporation Ltd. (2021b). Locations. *Lynas Rare Earths*. https://lynasrareearths.com/about-us/corporate-governance/

Malay Mail. (2013, April 8). Expert committee on Lynas established. *Malay Mail*. https://global.factiva.com/redir/default.aspx?P=sa&an=MALMAI0020130508e9480000f&cat=a&ep=ASE

Malaysian Insider. (2012, March 21). Let's de-politicise the Lynas issue — Stop Lynas coalition. *Malaysian Insider*.

Malaysian Investment Development Authority. (2021). Maritime Transport: Accelerating International Trade. *Malaysian Investment Development Authority*. https://www.mida.gov.my/maritime-transport-accelerating-international-trade/

Malaysian Investment Development Authority. (2022). Gearing Malaysia as a rare earth elements (REEs) powerhouse. *Malaysian Investment Development Authority*. https://www.mida.gov.my/gearing-malaysia-as-a-rare-earth-elements-rees-powerhouse/

Michigan State University. (2022). *Malaysia: Introduction*. globalEDGE. https://globaledge.msu.edu/countries/malaysia

Murugiah, S. (2021, September 20). Malaysia remains an attractive investment destination needed for growth — ASEAN-BAC. *The Edge Markets*. https://www.theedgemarkets.com/article/malaysia-remains-attractive-investment-destination-political-stability-needed-growth

Nazreen, M. (2014). Kuantan, Pahang: Revealing the ordinary. In M. L. Weiss (Ed.), *Electoral dynamics in Malaysia: Findings from the grassroots*. Institute of Southeast Asian Studies; Petaling Jaya, Malaysia: Strategic Information and Research Development Centre.

New Straits Times. (2018, May 10). Pakatan Harapan wins 14th General Election. *New Straits Times*. https://www.nst.com.my/news/politics/2018/05/367907/pakatan-harapan-wins-14th-general-election

Ong, H. S. (2015, October 10). High Court dismisses suits against Lynas by Kuantan folk. *The Star*. https://www.thestar.com.my/news/nation/2015/10/10/high-court-dismisses-suits-against-lynas-by-kuantan-folk/

Ong, H. S. (2018, September 24). Lynas worried that MP who had opposed its operations before is now evaluating it. *The Star*. https://www.thestar.com.my/news/nation/2018/09/24/lynas-worried-that-mp-who-had-opposed-its-operations-before-is-now-evaluating-it/

Onn, B. (2021, February 14). *Malaysia' FDI: Major factors and the way forward*. Malaysian Investment Development Authority. https://www.mida.gov.my/mida-news/malaysias-fdi-major-factors-and-the-way-forward/

Phua, K. (2016). Rare earth plant in Malaysia: Governance, green politics and geopolitics, *Journal of Southeast Asian Studies*, *2*, 443–462, https://www.researchgate.net/publication/312491211_Rare_Earth_Plant_in_Malaysia_Governance_Green_Politics_and_Geopolitics

Radin, S. (1960). Malay nationalism, 1896–1941. *Journal of Southeast Asian History*, *1*(1), 1–28. https://doi.org/10.1017/S0217781100000028

Raghu, A., & Koswanage, N. (2012, June 19). Malaysian lawmaker green light Lynas rare earths plant. *Reuters*. https://www.reuters.com/article/us-malaysia-lynas-idUSBRE85I0CN20120619

Reuters. (2018, September 24). Rare earth miner Lynas to face review in Malaysia — media. *Reuters*. https://www.reuters.com/article/lynas-corp-malaysia-idUKL4N1WA1IL

Reuters. (2019a, June 27). Rare earths producer Lynas secures better loan terms with Japanese backers. *Reuters*. https://www.reuters.com/article/uk-lynas-corp-japan-debt-idUKKCN1TS0FH

Reuters. (2019b, August 15). Malaysia extends license for rare earth miner Lynas' operations for six months. *Reuters*. https://www.reuters.com/article/us-lynas-corp-malaysia-idUSKCN1V5149

Reuters. (2020, March 1). Timeline: A week of political crisis in Malaysia. *Reuters*. https://www.reuters.com/article/us-malaysia-politics-timeline-idUSKBN20O1CP

Sanderson, H., & Palma, S. (2018, October 2). Malaysia to investigate Australian rare earth miner Lynas. *Financial Times*. https://www.ft.com/content/dccf3226-c636-11e8-ba8f-ee390057b8c9

Sipalan, J. (2021, March 13). Malaysia defends coronavirus fake news law amid outcry. *Reuters*. https://www.reuters.com/business/media-telecom/malaysia-defends-coronavirus-fake-news-law-amid-outcry-2021-03-12/

Steger, I., & Hoyle, R. (2013, May 6). Australia's Lynas seen a winner in Malaysia's election. *The Wall Street Journal*. https://www.wsj.com/articles/BL-MBB-995

Stratfor Worldview. (2019, August 25). How this one rare earth processing plant in Malaysia could change the US-China trade war. *The National Interest*. https://nationalinterest.org/blog/buzz/how-one-rare-earth-processing-plant-malaysia-could-change-us-china-trade-war-75931

Stutt, A. (2018, November 29). Lynas Corp's Malaysia shut down until 2019. *Mining.com*. https://www.mining.com/lynas-corps-malaysia-plant-shut-2019/

Sweetman, K. (2012, April 10). In Asia, power gets in the way. *Harvard Business Review*. https://hbr.org/2012/04/in-asia-power-gets-in-the-way#:~:text=Take%20Malaysia%2C%20for%20example.,the%20influence%20of%20the%20British

Tan, A. L. (2022, October 13). Malaysia unveils tighter 2023 Budget amid worries of slower growth. *The Business Times*. https://www.businesstimes.com.sg/international/malaysia-unveils-tighter-2023-budget-amid-worries-slower-growth

Tarrow, S. G. (2011). *Power in movement: Social movements and contentious politics* (Rev. & updated 3rd ed.). Cambridge University Press.

Teoh, S. (2019, August 15). Kuala Lumpur gives Lynas 6 months to finalise alternative to repatriating radioactive waste. *The Straits Times*. https://www.straitstimes.com/asia/se-asia/kuala-lumpur-gives-lynas-six-months-to-finalise-alternative-to-repatriating-radioactive

Teoh, S. (2022, November 26). Anwar Ibrahim sworn in as Malaysia's 10th prime minister, ending 24-year wait. *The Straits Times*. https://www.straitstimes.com/asia/se-asia/anwar-is-malaysia-s-10th-pm

The Straits Times (2019a, August 18). Hundreds of protesters gather to slam Malaysia's decision on Lynas. *The Straits Times*. https://www.straitstimes.com/asia/se-asia/hundreds-of-protesters-gather-to-slam-malaysias-decision-on-lynas

The Straits Times (2019b, August 27). Malaysia can't cast out rare earth producer Lynas as it creates jobs, says Mahathir. *The Straits Times*. https://www.straitstimes.com/asia/se-asia/malaysia-cant-cast-out-rare-earth-producer-lynas-as-it-creates-jobs-says-mahathir

The World Bank (2022, November 29). *The World Bank in Malaysia*. https://www.worldbank.org/en/country/malaysia/overview#1

Tim, Y., Pan, S. L., Bahri, S., & Fauzi, A. (2018). Digitally enabled affordances for community-driven environmental movement in rural Malaysia. *Information Systems Journal (Oxford, England)*, *28*(1), 48–75. https://doi.org/10.1111/isj.12140

Yang S-U., Kang, M., & Johnson, P. (2010). Effects of narratives, openness to dialogic communication, and credibility on engagement in crisis communication through organizational blogs. *Communication Research*, *37*(4), 473–497. https://doi.org/10.1177/0093650210362682

Yew, W. L. (2016). Constraint without coercion: Indirect repression of environmental protest in Malaysia. *Pacific Affairs*, *89*(3), 543–565. http://www.jstor.org/stable/24779694

Yew, W. L., & Azmil, T. (2019). Malaysia's green movement: Old continuities and new possibilities. In S. Lemière (Ed.), *Illusions of democracy: Malaysian politics and people* (pp. 287–304). Amsterdam University Press. https://doi.org/10.2307/j.ctvnjbgtv.20

Zain, N. (2022, June 15). Digital News Report 2022: Malaysia. *Reuters Institute*. https://reutersinstitute.politics.ox.ac.uk/digital-news-report/2022/malaysia

5

SINGAPORE

MNC Halts Retrenchment Over Employees' Anger

Clement Sim, Malcolm Teo, and Nicole Lee

Introduction

In 2020, the COVID-19 pandemic not only killed millions, but it also put millions out of jobs and threatened their livelihood as companies downsized to protect their businesses and sent home foreign workers. In Singapore, Eagle Services Asia (ESA), a joint venture between an American firm Pratt & Whitney (P&W) and SIA Engineering Company did just that. While the aviation company could claim that the series of retrenchment exercises was triggered by the COVID-19 pandemic, the backlash that it received in the cutback of workers was of its own doing. Our analysis of this crisis emphasizes the unique socio-economic and cultural environment of Singapore, including the strong influence of the Singapore government, juxtaposing it against the culture preferences of liberty and free market practices that American ownership enacts upon ESA.

Singapore is a small city-state located at the southern tip of the Malay Peninsula, with minimal natural resources and, a citizen population of only 3.5 million and a total population of 5.6 million as of June 2021 (Singapore Department of Statistics, 2022). Despite this lacuna, it has cemented its position as a global financial hub with its transparency and streamlined business environment, diverse investment ecosystem infrastructure, and low-tax rates. Additionally, Singapore is also frequently viewed as a hub where the "East meets West" (Singapore Corporation Programme, 2015). This transformation began in 1965 when Singapore gained independence from then Malaya. The GDP (Gross Domestic Product) per capita at that time was only US$517. By year 2000, when Lee Kuan Yew, the first Prime Minister acknowledged the transformation of Singapore from third world to first, Singapore had a GDP per capita of US$23,853

DOI: 10.4324/9781003411802-6

(Data Commons, 2021). Part of this transformation was no doubt due to Lee's leadership and pro-business policies. Then UN Secretary-General Ban Ki Moon highlighted this when he said that Lee "helped Singapore transition from a developing country to one of the most developed in the world, transforming it into a thriving business hub" (The Straits Times, 2015).

Today, Singapore is one of the few countries in the world to provide industry-specific tax deductions and incentives along with the exponential growth of Southeast Asia's investment and commercialize solutions for regional and international counterparts. With its precision engineering and innovation capabilities, Singapore is recognized as a global leader in high-value manufacturing across a variety of industries. In the current climate of global transparency, the city state continues to be a gateway to the region for top global multinational companies (MNCs) and foreign talent choosing to call Singapore home (EDB Singapore, n.d.).

The COVID-19 Pandemic

In 2020, the world was buffeted by the COVID-19 pandemic, and to protect citizens, lockdowns were implemented, and many industries came to an almost standstill. Singapore was no exception. The impact of COVID-19 on Singapore's economy has been significant. With the exception of online services, industries like food and beverage, manufacturing, retail, and in particular, travel-related sectors like air transport and tourism (Ministry of Trade and Industry, 2020) were severely impacted. The Singapore workforce suffered unprecedented losses, more so than any other crisis in the nation's young history. The city-state is heavily reliant on foreign workers – nearly 40% of the population comprises of immigrants – due to its internationalization and is thus vulnerable to fluctuations in the political or economic landscapes (Ching & Soon, 2000). The closure of borders and restriction of work visas resulted in manpower disruptions and overall contractions in employment, particularly in the construction, manufacturing, and service industries. In response to the predicted economic fallout, the government introduced several mitigating legislative and economic measures to protect the workforce, which included directives, guidelines, and pay-outs from the government.

In the early days of the pandemic, the Ministry of Manpower (MOM) – the government agency responsible for employment matters in Singapore – recognized that a more proactive stance towards affected parties would have to be taken, given the severe decline in revenues and disruption in supply chains. Directives and amendments of retrenchment recommendations were made to preserve jobs when faced with excess manpower (Ministry of Manpower, 2020). These amendments indicated that companies must notify the government in the event of any cost-cutting measures taken during the pandemic, with the intention of providing options to beleaguered employers as well as avoiding retrenchment as best as possible.

As for the impact of the pandemic on the aviation sector, international travel slowed and domestic arrivals plunged, and the country only saw 204,000 passengers in July 2020, as compared to 5.91 million the year before (Toh, 2021b). These circumstances hit the aviation sector hard, and many companies had to downsize. Pilots suffered pay cuts of 10% to 60%, and Singapore International Airlines (SIA), the flag carrier of Singapore, retrenched close to 2,400 employees (Meah, 2020). Fully aware that the aviation industry would suffer devastating losses, the Singapore government extended support to the sector through deferred loan payments, support packages, and cost relief schemes. Despite this, Eagle Services Asia laid off predominantly local employees in an exercise that was widely disapproved by the public and the agencies involved as it displayed discrimination against local employees versus expatriates.

Eagles Services Asia and Stakeholders

Incorporated in 1998, Eagle Services Asia (ESA) was a joint venture between American firm Pratt & Whitney (P&W) and SIA Engineering Company. It provides maintenance repair and overhaul (MRO) works for aircraft engines, and its ownership ratio of 51:49 gives P&W the position of majority shareholder.

Founded in 1925, P&W focuses on the design, manufacture, and servicing of aircraft engines (Pratt & Whitney, 2021). In 2019, P&W was one of the biggest market players, with about 17.5% of the world's aircraft engine market share (T4, 2020). It achieved 5.7% year-on-year revenue growth from 2010 to 2019 (Statistica, n.d.) and in December 2019, P&W's parent company Raytheon Technology Corporation traded at an all-time high on the New York Stock Exchange (Yahoo Finance, 2021). These figures highlighted P&W's status in the industry.

ESA's minor owner, SIA Engineering, is a subsidiary of the Singapore Airlines Group. The Group has over 20 subsidiaries, the most well-known of which is Singapore's flagship airline, Singapore International Airlines (SIA). A respected global brand, SIA was ranked 34th in *Fortune* magazine's 50 most admired companies, the only Southeast Asian company in the list (Toh, 2021a). As a partnership between two well-established players in the airline industries, ESA has cemented itself as one of Singapore's biggest players for MRO.

The Eagles Service Retrenchment and Aftermath

The COVID-19 pandemic prompted the government to enforce a rash of restrictions. The aviation sector bore the brunt of lockdowns, and many companies had to downsize. On July 22, 2020, 31 ESA employees were retrenched.

In interviews with the press, employees claimed they were asked to hurriedly pack their belongings and leave the office premises quickly. Some alleged they were barred from re-entering the premises. Two days later, 113 more ESA employees were retrenched (Azilah, 2020). The affected employees mentioned that they found the retrenchment process undignified, while those who remained in the company were anxious about their own positions (Yeo, 2020). Shortly thereafter, it was revealed that a majority of retrenched workers (56%) were Singaporeans (Azilah, 2020). This did not sit well with the public, with several expressing anger towards ESA's managing director on online forums as reflected in comments by the public on Facebook (FB) reacting to the news of "unfair retrenchment" skewed towards locals by ESA (Channel News Asia, 2020). A FB user wrote about how bosses would not hesitate in removing you if you had been in the company for many years. Another FB user implied that American companies are heartless, regardless of what the unions do.

This anger came amidst a backdrop of long-simmering tensions between Singaporeans and expatriate workers (Fenn, 2014). In recent years, Singapore has found it hard to balance the number of hirings of local and foreign workers. (Toh, 2014). In 2020, 28.9% of Singapore residents were non-citizens. In contrast, the highest recorded number of non-citizens residing in the United States was only 14.8% (Batalova et al., 2021). This comparison reflects the disparity in the level of competition between foreign and local workers, with foreigners seemingly having an advantage over locals. The discontent among locals for this situation has simmered for about two decades.

Organizing and Managing Retrenchment

On July 28, ESA clarified that affected staff had not been retrenched and that they had only been put on paid leave to await the outcome of negotiations between ESA and trade unions. Further, ESA denied that staff had been barred from re-entering the work premises (Yang, 2020a). However, on July 29, a joint statement by the representatives of multiple unions representing ESA employees as well as the National Trade Union Congress (NTUC), Singapore's national confederation of trade unions, contradicted ESA's original statements and highlighted that ESA had not followed due process in its retrenchment exercise. ESA had informed employees that they could be facing retrenchment before the names were finalized with the unions. This resulted in a phenomenon which does not often happen in Singapore – where NTUC and the other union groups stepped in to manage the ill-organized retrenchment process in order to protect the rights of Singaporean employees. Eventually, the list of people retrenched was revised, and the proportion of retrenched Singaporeans was reduced to 44% (from the proposed 56%). Additionally, those retrenched received a severance package of a month's salary for each year worked as well as retraining grants (Azilah, 2020).

Case Analysis

The unsatisfactory execution of ESA's retrenchment exercise and the outcome provide some context to the company's reputational crisis. Using Sriramesh and Verčič's (2020) Global Public Relations Framework and the five variables discussed in Chapter 1, we next analyze the communication by ESA with regard to its human capital management crisis from the forced retrenchment of employees.

Political System and the Labor Union

We have combined the political system of Singapore and the role of labor unions in the country, given that the two are tightly intertwined in the society and also in the current crisis. To understand the local political and labor union culture, it is important to first examine Singapore's unique relationship with the government, employers, and workers, who are represented by the National Trades Union Congress (NTUC) (Sharma, 2013).

The NTUC is a key component of Singapore's political system. It is the umbrella organization comprising 59 Trade Unions and 3 Trade Associations in Singapore, representing workers across various industries. The Singapore government has maintained close ties with NTUC by design, and the two have worked together on issues related to labor and employment. The relationship between NTUC and the government can be traced back to Singapore's early years of nation-building, when the government actively promoted industrialization and economic growth through various policies, including the encouragement of trade union formation. In 1961, the government established the Industrial Relations Department (IRD), which worked closely with NTUC to develop Singapore's industrial relations framework. The IRD was later renamed the MOM, which continues to play a central role in labor-related policies and regulations. Today, NTUC remains a major stakeholder in Singapore's political system, thereby encouraging a cooperative rather than contentious relationship between the government and labor unions. NTUC has representation in Parliament through its affiliated political party, the People's Action Party (PAP), and also participates in tripartite dialogues with the government and employers on issues such as wage policies, workplace safety and health, and training and development (Ng, 2019).

Singapore's political scene is hegemonized by the People's Action Party (PAP). One of the longest-surviving dominant parties in the world, the PAP received its mandate to rule in 1959 and has retained power in every election although of late the vote share has dropped. With such an extended rule, PAP has had the opportunity to enact policies that affect many generations. As a result of this, some of their policies have become slightly lost in translation over time (Mauzy & Milne, 2002). One such policy is Singapore's pro-immigration policy launched in the 1990s. This has resulted in the sizeable growth of its new immigrant population (Koh, 2003). The justification that foreign talent is necessary in response to the lack of in-demand skills from locals has not been well accepted by Singaporeans (Yang, 2018). In 1997, Singapore, through its Ministry of Manpower, launched six offices worldwide to facilitate the influx of foreigners into Singapore (Nathan, 1997). The project included a committee that was formed with the aim of attracting foreign talent to Singapore.

With expatriate workers assuming more professional roles, Singaporeans increasingly felt neglected, and those struggling to land jobs viewed the situation as unfair competition to locals. That perception resulted in locals blaming the government for not limiting the number of foreign professionals, managers, executives, and technical (PMET) and offering supporting data reflecting employers' preference toward foreign talent (Yeoh & Lam, 2016). This dissatisfaction also stemmed from the expectation that the government should prioritize the welfare of Singaporeans, which we shall further elaborate in the discussion on Societal Culture.

The failure to limit the number of foreign talents could arguably also stem from a separate underlying policy of encouraging meritocracy – a core value of the PAP when the country known as Malaya split into Malaysia and Singapore in 1965 (Ng, 2019). In post-independent Singapore, meritocracy was tied to the fight against a culture of patronage that existed in Malaya.

A policy that encouraged meritocracy and finding the best person for a job regardless of their country of origin resulted in discontent among Singaporeans toward the PAP and foreign workers. The COVID-19 pandemic aggravated these sentiments as overall unemployment peaked beyond that of the prior global financial crises and might have contributed to a lower percentage win for the PAP during the 2020 general election – which took place just weeks before the ESA crisis. Eventually, the NTUC proposed a Fair Retrenchment Framework, where the three key principles are to protect the Singaporean core of the workforce, preserve jobs, and provide job support (Choo, 2020). This was to support Singapore's reliance on manpower in order to grow its economy.

Economic System

Singapore's young history and lack of natural resources have paved the way for its reliance on foreign investment, where economic goals are prioritized by the government to ensure long-term viability and sustainability. As of 2019, there was an estimated S$2 trillion worth of Foreign Direct Investment in Singapore, with the United States as the largest investment partner. In its formative years, the government attracted foreign investment while maintaining a careful balance of "managed flexibility" and regulated unions through the promotion of a disciplined and hardworking workforce to deal with challenges that other developing countries were struggling to manage (Ching & Soon, 2000). Strict legislation reduced the political clout of unions and allowed companies to have free reign in the management of their human resources and technology. This approach has come with its boons and banes – while modernization frameworks prioritize national and economic growth as the catalyst for increasing the quality of life for individuals and communities (Sriramesh & Verčič, 2020), rational choice asserts that economic players will reliably and consistently maximize their self-interest based on rational calculations, which ESA attempted to do in its retrenchment in light of customer-driven volume decline (Yang, 2020a).

The ESA incident highlighted the long-standing issue of Singapore being a mere entry point for foreign corporations. Despite economic incentives, MNCs often used Singapore as the starting point for operations relocation within Southeast Asia before moving out to cheaper regional counterparts once operations had been tried and tested to cut costs and remain competitive (Ching & Soon, 2000). With the pandemic showing no signs of abating and organizations undergoing internationalization, the aviator sector as with all other sectors faced an uncertain future; this also resulted in lower job security for less-specialized workers, with MNCs regularly downsizing their existing workforce to replace them with contractual ones (Ching & Soon, 2000) to reduce costs. ESA's retrenchment exercise that resulted in local employees being disproportionately affected is likely due to the same reasons.

Pre-pandemic, there were close to 375,000 jobs in the aviation sector, approximately 10% of the workforce (Subhani, 2021). Recognizing the sector's importance to Singapore's positioning as a forerunner of global connectivity and its ability to function as a global aviation hub, the government provided the sector multiple lifelines throughout COVID-19. ESA's retrenchment, therefore, came as a rude shock to those involved as it was clear that sufficient government aid had been provided to the affected parties. For example, the S$870 million OneAviation Support Package for aviation companies comprised two components – enhanced manpower support and cost relief. Under the Jobs Support Scheme (JSS), aviation companies would receive 30% support for wages paid for the second quarter of 2021, and a grant that would provide 50% wage support specifically for local aviation employees from April to September 2021. It was during this wage support period that the layoffs occurred.

Additionally, the cost relief element of the package also extended existing rebates on operational costs to help aviation companies tide through the crisis (Ministry of Trade, 2020). Given the extensive government support provided to the sector, ESA failed to rationalize the timing and cost justification of the layoffs to its employees and members of the public. The three support schemes preceding the retrenchment had offered substantial financial support to the troubled aviation industry and were centered heavily around wage support and local worker welfare. The complexity of the situation resulted in the media picking up on it, which was amplified even further by affected employees and Singapore netizens who spoke up about their unhappiness towards the handling of the situation.

Media System

Sriramesh & Verčič (2009) suggested that communications practitioners must understand local patterns of *media control* when adapting global communications strategies. In Singapore, state control of media is an extension of the PAP's brand of soft authoritarianism (George, 2005; Kaur et al., 2016). PAP leaders have rejected Western notions of the media as the fourth estate in favor of the media adopting a nation-building role (Kaur et al., 2016). Various levers help exert control including the Newspaper and Printing Presses Act, while the companies that dominate Singapore's media scene – Singapore Press Holdings (SPH) and Mediacorp – have government links and are perceived as pro-government. An analysis of SPH's and Mediacorp's news coverage reveals how NTUC and its secretary general Ng Chee Meng (an ex-PAP politician) achieved dominant share-of-voice during the saga. From July 29 onward, NTUC's perspective enjoyed primacy in news headlines, which framed the incident as NTUC stepping in to protect workers from "unfair" retrenchments (see Table A.1).

As a result of NTUC stepping in to protect the rights of Singaporeans, the press inevitably supported that narrative and magnified ESA's internal organizational exercise into an issue of national importance: An errant company had flouted Singapore's tripartism framework and necessitated government and union intervention to safeguard Singaporean workers. The ESA case reflected the role of the press supporting Singapore's nation-building agenda – something which ESA's management appeared unprepared for as its communications did not effectively counter the messaging led by NTUC which, as highlighted above in our discussion, is tightly linked to Singapore's ruling political party.

Sriramesh (2009) also highlighted the importance of understanding *media diffusion* and *media access* in their communication strategies. It is worth noting that Singapore has the third-highest rate of Internet penetration in Southeast Asia, with 74% of the population being social media users (Müller, 2021). Angry employees and Singapore netizens added fuel to the fire by airing their grievances on social media, as mentioned above. Also salient is how the PAP has, in recent years, engaged in "authoritarian innovation" using digital marketing strategies to extend its online influence. For instance, hiring digital strategists and having politicians communicate directly with the masses via social media. Adopting such an approach allows the PAP to better shape public opinion in a more sophisticated manner (Tan, 2020).

ESA failed to grasp and navigate these trends. Its share-of-voice in mainstream coverage was limited to a few journalist-mediated soundbites such as how retrenchments were driven by "customer-driven volume decline," a robotic phrase which reinforced the perception of cold-hearted retrenchments (Yang, 2020b). It also failed to leverage its owned media channels. For example, its website was devoid of media statements. There was also no response to the ESA incident on parent company P&W's website. While P&W has a LinkedIn profile, the content is global-facing, and it is difficult to find localized Asian updates despite the company having seven offices in India, China, and Singapore. Given how digitally connected Singaporeans are, this is a glaring omission that led affected stakeholders to believe that ESA does not own any social media platforms that could have been used to convey its perspective.

In contrast, NTUC used the right platforms to address its target audience's concerns – PMEs experiencing job anxieties. In addition to a news release, NTUC adapted a bite-sized version for FB outlining how it had helped affected workers. Ng Chee Meng wrote a FB post, affirming the unions' commitment to workers, a move that bypassed journalistic gatekeepers, allowing him to communicate directly with social media users. Not only was his post quoted by mainstream media, but it also logged over 200 shares and almost 100 comments.

In a Facebook post, secretary general Ng 黄志明 (2020, July 29) wrote:

> About a week ago, I received messages from concerned workers and our unions about an unfair retrenchment exercise at Eagle Services Asia (ESA) Private Limited. I assured these workers and our unions that NTUC will intervene to protect them....
>
> ...We have since been able to reach an amicable agreement with the company on the retrenchment. By the time we concluded negotiations, we had jointly reviewed the name list of employees to be retrenched to ensure that the Singaporean Core is safeguarded to the extent possible, whilst giving due considerations to our foreign colleagues. In addition to receiving a fair compensation package for all affected workers, the unions had also further negotiated for an additional training grant for all affected union members. I look forward to renewing a collaborative approach with ESA for business continuity and success.... NTUC understands these are tough times. Nonetheless, there must still be fair play and proper process accorded to affected workers in any retrenchment. At the end of the day, while NTUC and our unions may not be able to save every job, we will do our best to protect the rights and interests of every worker. We will do so in a fair way to our employer partners as well...

"Eagle Services Asia" saw a spike in Google searches between July 26 and August 1, 2020, indicating strong public interest. NTUC's strong communications efforts meant that news coverage carried union-led messaging and shaped the trajectory of public discourse in social media and online forums. This was a missed opportunity for ESA. It released minimal public information, which might have satisfied online audiences' desire for information and restored trust. That information vacuum was filled by NTUC.

Media systems worked with other variables offered in the Global PR framework. ESA's retrenchments occurred in a highly charged political and economic context, after the PAP's less-than-stellar showing in the General Elections coupled with job market anxieties. This explains why NTUC and Ng Chee Meng mounted proactive efforts to show that the government was protecting the livelihoods of Singaporeans. Assertive stakeholders' communications, coupled with the levers of control available to the state, meant that ESA failed to own the narrative and was side-lined as the "bad guy." We feel that this setback was amplified to such an extent, largely because of the societal culture in Singapore, where people tend to look out for one another, especially fellow Singaporeans.

Societal Culture

Singapore is a multi-racial country made up of about 77% Chinese, 15% Malay, 6% Indian, and 2% other races. Examining its culture through Hofstede's (n.d.) framework of cultural dimensions, Singaporean melting pot culture is unique because it is the coming together of different cultures to form a new culture. It is described as a country with high power distance (74), a collectivistic society (20), leaning more toward a feminine society (48), has very low uncertainty avoidance (8), high long-term orientation (72), and a fairly balanced indulgent-restrained orientation (46).

The dimensions relevant to the ESA saga are power distance, collectivism, femininity, and long-term orientation. Many of these cultural dimensions are influenced and shaped by Singapore "Shared Values," which were crafted in 1988 to shape the Singaporean identity in order to unite the diversity of races and cultures to help Singapore succeed as a young nation (Singapore National Printers, 1991).

Singapore's collectivist culture was likely one of the strongest triggers behind the entire ESA episode. Collectivism is probably shaped by the first of five, "Shared Values — Nation before community and society above self." This collectivist identity extends even to the area of employment, where the government has had to carefully explain its policy vis-a-vis hiring foreign talent in a way that "requires employers to make jobs accessible to Singapore citizens" (Singapore Ministry of Communications and Information, 2020).

That reflects the importance and emphasis that Singapore places on taking care of the nation and its community. Another reason why the episode became such an intense crisis was also due to the nation's "power distance" culture, where citizens are deferential to those in authority (Sriramesh & Verčič, 2020). In March 2020, Members of Parliament (MPs) started a conversation about prioritizing Singaporeans for jobs (Aqil & Ahmad, 2020). ESA, however, did not consider this directive when it retrenched 144 workers, of whom more than half were Singaporeans (Low, 2020). This decision was made in spite of ongoing negotiations with other unions of the Singapore airline industry. The manner in which ESA disregarded authority and union negotiations resulted in an intense backlash from Singaporeans and several unions, including the NTUC, which stepped in publicly to censure the corporation for their decision in the retrenchment exercise (Lam, 2020).

The swift action taken by the unions to quickly arrest the issue to prevent further damage from being done and to seek an amicable way forward in the retrenchment exercise with ESA reflected the feminine dimension of Singapore society, where conflicts are avoided and the majority agreements are sought as much as possible. This dimension can also be paired with Singapore's view on placing greater emphasis on long-term goals like maintaining relationships and perseverance (Hofstede, n.d.) as well as communitarianism. Being unfamiliar with these dimensions, ESA's leaders made unilateral decisions that had little regard for an amicable decision-making process, prioritizing its bottom line above employee relationships. This damaged ESA's reputation and one can surmise that ESA's organizational culture was also influenced by P&W, the American aviation engineering company that owns 51% of ESA. The issue probably arose from the differences between the Singaporean and American cultural dimensions.

Responding to the situation, a P&W spokesperson stated that the need for retrenchment was due to decreasing sales and profits and how it continued to invest in employees to meet future challenges (Teo, 2020). What was revealing in its response was the individualist mindset and short-term orientation, which prioritized "self" and low-hanging goals like profits. Further, there was also a dissonance between the P&W's lower "power distance" orientation, where it did not have much regard for Singaporean authorities.

Having examined the differences in cultural dimensions between Singapore and P&W, it was little wonder that the leaders and citizens of Singapore generated such a strong reaction toward ESA's retrenchment exercise, which resulted in the loss of trust and reputational crisis for the company. The decision to retrench a portion of the workforce in itself was not the issue, but it was the way the company and P&W handled the process and communicated with its employees. The response reflected an insensitivity and lack of understanding of Singaporean culture.

Activist Culture

Unlike in the United States, protests are heavily restricted in Singapore by law. The primary reason provided by the Singapore government is that public order is essential to Singapore's economic survival and international standing (Ministry of Home Affairs, 2022). Hence, although the Labor Movement can be viewed as activism globally, NTUC adopted a different ideological position. The national confederation is closely linked with the nation's ruling political party, with senior positions including the Secretary-General appointment held exclusively by PAP MPs (Barr, 2000). Instead of directly fighting for workers' rights for higher wages and better conditions, NTUC supports tripartism – a strategic partnership between unions, employers, and the government – which is believed to allow Singapore to strengthen its economic competitiveness through harmonious labor-management relations and advance the nation's progress (Ministry of Manpower, n.d.). While tripartism secured the harmony of the nation's workforce for over 35 years, NTUC increasingly have difficulties attracting the fast-growing PME segment of the workforce. Beyond rank-and-file workers, NTUC seeks to be relevant to PMEs by championing their concerns, representing them in government policy formation, and protecting them against unfair labor practices (Ng, 2020).

With these factors operating against the backdrop of employment in Singapore, the ESA incident was the perfect opportunity for NTUC to showcase its relevance in protecting Singaporean workers against unfair retrenchment practices. NTUC orchestrated an aggressive communication plan showcasing how Ng Chee Meng, its secretary-general and an ex-PAP member, had rallied unions and workers to use legal industrial action to influence ESA to adopt fair negotiation. NTUC also emphasized how it fought a tough battle to ensure ESA preserved Singaporean jobs and retained a "Singaporean core" of workers. Retrenched ESA workers who were union members were not only given fair compensation, but they also received training grants. The incident also presented an opportunity for the government to re-emphasize that companies' retrenchment exercises needed to be aligned with the Tripartite Advisory on Managing Excess Manpower and Responsible Retrenchment, and it sternly warned companies against malpractices. In the process, the government also sought to gain brownie points with voters with regard to their stance on citizenry protection.

The government's agenda was further amplified by the country's regulated mainstream media, as discussed above. This means that any form of activism had to only come from independent sources of media – predominantly social media. Even so, false materials and fake information on social platforms are also subject to the inquiry of the Infocomm Media Development Authority (IMDA), a statutory board under the Singapore Ministry of Communications and Information.

IMDA plays an active role in censorship, especially in media sources that compromise the government's nation-building agenda. However, IMDA still allows room for individuals or groups to share their views for as long as it does not violate a standard list of guidelines that seek to protect racial, social, and religious harmony in Singapore (SG101, n.d.; Infocomm Media Development Authority, n.d.).

Conclusion

Viewing crisis communication from a socio-economic perspective helps highlight the real world challenges that Multinational Corporations face when operating in distant cultures. Cultural sensitivity is vital for businesses to prevent, or at least recover from, setbacks in overall performance. This is because crises rarely occur in isolation and are influenced by broader social, economic, and political forces.

In the case of ESA, the internal crisis reflected broader socio-economic issues such as the revelation of the subpar treatment of the local workforce in Singapore's aviation industry. Despite Singapore's reputation as a place where "East Meets West," the American-owned company could have better navigated the crisis by being more compassionate with its layoffs. Additionally, by not being cognizant and better aligned with Singaporean cultural values and more proactive in its communication and partnership with the unions, ESA broke employees trust and tarnished its corporate reputation.

The ESA crisis underscores the critical interplay between employee relations, communication strategies, and societal values. The heavy-handed treatment of what could have been a simple retrenchment exercise resulted in a rare case of union intervention – a consequence of the company management's failure to fully grasp Singapore's unique characteristics and confluence of the five socio-cultural factors. This crisis serves as a stark reminder of the essentiality of proactive, emphatic communication, with prevailing social ethos in navigating the complex landscape when managing global public relations challenges for foreign firms operating in a different market.

Annex

TABLE A.1 Summary of Selected Local News Headlines Around ESA Saga

Date	*Publication*	*Headline*	*Link*
July 27	Lianhe Wanbao	新航工程合资公司两轮裁员被指手段太 "激进" Translation: Two rounds of layoffs at Singapore Airlines Engineering joint venture accused of being too "radical"	https://www.zaobao.com.sg/znews/singapore/story20200727-1072375

(Continued)

TABLE A.1 (Continued)

Date	*Publication*	*Headline*	*Link*
July 28	The Straits Times	Eagle Services Asia says retrenchments not confirmed, all staff still on payroll	https://www.straitstimes.com/singapore/manpower/eagle-services-asia-says-retrenchments-not-confirmed-all-staff-still-on-payrolise
July 29	The Straits Times	NTUC, unions stepped in to stop unfair retrenchment by aircraft maintenance firm; industry action averted	https://www.straitstimes.com/singapore/ntuc-unions-stepped-in-to-ensure-fair-play-in-aircraft-maintenance-firms-retrenchment
July 29	The Business Times	NTUC, unions rebuke 'unfair' layoffs at P&W, SIA Engineering joint venture	https://www.businesstimes.com.sg/companies-markets/ntuc-unions-rebuke-unfair-layoffs-at-pw-sia-engineering-joint-venture
July 29	Channel News Asia	Unions halt "unfair" retrenchment by aerospace firm, industrial action averted	https://www.straitstimes.com/singapore/ntuc-unions-stepped-in-to-ensure-fair-play-in-aircraft-maintenance-firms-retrenchment
July 30	The Straits Times	Strike averted after unions get aviation firm to correct retrenchment process	https://www.straitstimes.com/singapore/strike-averted-after-unions-get-aviation-firm-to-correct-retrenchment-process
July 30	Today	Eagle services Asia had planned to axe more Singaporeans than foreigners before unions stepped in	https://www.todayonline.com/singapore/eagles-service-asia-had-plans-axe-more-singaporeans-foreigners-unions-stepped

References

Aqil, H. M., & Ahmad, Z. A. (2020). MPs call for firms to be more transparent on foreign hiring, make push to prioritise Singaporeans. *Channel NewsAsia*. https://www.channelnewsasia.com/singapore/foreigner-job-competition-singaporeans-employment-pass-638036.

Azilah, N. (2020, July 30). Eagle Services Asia workers on their 'rollercoaster' week of surprise layoffs. *Coconuts Singapore*. https://coconuts.co/singapore/news/eagle-services-asia-workers-on-their-rollercoaster-week-of-surprise-layoffs/

Barr, M. D. (2000). Trade unions in an elitist society: The Singapore story. *The Australian Journal of Politics and History*, *46*(4), 480–496. https://doi.org/10.1111/1467-8497.00109

Batalova, J., Hanna, M., & Levesque, C. (2021, February 11). Frequently Requested Statistics on Immigrants and Immigration in the United States. *Migration Information Source*. https://www.migrationpolicy.org/article/frequently-requested-statistics-immigrants-and-immigration-united-states-2020

Channel NewsAsia. (2020, July 29). https://www.facebook.com/ChannelNewsAsia/posts/on-jul-22-eagle-services-asia-informed-specific-workers-they-might-be-let-go-bef/10157643980127934/

Ching, Y. C., & Soon, L. G. (2000). Globalization, labour market deregulation and trade unions in Singapore. *Asia Pacific Business Review*, *6*(3–4), 154–173. https://doi.org/10.1080/13602380012331288512

Choo, Y. T. (2020, September 1). NTUC calls on firms to observe responsible retrenchment practices, keep Singaporean core. *The Straits Times*. https://www.straitstimes.com/singapore/manpower/ntuc-calls-on-firms-to-observe-responsible-retrenchment-practices-protect-workers

Data Commons. (2021). Singapore, Country in Asia. *Datacommons.org*. https://datacommons.org/place/country/SGP/?utm_medium=explore&mprop=amount&popt=EconomicActivity&cpv=activitySource,GrossDomesticProduction&hl=en.

EDB Singapore. (n.d.). Business-friendly environment. https://www.edb.gov.sg/en/why-singapore/business-friendly-environment.html

Facebook. (2020, July 29). Ng Chee Meng. Retrieved July 12, 2021 from https://www.facebook.com/NgCheeMengforSG/posts/about-a-week-ago-i-received-messages-from-concerned-workers-and-our-unions-about/3386022924751750/

Fenn, M. (2014, February 21). Singapore's Foreigner Problem. *The Diplomat*. https://thediplomat.com/2014/02/singapores-foreigner-problem/

George, C. (2005). The internet's political impact and the penetration/participation paradox in Malaysia and Singapore. *Media, Culture & Society*, *27*(6), 903–920.

Hofstede, G. (n.d). *What about Singapore*. Accessed October 17, 2021 from https://www.hofstede-insights.com/country/singapore/

Infocomm Media Development Authority. (n.d.). Political or religious content related to Singapore provided by individuals, groups, organisations, corporations. https://www.imda.gov.sg/regulations-and-licensing-listing/political-or-religious-content-related-to-singapore-provided-by-individuals-groups-organisations-corporations

Kaur, S., Tan, N., & Dutta, M. J. (2016). Media, migration and politics: The coverage of the Little India riot in the Straits Times in Singapore. *Journal of Creative Communications*, *11*(1), 27–43.

Koh, A. (2003). Global flows of foreign talent: Identity anxieties in Singapore's ethnoscape. *Journal of Social Issues in Southeast Asia*, *18*(2), 230–256. https://doi.org/10.1355/SJ18-2C

Lam, F. (2020, July 29). NTUC, unions rebuke 'unfair' layoffs at P&W, SIA Engineering joint venture. *The Business Times*. https://www.businesstimes.com.sg/companies-markets/ntuc-unions-rebuke-unfair-layoffs-at-pw-sia-engineering-joint-venture.

Low, Y. (2020, July 30). Eagle Services Asia had plans to axe more Singaporeans than foreigners before unions stepped in. *Today Online*. https://www.todayonline.com/singapore/eagles-service-asia-had-plans-axe-more-singaporeans-foreigners-unions-stepped.

Mauzy, D. K., & Milne, R. S. (2002). *Singapore politics under the People's Action Party*. Routledge. https://doi.org/10.4324/9780203471807

Meah, N. (2020, September 28). One sees his flying dream cut short, other SIA pilots become delivery drivers, retire early. *Today Online*. https://www.todayonline.com/singapore/one-sees-his-flying-dream-cut-short-other-sia-pilots-become-delivery-drivers-retire-early

Ministry of Home Affairs. (2022, May 12). *Ministry of Home Affairs*. Retrieved from Maintaining Public Order: https://www.mha.gov.sg/what-we-do/maintaining-law-and-order/maintaining-public-order

Ministry of Manpower. (2020, March 11). *Tripartite partners update advisory on managing excess manpower and responsible retrenchment in view of COVID-19*. https://www.mom.gov.sg/newsroom/press-releases/2020/0311-tripartite-partners-update-advisory-on-excess-manpower

Ministry of Manpower Singapore. (n.d.). *What is Tripartism*. https://www.mom.gov.sg/employment-practices/tripartism-in-singapore/what-is-tripartism.

Ministry of Trade and Industry Singapore. (2020, May 26). *Impact of the COVID-19 Pandemic on the Singapore Economy*. https://www.mti.gov.sg/Resources/feature-articles/2020/Impact-of-the-COVID-19-Pandemic-on-the-Singapore-Economy

Ministry of Trade Singapore. (2020, August 17). *Extension of support to the aviation sector*. https://www.mot.gov.sg/news-centre/news/Detail/extension-of-support-to-the-aviation-sector

Müller, J. (2021, September 10). *Singapore: Most used social media platform 2020. Statista*. https://www.statista.com/statistics/284466/singapore-social-network-penetration/.

Nathan, D. (July 31, 1997). New global drive starts, to attract foreign talent. *Straits Times*.

Ng, I. (2019). Industrial relations and the labour movement in Singapore. In L. K. H. Chua, & C. C. Ng (Eds.), *The Routledge Handbook of Contemporary Singapore* (pp. 141–156). Routledge.

Ng, J. S. (2020, August 27). As covid-19 puts more local white-collar jobs at risk, NTUC forms New Task Force to protect, push for their interests. *Today Online*. https://www.todayonline.com/singapore/covid-19-puts-more-local-white-collar-jobs-risk-ntuc-forms-new-task-force-protect-push

Pratt & Whitney. (2021, October 19). *About P&W*. Pratt & Whitney. https://prattwhitney.com/company/about-pratt-and-whitney

SG101. (n.d.). *Building a multi-cultural Singapore*. https://www.sg101.gov.sg/social-national-identity/multicultural/

Sharma, B. (2013). *Contextualising CSR in Asia: Corporate social responsibility in Asian economies and the drivers that influence its practice*. Lien Centre for Social Innovation, Singapore Management University.

Singapore Corporation Programme. (2015, January 24). *About Singapore*. Retrieved from Singapore Corporation Programme: https://archive.ph/20150124165252/http://www.scp.gov.sg/content/scp/about_us/about_singapore.html

Singapore Department of Statistics. (2022, September). Retrieved from Population in Brief 2022: https://www.strategygroup.gov.sg/files/media-centre/publications/Population-in-Brief-2022.pdf

Singapore Ministry of Communication and Information (2020). *Why do we need skilled foreign workers in Singapore*. Retrieved October 18, 2021: https://www.gov.sg/article/why-do-we-need-skilled-foreign-workers-in-singapore.

Singapore National Printers. (1991). Shared Values. *National Archives of Singapore*. https://www.nas.gov.sg/archivesonline/government_records/docs/a487bfde-7aea-11e7-83df-0050568939ad/Cmd.1of1991.pdf.

Sriramesh, K., & Vercic, D. (Eds.). (2009). *The global public relations handbook*, Revised and Expanded Edition: *Theory, research, and practice* (2nd ed.). Routledge. https://doi.org/10.4324/9780203889374.

Sriramesh, K., & Verčič, D. (2020). *The global public relations handbook: Theory, research, and practice*. Routledge.

Statistica. (n. d.). Pratt & Whitney's net sales from FY 2010 to FY 2020 (in million U.S. dollars). *Statistica*.com. https://www.statista.com/statistics/261858/net-sales-of-pratt-and-whitney/

Subhani, O. (2021, August 28). Covid-19 persistence makes domestic reopening critical for. *The Straits Times*. https://www.straitstimes.com/business/economy/covid-19-persistence-makes-domestic-reopening-critical-for-singapores-economic

T4. (2020, July 30). *Aircraft Engine Market Share, Market Size and Industry Growth Drivers, 2018–2025*. https://www.t4.ai/industry/aircraft-engine-market-share

Tan, N. (2020). Digital learning and extending electoral authoritarianism in Singapore. *Democratization*, *27*(6), 1073–1091.

Teo, G. (2020). NTUC and unions stepped in to halt retrenchment at Eagle Services Asia (Updated with ESA's response). Retrieved from: https://unscrambled.sg/2020/07/29/just-in-ntuc-and-the-unions-stepped-in-to-halt-retrenchment-exercise-at-eagle-services-asia/. Accessed date: October 18, 2021.

The Straits Times. (2015, March 24). Remembering Lee Kuan Yew — What world leaders say about Mr Lee Kuan Yew. *The Straits Times* https://www.straitstimes.com/singapore/what-world-leaders-say-about-mr-lee-kuan-yew

Toh, T. W. (2021a, February 2). SIA ranked 34th in Fortune magazine's list of 50 most admired companies. *The Straits Times. https://Www.Straitstimes.Com/Singapore/Transport/Sia-Ranked-34th-in-Fortune-Magazines-List-of-50-Most-Admired-Companies*

Toh, T. W. (2021b, September 2). Changi Airport T1 and T3 reopen to public 3 months after Covid-19 cluster found. *The Straits Times*. https://www.straitstimes.com/singapore/transport/changi-airport-t1-and-t3-reopen-to-public-3-months-after-covid-19-cluster-found

Toh, Y. C. (2014, February 16). Balance between local and foreign workers a 'tricky issue': Tan Chuan-Jin. *The Straits Times*. https://www.straitstimes.com/singapore/balance-between-local-and-foreign-workers-a-tricky-issue-tan-chuan-jin

Yahoo Finance. (2021, October 24). Raytheon Technologies Corporation. *Yahoo.com*. https://finance.yahoo.com/chart/RTX#eyJpbnRlcnZhbCI6IndlZWsiLCJwZXJpb2RpY2l0eSI6MSwidGltZVVuaXQiOm51bGwsImNhbmRsZVdpZHRoIjo2LjIwNjg5NjU1MTcyNDEzOCwiZmxpcHBlZCI6ZmFsc2UsInZvbHVtZVVuZGVybGF5Ijp0cnVlLCJhZGoiOnRydWUsImNyb3NzaGFpcnMiOnRydWUsImNoYXJ0U2NhbGUiOiJsb2ciLCJpbnRlcnZhbCI6IndlZWsiLCJ... hcnRUeXBlIjoibGl

Yang, C. (2020a, July 28). Eagle Services Asia says retrenchments not confirmed, all staff still on payroll. *The Straits Times*. https://www.straitstimes.com/singapore/manpower/eagle-services-asia-says-retrenchments-not-confirmed-all-staff-still-on-payroll.

Yang, C. (2020b, July 29). NTUC, unions stepped in to stop unfair retrenchment by aircraft maintenance firm; industry action averted. *The Straits Times*. https://www.straitstimes.com/singapore/ntuc-unions-stepped-in-to-ensure-fair-play-in-aircraft-maintenance-firms-retrenchment.

Yang, P. (2018). Desiring "foreign talent": Lack and Lacan in anti-immigrant sentiments in Singapore. *Journal of Ethnic and Migration Studies*, *44*(6), 1015–1031. https://doi.org/10.1080/1369183X.2017.1384157

Yeo, J. (2020, July 28). SIA Engineering joint venture reportedly retrenched 144 employees within 3 days in July. *Mothership*. https://mothership.sg/2020/07/sia-engineering-eagle-services-asia-retrench/

Yeoh, B. S. A., & Lam, T. (2016). Immigration and its (Dis)Contents: The challenges of highly skilled migration in globalizing Singapore. *The American Behavioral Scientist (Beverly Hills)*, *60*(5-6), 637–658. https://doi.org/10.1177/0002764216632831

6

JAPAN

Nike's Anti-Racism Ad Sparks Backlash

Yuri Okutsu, Daphne Zhiying Xu, Fiona Hui Ling Loi, and Stephanie Ai Ling Ng

Introduction

Japan is an interesting conundrum. It is steeped in history and heavily shaped by cultural traditions, yet adaptable to globalization and external economic influences for survival. This phenomenon has inevitably created tensions within Japan and her citizens – evident in the reactions observed when Nike launched a two-minute Japanese-language commercial titled "Nike Japan: The future isn't waiting" on November 28, 2020. This case study will analyze how a multinational brand like Nike was unable to replicate in Japan, the success of its social justice advertising strategy deployed in the United States, despite the good intentions to raise awareness on the rise in bullying and discrimination in the country. The main reason for the popular brand's failure lay in the different socio-cultural environment between the two countries.

The Nike Japan Crisis

In 2018, Nike partnered with activist and former NFL quarterback Colin Kaepernick as the face of its 30th anniversary "Just Do It" campaign. This was a bold and deliberate move that signaled Nike's commitment to integrate social justice in its marketing strategy in the United States. Even though Nike stocks dipped immediately following the announcement, sales subsequently rose by 31%, reflecting a consumer base that resonated with Nike's social commentary (Trussell, 2018). In November 2020, six months prior to the Tokyo 2020 Olympics, the Tokyo arm of the global advertising agency, Wieden+Kennedy decided to replicate Nike's tried and tested social justice playbook and conceptualized an

DOI: 10.4324/9781003411802-7

anti-racism campaign for launch in Japan. Reflecting true stories and encounters, the creative strategy was inspired by a record high number of bullying cases in Japan in 2019, as well as findings from interviews that Wieden+Kennedy had conducted with over 20 young females, aged 18 to 22 who indicated that they hoped to see a change in Japanese culture and an end to bullying (WARC, n.d.). The commercial that featured Rui Hachimura and other athletes centered around three female teenagers of Japanese, ethnic Korean, and mixed heritage who faced bullying and discrimination, but subsequently found confidence and determination to embrace their identities through their passion in sports. Naomi Osaka, Japanese international tennis star, four-time Grand Slam winner and Nike ambassador, made a cameo appearance in the advertisement. In previous interviews, Osaka had shared that she had to deal with racial insensitivity in Japan due to her biracial ethnicity. Thus, her involvement further lent credibility to Nike Japan's intent of pushing for inclusion, respect, and fairness for everyone. The video was also accompanied by the hashtag #YouCantStopUs – which went viral in Japan almost immediately after the video premiered.

By December 2, 2020, the commercial had garnered approximately 25 million views on social media and close to 80,000 shares. It sparked a debate on Twitter and YouTube, drawing local and international media coverage especially online. On the surface, the video seemed similar to past Nike advertisements, featuring stories of athletes overcoming the odds and thriving. However, the message of having to battle racism and bullying in Japan was too provocative for the local populace, especially when conveyed by foreigners and through a high-profile mouthpiece – American brand Nike. Thus, one reason why the video went viral quickly was that it was uncommon to speak out against racism and discrimination in Japan, and many Japanese do not even think that discrimination exists in Japan (Denyer & Kashiwagi, 2020). Additionally, featuring a teenager of Zainichi Korean ethnicity created a furor as it outright implied ethnic discrimination, offending Japanese viewers and causing them much discomfort.

Online sentiments were mixed – drawing both applause and outrage. On the one hand, some were receptive and praised Nike for using sports and an inspirational video to encourage the Japanese to embrace diversity and have an open discourse on inclusivity. On the other hand, some viewed the advertisement as insensitive and malicious as it was a misrepresentation and exaggeration of discrimination in Japan, and questioned a foreign conglomerate's motive in casting Japan in a negative light. Some of these negative sentiments also led to public calls for a boycott, with netizens posting their views with hashtags such as #ナイキ不買運動 (Nike boycott)#ナイキの印象操作に抗議する(protest against Nike's impression manipulation), vowing to never buy Nike products again. In a Twitter analysis by a local marketing agency, mentions of the advertisement peaked on November 30, 2020 with nearly 80,000 posts. During its second peak on December 3, 2020, there were around 70,000 mentions with a mix of positive and negative sentiments. The backlash, which primarily took place online with limited broadcast coverage, lasted about 11 days (Shimazu, 2021) and tapered off quickly.

Despite the online backlash, Nike Japan did not immediately respond to a request for comment. When Nike Japan responded a few days later, it adopted a defensive strategy, reaffirming its firm stance on social justice and the intent to continue tackling socio-political issues. Nike Japan's senior marketing director Barbara Guinet said: "Nike for a long time has listened to minorities, supported them and voiced our views about causes that meet Nike's values." Nike communications vice-president Kate Meyers added, "Because of the controversial content in a country that prides itself on social harmony, the video garnered immediate attention – even before Nike completed its five-day distribution efforts across multiple communications platforms, i.e., Nike.com, the Nike app, Twitter, YouTube, Instagram and the media platform Teads" (Hengst, 2021). Nike Japan's course of action, or lack thereof, was anchored on their belief that "sports have the power to show what a better world looks like and can serve as a driving force for prompting positive changes that help bring the world forward," and that they will "continue calling loudly for inclusion, respect and fairness for all people" (The Asahi Shimbun Asia & Japan Watch, 2020). Despite calls to boycott Nike, the American brand has a strong reputation in the country, and impact to sales was minimal and it remained a leading sportswear brand in Japan (Euromonitor International, 2023). Even though there were no immediate or significant financial repercussions, the extent of the public anger showed that Nike had crossed the line with Japanese consumers, who are known not to voice their outrage out of politeness (Regaldo & Shibata, 2020). Crossing such lines could instead have longer-term reputational repercussions that would eventually result in financial implications given that 55% of Japanese consumers in a survey said they would choose, avoid, or boycott products according to a brand's attitude towards social issues (Matsuura et al., 2020 as cited in Salenius, 2023). What this implies is that it would not be inconceivable for even a well-loved brand like Nike to lose support from Japanese consumers over time should they continue to push for controversial views on social issues that the Japanese might frown upon.

Understanding Japan and Its Socio-cultural Environment

Why was Nike's neoliberal global message, which drew upon the American's symbolic meanings of liberalism and color blindness, rejected in Japan? Firstly, Japan is a homogenous society with little ethnic or racial diversity. As of 2022, 97.6% of the total population – 124.49 million are Japanese (Immigration Service Agency, n.d.) and foreign residents in Japan was a record high of 3 million at the end of 2022 (Japan Times, 2023).

On the definition of being Japanese, Article 10 of the Constitution of Japan defines the term "Japanese" based on Japanese nationality. The Nationality Law Article 2 defines Japanese national as: (1) When, at the time of one's birth, the father or the mother is a Japanese national; (2) When the father who died prior to the birth of the child was a Japanese national at the time of his death; (3) When both parents are unknown or have no nationality in a case where the child is born in Japan. Japan does not allow dual citizenship and citizens are required to renounce either their Japanese or foreign nationality before turning the age of 20 (The Ministry of Justice. (n.d.)). The Japanese Statistics Bureau only focuses on one's nationality. "*Hafu*" – or "half" in English, to refer to people who are ethnically half Japanese, mixed-race Japanese (Narain, 2019). While some Japanese nationals are ethnically or racially from diverse backgrounds, this diversity (i.e., distinctions in ethnicity) is not recognized officially. Thus reinforcing the idea that the "Japanese" refers to a single ethnic group, and that Japan's population only comprises a dichotomy of monoracial Japanese people and non-Japanese people.

A survey by Ishida in 2016 with 2,000 respondents living in Japan found the condition of blood as a necessary factor for one to be deemed Japanese, reflecting the concept of jus sanguinis (i.e., inherited nationality from one's parents). A Japanese national is raised and educated overseas would be perceived as being "diluted" – with a poorer ability to speak the language and lesser understanding of Japan's cultural background or the insensitiveness of the Japanese context. This is a critical factor as the Japanese language is highly contextual; dependent on one's social status and involves non-verbal signals. The communication style is indirect and implicit, requiring speakers to understand the cultural background to obtain the full command in Japanese language (Ishida, 2016; World Population Review, 2022). However, with greater contact with foreigners and higher socio-economic status, the younger generations are shifting their mindsets on such a definition of being Japanese over time.

Yet when we consider the actual racial and ethnic makeup of people living in Japan, the reality is far more complex. There are in fact differential undertones in the terminologies used in the discourse on Japanese identity and history. The term *nikkeijin* refers to Japanese people who emigrated from Japan and their descendants. "*Nikke*i" means "Japanese descent" and broadly refers to Japanese people who have relocated overseas on a permanent basis, irrespective of their current nationality and degree of Japanese ethnicity. Minority communities in Japan are perceived differently and have to strive hard for social acceptance (Yoon, 2015). For example, *"Zainichi,"* meaning "living in Japan," commonly refers to ethnic Koreans who have been living in Japan since 1910. Lastly, there is an inherent Japanese attitude of exclusivity that is pervasive and stems from two key aspects: The country's geographic isolation of an island nation, and *Sakoku* (Itoh, 1996). *Sakoku*, an isolationist foreign policy of the Japanese

Tokugawa shogunate that lasted over 200 years during the Edo period, limited trade and prevented the Japanese from traveling abroad and restricting the presence of foreigners in Japan. The initial intent of *Sakoku* was to limit Christian incursions in the country (Kazui & Videen, 1982).

The combination of natural and voluntary isolation facilitated a uniquely homogenous culture and mentality that underlie modern Japanese behavior and business practices (Reischauer & Jansen, 1995). What further preserved and reinforced traditional attitudes and ways of thinking are the country's government policies and group-oriented culture. Thus, even though the Japanese generally support multiculturalism, as mentioned, they prefer to maintain the image of national homogeneity (Nagayoshi, 2008). This likely stems from a strong sense of national and group identity, and what it means to "be Japanese" as ingrained over generations. The strong sense of national identity could have been compounded by Japanese politicians' assertions over the years about Japan being a "homogeneous society" and that the distinct nature of the country comes from being "one nation, one civilization, one language, one culture and one race"; further reinforcing a sense of homogeneity in the public's minds (Hellyer, 2002).

After Japan's declaration of independence in 1868, racial classification was anchored on the notion that race and ethnicity would be based on a common "blood," imagined ancestry, and shared national identity. Additionally, nationalism continued to build up – such as in the form of Japanese national language education (Stockwell, 2021) and an emphasis on cultivating a patriotic spirit in learners throughout the Meiji Restoration until World War II (Himeno et al., 1998; Kurasawa, 1994). After WWII, "*Nihonjinron*," meaning "sociology of race" was popularized in the discourse on the Japanese national and cultural identity, viz., essential aspects of the character, behavior and features unique to Japan (Stockwell, 2021). This drove an intense belief that the in-group's cultural and psychological characteristics were to be homogenous and a shared uniqueness of being Japanese. Despite the less frequent reference to *"Nihonjinron"* over time, the same concept of homogeneity continued to be promulgated in mainstream politics (Burgess, 2004). Furthermore, Japan is one of the few countries in Asia that was never ruled or colonized by Western powers. Thus, it is unsurprising that the country has been uncompromising in developing its economy and industry with strong protectionist policies (Fukurai & Yang, 2018), further enhancing Japan's insularity and homogeneity.

Political System

Japan is a bicameral parliamentary constitutional monarchy, in which the Emperor is the head of state – "the "symbol of the state and the unity of the people," and the Prime Minister is the head of government, and the head of the Cabinet, which directs the executive branch. Legislative power is vested in the National Diet (*Kokkai*), which consists of the House of Representatives and the House of Councillors. Judicial power is vested in the Supreme Court and lower courts, and sovereignty is vested in the people of Japan by the 1947 Constitution (Ministry of Internal Affairs and Communications, 2007; Web Japan, n.d.).

Japan's constitution was promulgated in 1946 and came into force in 1947, superseding the Meiji Constitution of 1889. This new constitution introduced two pivotal changes when compared to its predecessor: A revised concept of sovereignty and an explicit commitment to ensure Japan's enduring status as a peaceful and democratic nation (Ministry of Internal Affairs and Communications, 2007). Japan has since steadfastly adhered to its commitment, actively contributing to the promotion of peace and stability in both the Asia-Pacific region and the global community. Japan's encounter with the world, during a period marked by nationalism and imperialism, compelled the integration of traditional values and norms into what was termed a "national value system" (*Kokutai*) and further perpetuated by the national characteristic (*Kunigara*). National policies are orchestrated to serve the country's interests, and they in turn influence economic growth and education with the aim of cultivating model Japanese citizens. By fostering disciplined individuals, the nation reaps economic benefits, and society functions effectively (Rohlen, 1989).

Keeping the Japanese cultural identity intact is a priority for the Japanese government and as such, accepting immigrants would be feasible only if doing so does not damage Japanese cultural identity. Japan has frequently been criticized for its lack of multicultural policies due to the adoption of the bilineal *jus sanguinis* principle under the "Nationality Law." Japan had promoted ethnic homogeneity and its own culture by discouraging immigrants through their labor migration policy. Japan's labor migration policy is highly selective, prioritizing those in professional occupations and with higher education credentials (Akashi, 2010; Murata, 2010; Oishi, 2012; Tsukasaki, 2008). Over the past two decades, Japan had made only incremental reforms to its immigration policies that fall short of alleviating labor shortages and fiscal burdens of maintaining a large elderly population (Chung & Kim, 2012), where elderly households accounted for 40.7% of the total households (Statistics Bureau of Japan, 2021). For decades, immigration was a political taboo, with concerns about culture and ethnic homogeneity often by Japan's powerful right-wing. The country accepted only modest numbers of immigrants, often making strict requirements of them. Only select groups such as families and descendants of Japanese emigrants were offered permanent residency (Taylor, 2021). This was especially evident during the COVID-19 pandemic – while many countries closed their borders to foreign visitors to stem the spread of the virus, Japan went further by banning not only foreign visitors, but even foreign residents from re-entering the country (Murakami & Lies, 2021; Okutsu & Regalado, 2020). The country's COVID-19 foreign entry policies exacerbated pre-existing xenophobic sentiment and incited discourse among those who do not hold Japanese citizenship.

Considering all these factors, Nike's advertisement was controversial as an external company unveiled the evident racism and discrimination embedded within the country's policies and census. Though its homogeneous society has long been criticized for being discriminatory towards mixed-race individuals, Nike's advertisement forced the Japanese government to acknowledge racism and discrimination as an issue to be tackled by society. Some conservative politicians have criticized Nike for interfering in local domestic affairs and promoting Western values. However, the overall government response was deemed to be reserved throughout the episode, without official statements released or actions taken regarding the advertisement or company.

Economic System

Japan is known for its economic and business prowess, rich culture, and technology. It is the third largest and most developed economy in the world, with a well-educated and industrious workforce. Its large affluent population makes it one of the world's biggest consumer markets. Japan's infrastructures and well-established financial markets are conducive to the operation and potential success of multinational corporations. The legal and regulatory climate is highly supportive of investors in many respects. Capital markets are deep and broadly available to foreign investors. The country also maintains strong protections for intellectual property rights with robust enforcement. Corruption is low, but deep relationships between firms and suppliers may limit competition in certain sectors and inhibit the entry of foreign firms into local markets.

Although the extent of direct state participation in economic activities is limited, the government's control and influence over business is stronger and more pervasive than in most other countries with market economies. This influence primarily manifests through ongoing government-business consultations and the deep, indirect involvement of authorities in the banking sector. Collaboration occurs predominantly via joint committees and groups responsible for monitoring and establishing performance targets across nearly every branch and sector of the economy. Japanese bureaucrats wield considerable discretionary power instead of relying on explicit directives, offering what is termed "administrative guidance" when interacting with the private sector to implement official policies. Nevertheless, since the early 1990s, concerted efforts have been underway to curtail the use of such informal directives, as they have faced criticism for fostering a perception of collusion between government entities and large corporations. In 2021, Japan's GDP was estimated to be close to US$5 million, just behind the United States and China.

However, due to the decline of the working population, its per-capita income is US$39,285.20, placing it 28th in the world. Following the period of economic stagnation in the 1990s and the economic impact caused by various global recessions, the country has managed to see an uptick in its economy in recent years. This was driven by strong cooperation between government and industry, and advanced technological know-how. MNCs see Japan primarily as a stable, slow growth but highly profitable market with extremely sophisticated consumers (Marshall & Koshino, 2018). Government policies on foreign direct investments (FDI) were especially crucial to Japan's development. Nike, being an American MNC, indirectly benefitted from the sound relationship Japan holds with the United States, becoming amongst the top activewear brands in Japan in terms of market share (Bloomberg, 2020). However, as with all countries worldwide, the COVID-19 pandemic greatly affected Japan, and massive government support was required to buffer the nation against the pandemic's impact. The COVID-19 pandemic had affected Japan's economy significantly. In 2020, GDP fell by 3.6%, the volume of trade declined by 5.3%, and FDI flows dropped by 42%. Due to global travel restrictions, the number of foreign visitors to Japan dropped by 73% as compared to the previous year (UNWTO, 2021). Domestic tourism fell by 50%.

Since the 1970s, there has been reduced visibility of social movements in Japan. Labor unions are seeing a fall in membership rates, and the political scientist Chigaya Kinoshita noted that, at universities, student groups including councils and clubs were also in decline. There had also been a drop in the number of protests, and labor and civil movements were therefore less visible. Under such circumstances, it is difficult for young people to find ways to criticize or oppose society, and they have trouble believing their actions could change anything (Kyoko, 2021).

The proliferation of technology and social media has led to a high acceptance of "Americanization" globally, and even more so in Japan, given Japan's history of interaction with the United States after WWII. This undoubtedly contributed to the popularity of Nike in Japan. Despite the controversial advertisement, Nike remains the most popular sports brand in Japan in 2022 with 38.8% of respondents indicating that it was their favorite brand (Statista, 2022a). Nike was the favorite sports brand for adults up to 49 years and for the elderly aged 60 to 69 years. The revelation of the controversial advertisement did little to dampen the image of the Nike brand in the eyes of the Japanese, who had cleverly placed their cards on the immensely popular Naomi Osaka, especially the youth. Hence, even though the advertisement faced some initial backlash from some consumers who felt that the company was promoting a political agenda rather than selling its products, Nike Japan had gained a positive economic impact on its sales.

Due to its trend popularity and upbeat promotional tactics, the company's sales increased significantly, and the advertisement was well received by a majority of its consumers.

Media System

Consumption of news has always been primarily via print media and its nationwide television (TV) networks (Sawa & Saisho, 2022). The print media consists of five national newspapers – the Yomiuri Shimbun, Asahi Shimbun, Mainichi Shimbun, Sankei Shimbun, and the Nikkei (the Nihon Keizai Shimbun). These newspapers primarily cover factual news with limited opinion-based pieces. According to Statista (2021), newspaper circulation was approximately 35 million in 2021. Magazine circulation is also widespread, with the top 10 magazines being comic or graphic novel *(manga)* magazines. As for broadcast media, TV remained the largest medium (Statista, 2022b) and is often considered an important means to establish social trends (Kyodo, 2019). There are currently seven country-wide television networks in Japan including two owned by Japan's national public broadcaster NHK. While there are regulations to govern cross-media ownership, most of Japan's main newspaper groups have a majority stake in their affiliated TV networks, either through direct or partial ownership. According to "Reporters Without Borders" (2021), Japan is ranked 67 in the 2021 World Press Freedom Index.

While the country embraces the principles of media freedom and pluralism, media practitioners believe that total editorial freedom does not exist due to the influence of tradition and business interests. Japan's unique "*kisha clubs*" (press clubs) system is known to discriminate against freelancers and foreign reporters and is a channel for official sources to control the information they provide to the media (Kingston, 2016). Aligned with global trends, consumption of traditional media has been declining since 2000s as the Internet has become more prevalent. Although Japan has seen increased use of digital and social media, a media awareness survey conducted by The Nippon Foundation (2019) found that TV remains the main information source for young Japanese, with social media at 47.1%, news websites at 45.1%, and video streaming and sharing websites at 36.4%.

According to the "Digital 2020" report by Hootsuite (Kemp, 2020), social media penetration in 2020 was low (65%) relative to the rest of the world, and in January 2020, there were 82 million active social media users. Based on monthly active user numbers, YouTube was the top social media platform in the year the Nike advertisement was aired on YouTube, and with most YouTube users then being in their 40s and 50s. Thus, given that the controversial commercial accompanied by the hashtag #YouCantStopUs was first uploaded on YouTube, it would be hard for the video to have gone unnoticed. Between November 30 and December 2, 2020, there was an intensive debate on social media as the Japanese are not accustomed to discussing sensitive issues like racism publicly. The controversy also sparked discussions about racism and discrimination in the country, as well as whether corporations should even be promoting social justice.

Many online commentators opined that Nike had exaggerated the scale of racial discrimination in Japan and questioned if Nike, as a foreign brand, had the right to weigh in on such domestic issues. The incident was also covered by both local and international media such as Bloomberg, BBC, and The Washington Post within the first week of the commercial's debut, with coverage driven by extensive online debate. However, within Japan, the backlash and debate were primarily contained in social media as the advertisement was mostly talked about online with limited coverage on television (Shimazu, 2021). Additionally, despite the calls for the boycott of Nike products, Ikuo Gonoi, a business professor at Takachiho University, noted that the people calling for the boycott were "not the same group of people who prefer to buy Nike, and some of them may have never bought Nike in the past" (Regaldo & Shibata, 2020). Indeed, Nike only suffered a brief reputational dip and remains one of the leading sportswear brands in Japan. Because Nike's customers are predominantly in the 15 to 45 year range (Start.io, 2022), and most Japanese YouTube users are in their 40s and 50s, the negative sentiments from existing Nike customers would not have formed the majority. Thus, with Nike's popularity and large consumer base, and with the backlash primarily contained on social media, response to the calls for a Nike boycott was muted and short-lived. Additionally, since TV and newspapers are the primary sources of media that the Japanese – including the young – trust and rely on for essential information, the advertisement on YouTube had little impact on the public as compared to if it were shown on TV (Nippon.com, 2019).

Societal Culture

Culture is a "silent language" (Hall, 1973) that can be regarded as a key "environment" that public relations practitioners need to navigate. In analyzing the Nike backlash crisis, one cannot overlook Japan's societal culture. On Hofstede's dimensions of culture, Japan scores high in masculinity (95), uncertainty avoidance (92), and long-term orientation (88), and medium levels of power distance (54), individualism (46) and indulgence (42) (Hofstede Insights, 2021). In relation to Nike's incident, of primary relevance are the dimensions of low individualism (i.e., high collectivism) and high uncertainty avoidance. Although Japan is one of the world's most masculine societies, any emphasis on competition and achievement at the individual level may potentially be eclipsed by its high sense of collectivism. Japanese are taught early to conform to societal standards and norms, and to prioritize group harmony above individual expressions of opinions (Scribner, 2007; Web Japan, 2020). Individuals that stand out (e.g., in terms of ethnicity, deviant behaviors, etc.) may become potential targets of bullying in schools, and per Japan's high-context culture, bullying often takes the form of indirect words or gestures as reflected in the Nike advertisement.

The importance of group harmony over individual desires and opinions is evidently emphasized through various notions. Firstly, there is the common Japanese saying, "the nail that sticks out gets hammered down." It emphasizes the potential difficulties and resistance individuals may face from being different from the norm. Next, the concept of *honne* and *tatemae* – a Japanese cultural paradigm between what is publicly stated versus what is the true motive or intent. It describes the tendency to hide one's true feelings and preferences to minimize direct confrontation and disagreements in social situations (Doi, 1986; Sriramesh & Takasaki, 1999). This also explains why Japanese accounted for the second largest Twitter user cluster, after the Americans, with 58.96 million accounts in 2022 (Tamura, 2022), given that this social media platform serves as an anonymity mouthpiece (75.1% of Japan's Twitter accounts are anonymous) for Japanese users to voice their views, beyond the façade of *tatemae*. Also, high-context language is a great fit with 140 characters limitation and can tell much richer information compared to other language, such as English (Tamura, 2022).

Japan is a collectivistic culture with the concept of "*wa*" i.e., harmony, being integral to public discourse and interactions. The individual is expected to prioritize group values and community welfare over one's own desires and ambitions for the good of society (Alston, 1989). The concept of *wa* is often translated as cooperating to achieve collective goals, maintenance of group unity and peaceful conformity in public circumstances, and even the suppression of individual goals in favor of the group. *Wa* highlights the importance of group membership, and Japanese are expected to temper the bluntness and negativity if they are to express a truth that might affect harmony (Alston, 1989; Midooka, 1990). As the message conveyed through Nike's advertisement was sensitive, direct, and in-your-face with the potential of threatening *wa*, coupled with Nike being an outsider, it was inevitable that there would be backlash and accusations of Nike portraying Japan as racist and discriminatory to the rest of the world.

However, while the Japanese emphasize harmony, most Japanese people are at worst passive racists, making racism in Japan less apparent than it truly is. McNeil (2018) highlighted that discrimination in Japan is not just about hatred and violence, but it could be anchored on fear or a lack of understanding. Thus, when asked if they are racist, the Japanese are more likely to disagree, whereas if questioned whether they are afraid of foreigners, they would likely respond in the affirmative. To add, such fear primarily stems from a lack of communication experience with foreigners and/or having a language barrier.

Uncertainty avoidance refers to "the extent to which the members of a culture feel threatened by ambiguous or unknown situations" (Hofstede et al., 2010). Japan's score on uncertainty avoidance is one of the highest globally, and this is often attributed to the country's frequent experience of natural disasters. This has resulted in a societal tendency to always be prepared for uncertainties and extends beyond emergency planning and precautions for natural disasters to also include every other aspect of the Japanese's way of life (Hofstede Insights, 2021). Given Japan's high uncertainty avoidance, citizens are generally risk-averse and encounter discomfort in ambiguity. Coupled with their sense of collectivism, it follows that members tend to embrace group standards, norms, and behaviors as they provide predictability, certainty and security (Triandis, 1989). Furthermore, as Japan sees itself as largely monoethnic and culturally homogeneous with a strong sense of national identity, racial divisions are commonly deemed sensitive and open discourse could potentially destabilize Japan's social fabric and the common perception that there is little or no discrimination in the country.

The actions and efficiency of the Japanese government in addressing diversity and inclusion matters may also be a telling reflection of the society's prevailing perceptions towards racism and discrimination. Despite the long existence of various minority ethnic groups and the known attitudes and behaviors towards them, the Japanese government only initiated the Multicultural Coexistence Promotion Plan in 2006 (Demelius, 2021) and passed the Hate Speech Act in 2016 to comply with the International Convention on the Elimination of All Forms of Racial Discrimination (ICERD) rolled out by the United Nations. However, there remains no official ban on hate speech and no penalties for individuals or organizations that run afoul of the convention (Osaki, 2016). While one could argue for considerations on freedom of speech and the need to maintain unity (Fukurai & Yang, 2018), it could also imply the inherent perceptions on the extent of racism and discrimination in Japan. Looking at the need to maintain harmony even in the face of negativity, regardless if it is true, this circles back to the point on why a high-context society like Japan rarely engages in direct expressions – especially negative ones – with messages often implied and inferred through indirect communication styles (Lufkin, 2020). Thus, when an outsider or foreign brand like Nike stirs up the hornet's nest in a way that the Japanese find confrontational, disrespectful, and even somewhat misleading, backlash inevitably will ensue.

Given how the different yet important environmental constructs have played out in the case of Nike's controversial commercial, there are lessons to be learned for crisis communication professionals. In view of the uproar that was amplified through social media, could Nike Japan have adopted a more strategic or sensitive communication stance, or responded more in alignment with the socio-cultural variables? By developing controversial advertisements to make a social statement or to shape consumer response toward corporate social advocacy (e.g., Nike's Colin Kaepernick's campaign against racial inequality and police brutality), Nike might have fared well and achieved the desired outcomes in its home country or in other Western countries. Li et al. (2022) found that people would validate why companies are supporting a socio-political cause, i.e., are companies getting involved because what they advocated is in line with their values. However, are the rest of the world equally prepared for such direct social statements despite globalization? Therefore, to avoid potential backlash or unnecessary downstream crisis communications, strategic communicators would need to consider the socio-cultural context and generate content that is both targeted and meaningful.

Culture is an important influencer of both communication and relationships, and it is important for MNCs to tread carefully on sensitive topics such as racism, especially in an age where social media can easily amplify sentiments. Emotions can also be magnified in the digital space and eventually drive online discourse to offline activism. This was apparent in recent social movements such as #BlackLivesMatter, which successfully transitioned from debates on Twitter to protests on the streets (Carney, 2016, p. 180). In the case of the advertisement in Japan, the consequence was less dire given the cultural aspects overriding the extent of activism observed. Further, considering Japanese's preference to remain polite and avoid conflict, it would be challenging to assess the true extent of unhappiness felt by the public, or whether resentment towards Nike might breed and fester over time. Thus, while the immediate damage to Nike's reputation might have seemed minimal and short-lived, it would be remiss of anyone to assume that Nike had gone completely unscathed from the episode.

Activism in Japan

Japan has seen a resurgence in student activism in recent years both in the form of participation as well as the ways they have leveraged technology, branding, and even pop-culture to mobilize the masses. Groups savvy in new media have also emerged over the last decade, including anti-nuclear activists following the Fukushima disaster in 2011 as well as the rise of the group known as Students Emergency Action for Liberal Democracy (SEALDs) in 2015 to resist controversial Constitutional interpretations by the Shinzō Abe government viz., the proactive actions on the part of the Japanese Self-Defense Forces (Smith, 2020).

However, activism remains relatively uncommon in Japan. This is unsurprising as the Japanese value the concept of *wa* and is inclined to avoid direct confrontation and disagreements. This is supported by The Asahi Shimbun (Fujisaki, 2021) report from a survey by Japan's largest labor organization, Rengo (Japanese Trade Union Confederation), that young Japanese are not in favor of activities such as demonstrations, boycotts, and traditional social movements, preferring instead to leverage social media to bring about change.

Additionally, Japanese generally do not deem it beneficial to prolong discourse on topics that are considered controversial or sensitive or to even go deep into the issue of ethnic minority discrimination in a public setting. In the Nike crisis, the impact of activism was limited mainly to some online calls for boycotts with no reports of physical or violent demonstrations. Even the online calls for a boycott with hashtag activism were short-lived and muted, with little impact on Nike's subsequent sales performance and share price. Such an observation reinforces the plausible interplay of factors pertaining to Nike's sufficiently strong consumer loyalty and Japanese cultural idiosyncrasies, preventing the backlash from evolving into full-scale activism. Interestingly, perhaps it was the lack of activism and impact that might have led to Nike Japan adopting an approach of inaction in dealing with the crisis, with a preference to stand by their advertisement and stance on addressing social justice issues to promote positive change.

Kobayashi (2012) suggested that rather than preconditioning non-Western individuals to be passive "others," it is important not to neglect how their identities and cultures make profound impact on global media representation and consumption as well as how they are at the same time shaped by the regulations and cultural norms of Western corporate practices. Communication practitioners ought to acknowledge that non-Western cultural intermediaries deserve more attention in studies of sport, media, and cultural identity articulated in the global cultural economy. This translates to further implications and additional efforts on MNCs' communication professionals who have to market brands across cultural and national boundaries. Agility and flexibility on the part of crisis communication professionals while being sensitive to local culture when meeting organizational goals is necessary. This is especially so considering that stakeholder activism is on the rise, and ease of information and news being spread at breakneck speeds. Alternative means and positivity could still be advocated through Nike's commercials as the company has all along embarked upon emotional advertising strategy – a technique that aims to arouse strong positive emotion from audiences by triggering nostalgic, motivating, inspiring or aspiring images and narratives (Kim, 2020).

Conclusion

Japan's rich history, cultural foundations, and societal values that have centered around homogeneity, collectivism, and harmony for centuries will endure for the foreseeable future, even if with some changes due to modernization. Foreign companies need to be acutely aware that beneath the stoic surface lies a complex tapestry of individual perspectives muted by Japanese societal norms that emphasized harmony. However, Nike has taken a bold step in its "The Future Isn't Waiting" campaign, challenging societal norms in Japan. The commercial triggered a crisis and calls for a boycott, while also successfully igniting public conversations on diversity and inclusion.

From the confluence of the five dimensions prescribed in the Global PR Framework (Sriramesh & Verčič, 2020), it might appear that Nike emerged unscathed from this communication crisis with no substantial impact on its sales, owing to the strong societal cultural fabric that helped to quell and mitigate the backlash. While the campaign has yet to improve racism in Japan, it steered a need to discuss a sensitive topic in the country. Yet, this uncalled "attack" on society may be fueling a slow burn for long-term reputational damage for Nike Japan.

The backlash was short-lived likely because a homogeneous Japanese society is not comfortable about speaking up and adopts "*Gaman*" or the virtue of patience and perseverance, particularly when faced with unexpected or difficult situations (Littler, 2019). However, this behavior may change if the Japanese face "*Gaman no genkai*," that is, when Japanese pride is threatened or put down. Once the perception pivots to a negative angle, the entire collectivistic society might stand against the brand that caused the "discord." In retrospect, companies should weigh in on underlying factors that may be deep-seated in target markets' local environments and save the need to repair damaging and harmful disruptions that threaten the survival of an organization.

References

Akashi, J. (2010). *Imin kennkyū to nyūkoku kanri: Nyuukok ukanri seisaku-1990 nentaisei no seiritsu to tenkai [Japan's immigration control policy: Foundation and transition]*. Nakanishia Sh.

Alston, J. P. (1989). Wa, guanxi, and inhwa: Managerial principles in Japan, China, and Korea. *Business Horizons*, *32*(2), 26–31. https://doi.org/10.1016/S0007-6813(89)80007-2

Bloomberg. (2020). Nike sales trends outstrip rivals 'by far,' Credit Suisse says. https://www.bloomberg.com/news/articles/2020-05-14/nike-sales-trends-outstrip-rivals-by-far-credit-suisse-says

Burgess, C. (2004). Maintaining identities: Discourses of homogeneity in a rapidly globalizing Japan. *Electronic Journal of Contemporary Japanese Studies*. *5*(3), Article 1. https://www.japanesestudies.org.uk/articles/Burgess.html

Carney, N. (2016). All lives matter, but so does race: Black lives matter and the evolving role of social media. *Humanity & Society*, *40*(2), 180–199. https://doi.org/10.1177/0160597616643868

Chung, E. A., & Kim, D. (2012). Citizenship and marriage in a globalizing world: Multicultural families and monocultural nationality laws in Korea and Japan. *Indiana Journal of Global Legal Studies*, *19*(1), Article 8.

Demelius, Y. (2021). Thinking through community spirit: Zainichi Koreans in post-Korean wave Japanese communities. *Japanese Studies*, *41*(1), 93–112. https://doi.org/10.1080/10371397.2021.1893673

Denyer, S., & Kashiwagi, A. (2020). Nike ad showing racial discrimination faced by Japanese girls provokes backlash. https://www.washingtonpost.com/world/asia_pacific/nike-ad-japan-naomi-osaka/2020/12/01/cf310a2a-3387-11eb-9699-00d311f13d2d_story.html

Doi, T. (1986). *The anatomy of self: The individual versus society*. Kodansha International.

Euromonitor International. (2023, January). Sportswear in Japan. *Euromonitor*. https://www.euromonitor.com/sportswear-in-japan/report

Fujisaki, M. (2021). Japan teens turn to activism but no public display of protest. *The Asahi Shimbun*. https://www.asahi.com/ajw/articles/14342207

Fukurai, H., & Yang, A. (2018). The history of Japanese racism, Japanese American redress, and the dangers associated with government regulation of hate speech. *Hastings Constitutional Law Quarterly*, *45*(3), 533.

Hall, E. (1973). *The silent language*. Anchor Press/Doubleday.

Hengst, C. (2021, March 18). Nike: "The future isn't waiting." Ad Week. Retrieved on October 25, 2021, from https://www.adweek.com/adw_slide/nike-the-future-isnt-waiting-wiedenkennedy-tokyo/

Himeno, M., Kobayashi, Y., Kaneko, H., Komiya, T., & Murata, M. (1998). *Kokokara hajimaru nihongo kyoiku*. Hitsuji Shobo.

Hellyer, R. (2002). Historical and contemporary perspectives on the sakoku theme in Japanese foreign relations: 1600-2000. *Social Science Japan Journal*, *52*, 255–259.

Hofstede, G., Hofstede, G. J., & Minkov, M. (2010). Cultures and organizations: Software of the mind.

Hofstede Insights. (2021). Country Comparison. https://www.hofstede-insights.com/country-comparison/japan,the-usa/

Immigration Services Agency. (n.d.). 統計｜出入国在留管理庁. Retrieved on August 23, 2023, from https://www.moj.go.jp/isa/policies/statistics/

Ishida, A. (2016). Imagined conditions of the "Japanese. *Japanese Sociological Review*, *67*(2), 182–200. https://doi.org/10.4057/jsr.67.182

Itoh, M. (1996). Japan's abiding sakoku mentality. *Orbis*, *40*(2), 235–245. https://doi.org/10.1016/S0030-4387(96)90062-9.

Japan Times. (2023). Number of foreign residents in Japan rises to record 3.2 million. Retrieved on August 23, 2023, from https://www.japantimes.co.jp/news/2023/10/14/japan/society/japan-foreign-population/

Kazui, T., & Videen, S. D. (1982). Foreign relations during the Edo period: Sakoku reexamined. *The Journal of Japanese Studies*, *8*(2), 283–306. https://doi-org/10.2307/132341.

Kemp, S. (2020). Digital 2020 (Japan). Hootsuite. https://datareportal.com/reports/digital-2020-japan

Kim, M. (2020). How Phil Knight made Nike a leader in the sport industry: Examining the success factors. *Sport in Society*, *23*(9), 1512–1523.

Kingston, J. (Ed.). (2016). *Press freedom in contemporary Japan*. Taylor & Francis.

Kobayashi, K. (2012). Globalization, corporate nationalism and Japanese cultural intermediaries: Representation of bukatsu through Nike advertising at the global–local nexus. *International Review for the Sociology of Sport*, *47*(6), 724–742.

Kurasawa, E. (1994). *Kokusai rikai kyoiku to kyoiku jissen: Kokugo ni okeru kokusai rikai kyoiku (educational theories and practices: Globalization and Japanese language education for Japanese children)*. Emutei Shuppan.

Kyodo, P. R. (2019). Japan market and media overview. https://kyodo-pr.com/japan-market-media-overview/

Kyoko, T. (2021) Why are Japanese youth distancing themselves from social activism? Nippon.com. Retrieved on August 19, 2022, from https://www.nippon.com/en/in-depth/d00668/.

Li, J. Y., Kim, J. K., & Alharbi, K. (2022). Exploring the role of issue involvement and brand attachment in shaping consumer response toward corporate social advocacy (CSA) initiatives: The case of Nike's Colin Kaepernick campaign. *International Journal of Advertising*, *41*(2), 233–257.

Littler, J., (2019, March 20). The art of perseverance: How gaman defined Japan. *BBC.com*. https://www.bbc.com/worklife/article/20190319-the-art-of-perseverance-how-gaman-defined-japan

Lufkin, B. (2020). How "reading the air" keeps Japan running. *BBC.com*. https://www.bbc.com/worklife/article/20200129-what-is-reading-the-air-in-japan

Marshall, R., & Koshino, H. (2018). The challenge for multinationals in Japan White paper. Odgers Berndtson. Retrieved on August 18, 2022, from https://www.odgersberndtson.com/media/6335/odgers-berndtson-the-challenge-for-multinationals-in-japan-whitepaper.pdf.

Matsuura, Y, Kahn, S., Kimura, E., & Deguchi, R. (2020). Daibashiti ando inkurujon jidai ni okeru black lives matter to kohkoku komyunikeshon [black lives matter and advertisement communication in the era of diversity and inclusion] *JAA* 108. 770: pp. 4–8.

McNeil, B. (2018, June 16). 日本人が知らずにしている人種差別の「正体」. 東洋経済オンライン. https://toyokeizai.net/articles/-/225393?page=2

Midooka, K. (1990). Characteristics of Japanese-style communication. *Media, Culture & Society*, *12*(4), 477–489.

Ministry of Internal Affairs and Communications. (2007). Organisation of the Government of Japan. Retrieved on August 5, 2022, from https://japan.kantei.go.jp/constitution_and_government_of_japan/fundamental_e.html

Murakami, S., & Lies, E. (2021, December 1). Japan escalates Omicron emergency as airlines halt reservations, 2nd case found. *Reuters*. https://www.reuters.com/world/asia-pacific/japan-expand-travel-ban-some-foreigners-with-resident-status-2021-12-01/

Murata, A. (2010). "Gaikoku koudo jinzai no kokusai idō to rōdō – Idojin IT en-jinia no kokusai idō to ukeoi rōdō no bunseki Kara" [International migration of highly skilled workers: Analysis of the temporary migration of Indian IT engineers and contract labor in Japan]. *Migration Policy Review*, *2*, 74–89.

Nagayoshi, K. (2008). The influence of the perceived threat and contact in Japanese anti-immigrant attitude: Analysis of JGSS–2003. *JGSS Research Series*, *7*, 259–270.

Narain, A. (2019, April 1). *Daburu bind: Perceptions of the speech of mixed race Japanese.* Copyright © 2007–2008. http://id.nii.ac.jp/1130/00004542/

Nippon.com. (2019). Young Japanese still trust TV and newspapers more than online media. Japan Data in Nippon.com Society. https://www.nippon.com/en/japan-data/h00577/young-japanese-still-trust-tv-and-newspapers-more-than-online-media.html

Oishi, N. (2012). The limits of immigration policies: The challenges of highly skilled migration in Japan. *American Behavioral Scientist*, *56*(8), 1080–1100.

Okutsu, A., & Regalado, F. (2020, September 1). Japan finally lifts COVID-based reentry ban for foreign residents. *Nikkei Asia*. Retrieved on August 5, 2022, from https://asia.nikkei.com/Spotlight/Japan-immigration/Japan-finally-lifts-COVID-based-reentry-ban-for-foreign-residents

Osaki, T. (2016). Diet passes Japan's first law to curb hate speech. *Japan Times*. https://www.japantimes.co.jp/news/2016/05/24/national/social-issues/diet-passes-japans-first-law-curb-hate-speech/

Regaldo, F., & Shibata, N. (2020). Nike shrugs off Japan boycott threats after controversial ad. *Nikkei Asia*. https://asia.nikkei.com/Business/Business-trends/Nike-shrugs-off-Japan-boycott-threats-after-controversial-ad

Reporters Without Borders. (2021). Japan. Retrieved from https://rsf.org/en/japan

Reischauer, E. O., & Jansen, M. B. (1995). *The Japanese today: Change and continuity*. Belknap Press of Harvard University Press. https://books.google.com.sg/books?id=BTPNlLIy2soC

Rohlen, T. P. (1989). Order in Japanese society: Attachment, authority, and routine. *Journal of Japanese Studies, 15(1),* 5–40. https://doi.org/10.2307/132406.

Sawa, Y., & Saisho, R. (2022). *Japan Digital news report. Reuters institute for the study of journalism*. University of Oxford. https://reutersinstitute.politics.ox.ac.uk/digital-news-report/2022/japan

Salenius, S. (2023). *Gender in Japanese popular culture: Rethinking masculinities and femininities*. Springer Nature.

Scribner, S. (2007). Civic and moral education in Japanese public schools. *Leadership for Student Activities*, *35*(5), 30–40.

Shimazu, K. (2021, November 12). 【SNS分析】NikeのCMは「炎上」なのか?データから広報・マーケ担当が学ぶべきことを考察. サードオピニオン（β）. https://3rd-opinion.net/article/312/

Smith, N. M. (2020). Vigilante video: Digital populism and anxious anonymity among Japan's new netizens. *Critical Asian Studies*, *52*(1), 67–86.

Sriramesh, K., & Takasaki, M. (1999). The impact of culture on Japanese public relations. *Journal of Communication Management (London, England)*, *3*(4), 337–352. https://doi.org/10.1108/eb023497

Sriramesh, & Verčič, D. (2020). *The global public relations handbook: Theory, research, and practice*. Taylor & Francis Group. https://doi.org/10.4324/9781315173290

Start.io. (2022). Nike target market segmentation – customer analysis and marketing goals for 2022. https://www.start.io/blog/nike-target-market-analysis/

Statista. (2021). Japan newspaper circulation. Retrieved from https://www.statista.com/statistics/652352/japan-newspaper-circulation/

Statista. (2022a). Most popular sports brands in Japan by age group. https://www.statista.com/statistics/735053/japan-popularity-of-sports-brands/#:~:text=According%20to%20a%20survey%20conducted,was%20Asics%2C%20with%2024.4%20percent.

Statista. (2022b). Media industry in Japan — statistics and facts. https://www.statista.com/topics/7407/media-industry-in-japan/#dossierKeyfigures

Statistics Bureau of Japan. (2021, December 10). 全国社寺教会等宗教団体・教師・信者数. E-stat. Retrieved on September 10, 2022, from https://www.e-stat.go.jp

Stockwell, E. (2021). In principle or in practice? Investigation of Japanese university students' perceptions and attitudes toward multiculturalism in Japan. *Journal of International and Intercultural Communication*, *14*(2), 164–183. https://doi.org/10.1080/17513057.2020.1772343

Tamura, Y. (2022, June 9). Here is why Japanese people are addicted to Twitter. *Medium.com*. https://medium.com/illumination/here-is-why-japanese-people-are-addicted-to-twitter-e74ec7ac863e

Taylor, A. (2021). Long closed to most immigration, Japan looks to open up amid labor shortage. *Washington Post*. Retrieved on August 15, 2022, from https://www.washingtonpost.com/world/2021/11/18/japan-labor-shortage-immigration/.

The Asahi Shimbun Asia & Japan Watch. (2020, December 24). Nike Japan ad on discrimination draws applause and outrage. https://www.asahi.com/ajw/articles/13993062

The Ministry of Justice. (n.d.). *The Ministry of Justice: The Nationality Law.* Retrieved on August 23, 2023, from https://www.moj.go.jp/ENGLISH/information/tnl-01.html

The Nippon Foundation. (2019). Awareness survey of 18-year-olds. Retrieved on August 22, 2023, from https://www.nippon-foundation.or.jp/en/news/articles/2019/20191225-39458.html

Triandis, H. C. (1989). The self and social behavior in differing cultural contexts. *Psychological Review*, *96*(Jul 89), 506–520.

Trussell, C. (2018). Nike's revolution: From sweatshops to social justice activists. LinkedIn. https://www.linkedin.com/pulse/nikes-revolution-from-sweatshops-social-justice-cassy-trussell/

Tsukasaki, Y. (2008). *Gaikokujin senmonshoku gijutsushokuno koyou mondai [employment problems concerning foreign professionals and engineers]*. Tokyo, Japan: Akashi Shoten.

UNWTO (2021, January). World Tourism Barometer and Statistical Annex. Retrieved on August 17, 2022, from https://www.e-unwto.org/doi/abs/10.18111/wtobarometereng.2021.19.1.1.

WARC. (n.d.). Nike Japan: The future isn't waiting | WARC. Retrieved on October 25, 2021, from https://www.warc.com/content/paywall/article/youtube-works/nike-japan-the-future-isnt-waiting/en-gb/138675

Web Japan (n.d.) Introduction of Japan—Japan fact sheet. (n.d.). Web Japan. Ministry of Foreign Affairs of Japan. Retrieved on August 4, 2022, from https://web-japan.org/factsheet/

Web Japan. (2020). Mass media. Japan fact sheet. https://web-japan.org/factsheet/en/pdf/e41_mass.pdf

World Population Review. 2022 World population by country. Retrieved on August 30, 2022, from https://worldpopulationreview.com/

Yoon, K. (2015). 「在日」の精神史. 岩波書店. 出入国在留管理庁ホームページ. (n.d.). 出入国在留管理庁ホームページ. Retrieved on August 29, 2022, from https://www.moj.go.jp/isa/index.htm

7

CHINA

H&M "Canceled" by Chinese Consumers Over Uyghur Cotton

Kathy Chengshuang Zhang, Sam Ahmed, Celest Quek, and Elle Ning Jin

Introduction

In March 2021, high-profile foreign retailers including Adidas, Burberry, Nike, and H&M faced widespread boycotts in China after they spoke out against what they termed as forced labor in Xinjiang, home to the predominantly Muslim Uyghur people. Following this incident, H&M faced unprecedented public backlash as the company's comments spread like wildfire on Chinese social media. Angry Chinese netizens criticized H&M for interfering in Chinese domestic affairs while profiting from its business operations in the world's second-most populous country. H&M's business subsequently plummeted in China; its number of stores shrank to 380 from 500, and on Douyin, the Chinese version of TikTok, the H&M brand continues to be boycotted by tens of thousands of netizens in 2023 (Zhao, 2023). While companies such as Nike, Adidas, and Uniqlo, which echoed H&M's narratives, were able to avoid severe retaliation, the Swedish fast-fashion clothing found itself singularly targeted as it was not valued by local authorities, resulting in a near collapse of the retail giant's operations in China. H&M's failure in not prioritizing relationship building with key Chinese business partners and authorities was a costly mistake as such relationships can make or break businesses in China (Wei et al., 2022).

The H&M Xinjiang Cotton Saga

Hennes & Mauritz (H&M) was founded by Erling Persson in 1947 and is headquartered in Stockholm, Sweden. The mass-market retailer of men's, women's, and children's apparel, and accessories is the world's second-largest

DOI: 10.4324/9781003411802-8

clothing retailer, and it has over 150,000 employees worldwide. The Persson family is Sweden's richest family, ranked 94 globally in the 2022 Forbes Global Billionaires List, and holds a 36% ownership stake in H&M. H&M had 500 stores in China, which made China the company's fourth largest market after Germany, the United Kingdom (UK), and the United States (US). China alone accounted for 5.2% of net sales while also being one of the main suppliers to H&M (Tan, 2021).

In September 2020, H&M announced that in accordance with the Better Cotton Initiative (BCI), it would no longer buy cotton from the Xinjiang province in China. The company felt that the local Uyghurs were forced to work in the cotton industry under unfair conditions, a claim denied by China. The H&M announcement did not attract much interest, until March 2021 when sanctions were imposed on China by several Western nations such as the European Union, UK, US, and Canada in response to the human rights violations against the Uyghurs (BBC News, 2021).

On March 24, 2021, the Chinese Communist Youth League (CCYL) uploaded a post on the popular Chinese social media platform Weibo, claiming that H&M had made false allegations against China and had spread rumors about forced labor in the Xinjiang cotton industry (Exhibit A). During this time, Chinese state media outlets launched campaigns refuting forced labor accusations in Xinjiang. China Global Television Network shared a video on Weibo showing how automation was employed to harvest cotton in Xinjiang instead of physical labor. Seemingly healthy and satisfied Uyghur cotton farmers were also featured in the interview to debunk claims of forced labor (BBC News, 2021). China Central Television Station slammed H&M for making unfounded accusations against China and labeled H&M as "荒谬" (pronounced as huang miu), which means absurd. On Chinese Internet portals, articles were rife that H&M's boycott was in fact a conspiracy employed by Western intelligence to destabilize China (Baidu, 2021).

The crisis also affected stakeholder groups such as H&M's trading e-commerce partners and its celebrity ambassadors. The company faced a nation-wide boycott with its products being removed from all major Chinese e-commerce platforms, and Chinese celebrities publicly cut ties with the brand. H&M's sales in China plummeted 23% in the second quarter of 2021 compared to the previous year (He & Lee, 2021). H&M's action not only called into question Chinese industry practices but also cast a shadow on the Chinese government and its policies toward the Uyghurs. H&M had commented on the human rights abuses in Xinjiang echoing a report in a US government website that the regional Chinese authorities showed extraordinary hostility toward the Islamic faith and local Uyghur population. The report also cited what it called the "three evils" of "ethnic separatism, religious extremism, and violent terrorism" as China's justification for enacting and enforcing restrictions on religious practices of Muslims and non-Muslim religious minorities (United States Department of State, 2021).

China denied all allegations and its foreign ministry spokesman told the media that anti-China voices were out to smear China; Xinjiang enjoyed stability and prosperity, and residents were living happy, fulfilling lives. China asserted that the crackdown in Xinjiang was necessary to prevent terrorism and root out Islamist extremism and that the camps were an effective tool for re-educating inmates in the government's fight against terrorism (Ministry of Foreign Affairs of the People's Republic of China, 2021).

The Uyghur Conflict

At the heart of the H&M Xinjiang Cotton saga is the Uyghur conflict, which has been an ongoing ethnic conflict since the region failed to form a confederation within late Chairman Mao Zedong's People's Republic of China (PRC) after its establishment in 1949 (Dwyer, 2005). Although Xinjiang is labeled an autonomous region, it is still subject to significant regulations from the Chinese government. The conflict revolves primarily around Uyghur grievances of ethnic discrimination and cultural and religious suppression (Dwyer, 2005) as the indigenous Uyghurs are Muslims. Since gaining control over the region in the 1950s, the Chinese government has carried out a mass state-sponsored migration of Han Chinese into the province and implemented government policies promoting Chinese cultural unity (Dwyer, 2005). This caused friction between the Han, now a majority, and the Uyghurs, who had become a minority, as the influx not only intensified competition for Xinjiang's economic resources but also marginalized minority languages and cultures (Fuller & Starr, 2004).

The government argues that ethnic minorities are given preferential treatment in China such as priority in college admission (Leibold, 2016). To increase employment prospects, like other ethnic minorities, the Uyghurs are required to master the official Chinese language, Mandarin Chinese. This meant that Uyghur children needed to learn Mandarin Chinese in addition to Uyghur language although the Uyghurs have contended that their children are losing out on learning their mother tongue. The Chinese government says it is invested in alleviating Xinjiang from abject poverty and by studying a unified language, the Uyghurs would be able to interact with the world at large (Fuller & Starr, 2004).

However, there exists a deep mistrust amongst the Uyghurs with the Chinese idea of a multi-ethnic society coupled with their fear of being assimilated into a Han Chinese world and thereby losing their own cultural identity. After the collapse of the Soviet Union and the emergence of independent Muslim states in Central Asia in 1990s, open support for separatist groups increased, which resulted in massive street protests, even in the run-up to the Beijing Olympics in 2008 (BBC News, 2014). Things escalated in 2009 when about 200 people died, and about 1700 were injured in ethnic riots between the Han majority and Uyghur minority in Urumqi, the capital city of Xinjiang autonomous region.

The Xinjiang Cotton Controversy

On March 1, 2020, an investigative report titled “Uyghurs for sale – ‘re-education’, forced labor and surveillance beyond Xinjiang” was released by the Australian Strategic Policy Institute (ASPI). The report alleged that the Chinese government facilitated the mass transfer of at least 80,000 Uyghur and other ethnic minority members from the far west region of Xinjiang to factories across China, under conditions that strongly suggested forced labor. According to the report, 82 well-known global brands in clothing, technology, and automotive sectors including Apple, Adidas, BMW, Gap, H&M, Huawei, Nike, Samsung, Sony, Volkswagen, and Uniqlo (Xu et al., 2020) had directly or indirectly sourced products from the factories that employed forced labor. The report further stressed that companies using forced Uyghur labor in their supply chains could find themselves in breach of laws that forbid goods made with forced labor or mandate disclosure of forced labor. On March 30, 2020, BCI announced suspension of its sourcing activities in Xinjiang due to concerns over the prevalence of labor abuses in the region (Business & Human Rights Resource Centre, 2020b). BCI is a global cotton supply chain initiative set up for smallholders, large farms, and cotton-growing communities to survive and thrive while protecting and restoring environment for sustainable farming (Better Cotton, 2023).

Today, BCI has become the world’s largest cotton sustainability program, supporting 2.2 million licensed cotton farmers in developing countries for 20% of global cotton production. H&M, along with many global brands are members and supporters of BCI. In March 2020, Business & Human Rights Resource Centre claimed that they had reached out to 83 brands (instead of 82 brands identified in the ASPI report) that were implicated in the report. While 14 brands including Adidas, Gap, H&M, Nike, Uniqlo responded, Apple, Esprit, and Fila did not. The 14 brands that responded either denied their associations with forced labor or announced that they were taking decisive steps to decouple their sourcing practices from the alleged labor abuse while openly expressed concerns about the reported human rights saga (Business & Human Rights Resource Centre, 2020a).

Case Analysis

More than three years have passed since the onset of the crisis, and global brands such as Adidas, Nike, and Uniqlo have recovered or are on the way to recovery, while H&M announced closure of its flagship Shanghai store in June 2022.

Further, it shuttered its flagship Beijing store in 2023 with a lackluster offline presence owing to the continued online boycott by Chinese netizens (Reuters, 2023; Zhao, 2023). Our analysis of the H&M case is informed by the interplay of the five socio-cultural systems, namely, political, economics, media, culture, and activism systems offered by Sriramesh and Verčič's (2020) and discussed in Chapter 1.

In the context of China, the political system overarches the rest of the four environmental systems. For any MNC, hubris in such an environment could lead to a permanent ban by Chinese consumers. A look at H&M's statement on the incident would provide a glimpse of insights to the socio-cultural systems at play in China, which spells the continued unforgiveness of the Chinese consumers toward H&M.

H&M's response on March 23, 2020 to ASPI, "H&M Group strictly prohibits forced labour and any form of discrimination in our supply chain and we are deeply concerned by reports from civil society organisations and media that include accusations of forced labour and discrimination of ethnoreligious minorities in Xinjiang."

Political System

The Xinjiang cotton crisis broke out in March 2020, just after the turmoil of the Hong Kong (HK) unrest in 2019 – triggered by HK's extradition law – which was directly targeted at the human rights track record of the Chinese government. A series of protests against the HK government's introduction of the bill to hand over fugitive offenders to countries broke out in June 2019. The bill was withdrawn in September but protests became increasingly violent. An 18-year-old was shot in the chest as protesters clashed with police (BBC News, 2019). While the incident in HK happened before the ban on MNCs using Xinjiang cotton, it underscored the already fragile relationship between China and the West. Human rights are at the center of the conflicts, and the sentiments of Chinese citizens toward the West have since changed from the bygone days of admiration (M. Wang, 2021) as China denied all allegations of human rights violations, including Xinjiang (Ministry of the Foreign Affairs of the People's Republic of China, 2021).

To understand the collective sentiments of the Chinese consumers toward human rights, one needs to dive deeper to the political system of the PRC. Since the establishment of the PRC in 1949, the Chinese Communist Party (CCP) has ruled China for 74 years. Under current President Xi Jinping, the CCP has gradually transformed itself from a Marxist ideology to one that attempts to walk the fine line between its Communist ideals, traditional Chinese values, and economic pragmatism. (Yan, 2018). Xi Jinping's style has shown a preference for high-level centralized control, while expanding Chinese political and economic influence to the rest of the world through the Belt and Road initiative launched in 2013.

Ideological Dichotomy

A common fallacy in the West had been that economic liberalization would also result in political liberalization (Rankin, 2004). On the contrary, the communist system of centralized power has proven to be stable and effective, and the popular view amongst its citizens is that the country's recent economic leapfrog came about because of China's authoritarian government (Mitter & Johnson, 2021). The authoritarian government's legitimacy is rooted in the history of the CCP's role in "liberalizing" the Chinese people after a century of "humiliation" by Western powers starting with the Opium War. This hard-won victory cemented the CCP's legitimacy as the ruling party (Mitter, 2020). National pride and patriotism have grown in the era governed by President Xi Jinping. In his fourth volume of *Xi Jinping: The Governance of China*, President Xi emphasizes: "We will stay true to the Party's original aspiration and founding mission and do solid work, generation after generation so that by the centenary of the PRC 2049, our nation will stand taller and stronger in the East and mark a greater contribution to humanity."

Behind these rising nationalist sentiments, Chinese society is driven by three key values interplayed with ascending priority since 1978, when the country opened its door to the West. First, economic pragmatism which "regards the economy as the basis for national comprehensive strength" and thus stresses the importance of global trade and foreign investment in China (Yan, 2018). This was the basis for CCP's reform and open-door policy in 1978, led by the late leader, Deng Xiaoping. Second, embracing traditional values of "harmony," "good neighborliness," and "mind one's own business" as stated by the former Chinese Foreign Minister Wang Yi at the World Peace Forum in 2013. H&M's public criticism of China's internal affairs, seen as being disrespectful to traditional Chinese values, resulted in a rebuke by the Chinese government (Ministry of the Foreign Affairs of the People's Republic of China, 2013). Finally, the importance of Marxist-Leninist ideology, which is deeply embedded in China's society. Chinese leadership is not simply concerned with economic growth but also with direct control and capital ownership by the state. This last value is of the highest priority under President Xi's leadership. By questioning China's political sovereignty, where human rights issue is concerned, H&M has incurred the wrath of the Chinese government (The State Council Information Office The People's Republic of China, 2003).

To worsen the situation, an H&M review found that the fast-fashion giant was not particularly valued by local Chinese authorities (Wei et al., 2022). The tax that the company paid was considered insignificant, and it was also negligent in cultivating good government relations by failing to sponsor government-backed events. This is in stark contrast to Uniqlo, whose parent company Fast Retailing Co., for instance, would rent a booth bigger than any other clothing brand at China's International Import Expo almost every year since the event's inauguration in 2018 in Shanghai (Wei et al., 2022).

Hence, it is unsurprising that CCYL, the Chinese communist party's youth league uploaded a post on popular Chinese social media platform Weibo to accuse H&M of making false allegations against China. To them, H&M's had not only questioned Chinese industry practices but also criticized the government and its policies toward the Uyghurs. H&M had either failed to realize or deliberately ignored that the issue in question was not the alleged persecution of the minority group by the Chinese authorities but rather a direct challenge to the authority of the Chinese government in managing its own affairs. H&M's stance was tantamount to "suicide" in the Chinese socio-cultural environment.

Economic System

Economic liberalization is a hallmark of modern China under its overarching political system. Economic liberalization started in 1978 under the late Deng Xiaoping. Prior to this, the ill-planned state and economic policies of Chairman Mao Zedong such as the Great Leap forward caused the death of approximately 30 million Chinese between 1959 and 1961 (Smil, 1999). Amongst Deng's many initiatives to reform the economy was the creation of Special Economic Zones (SEZs) in 1980, which was motivated by a need to open up China's domestic economy and "to attract foreign investors and integrate China into the global trade system" (Autor et al., 2016). The two decades that followed saw a large influx of foreign MNCs such as Coca-Cola, Motorola, NEC, and Philips entering China, where "they were revered by the government and consumers alike" (Park & Vanhonacker, 2007).

However, as the economy grew and the GDP per capita reached the US$1,000 mark, and later broke the US$10,000 mark in 2018 (Textor, 2023), the Chinese government began to change its approach toward foreign MNCs, and a host of regulations on employment and environmental standards were imposed. As for Chinese consumers, there was a marked shift with the younger generation embracing national identity and domestic brands, with 85% of the domestic respondents preferring local brands (Hu et al., 2020). Today, China is the world's second-largest economy and is expected to become the world's largest economy by 2028 (BBC News, 2020). The prospect of reaching one-fourth of the world's population with rapidly increasing disposable income has attracted many international companies to converge in China. Economic development brings challenges for MNCs and so they "must invest heavily in communication campaigns to establish strong relationships with consumers" (Sriramesh & Vercic, 2009).

However, when H&M chose to boycott Xinjiang-produced cotton, they might have overlooked two critical factors: How MNCs are perceived in China's economic context and the role of corporate communication in China.

Corporate Values of MNCs and Their Impact on Communication

H&M prides itself as a company driven by its corporate values and actively works at recruiting and keeping employees that match its corporate values (Batyalova & Bucht, 2015). One such core value displayed on its corporate website is "straightforward and open-minded" and that "employees should be honest and unafraid of talking to someone directly, openness for new ideas is central and right or wrong should not be emphasized." Such values are not compatible with Chinese norms, which focus on "avoiding creating negative emotions among others" (Javidan et al., 2006). Despite the progress made by China on the economic front and the subsequent invitations for MNCs to set up businesses in the country, the overall sentiment toward MNCs turned negative since 2018 (M. Wang, 2021). To remain competitive and relevant, organizations need to constantly assess their business strategies against evolving stakeholders' perceptions. A case in point is Shien – China's homegrown fast fashion brand – which has since overtaken direct competitors like H&M and Zara to become the world's largest online fashion company (Gonzalez-Rodriguez, 2021). As such, the tables have turned, and while MNCs like H&M cannot afford to lose the vast Chinese consumer market, Chinese consumers can afford to forego the likes of H&M. H&M underestimated the deep-seated Chinese cultural values based on centuries of Taoism, Confucianism, and Buddhism (Li, 2022). Despite the rapid economic development, Chinese society has become increasingly less tolerant of Western ideology of issues such as human rights. And trade and technology sanctions against China by the Trump and Biden administrations have further exacerbated the negative sentiments Chinese have toward the US and the West.

Media System

Like everywhere in the world, traditional media in China are declining while social media are thriving. Nevertheless, there were over 1,900 newspapers, which form the traditional media in China, sponsored by or controlled by the government as of 2019 (BBC News, 2022). No private citizen or private entities are allowed to operate newspapers in China, while political news reporting is controlled by the central government, with only 13 licenses granted (BBC News, 2022). On the other hand, China ranks high in mobile digital connectivity and social media play a big part in the online landscape, with a 72% penetration rate. Surveys show that 98% of Chinese users visit a social network or messaging service regularly, while 89% are actively engaged on social media (Kemp, 2020). With Chinese consumers spending more time on their smartphones, the print media industry has seen a moderate decrease over the years and many print media companies have shifted to social media, publishing content on platforms such as WeChat, Weibo, Douyin, Kuaishou, and Xiaohongshu (Thomala, 2021).

China has a classic top-down media system; all media operate as a mouthpiece of the Chinese government. State-owned media control the direction of narratives and influencers are called DaVi or Big Vs – Chinese equivalent of key opinion leaders – who spread the state narratives in everyday lives on social media. For every popular global site in the world, there is a Sino-doppelganger behind the Great Firewall of China, i.e., Taobao, Youku, Sina Weibo, WeChat, and Baidu. The Google Search equivalent for China is Baidu; Alibaba is its Amazon-equivalent, while Weibo and WeChat are the social media platforms for China. Global companies operating in Internet search, e-commerce, news, and social media such as Google, Rakuten, Facebook, YouTube, and Twitter are blocked by the CCP's Internet censorship body (Reddy et al., 2015). The government exercises tight control over public opinion, designating many areas off-limits for public discussion and imposing penalties to restrict editorial freedom (He, 2004). Politics-related discussions such as human rights are part of these off-limits topics. Most commercial web portals like QQ.com or Sina.com.cn can only repost news from official state-owned news sources and are not permitted to publish original news and political articles (PR Newswire, 2017). The government also keeps a tight rein via the Cyberspace Administration of China with rules governing public social media accounts to avoid potential opposition of its authority, and crack down on fake news and other online activities perceived to be harmful (Deng & Hu, 2021).

How the H&M Crisis Unfolded on Chinese Media and Its Impact

The firestorm of nationalist fury over H&M erupted on social media after CCYL's post on Weibo. The CCYL's post was adamant about the wrong stand that H&M took to echo ASPI's allegation on forced labor in Xinjiang. The post generated widespread outrage on the Internet and garnered 383,000 likes within a day, with tens of thousands of users calling for a boycott of H&M (Sogou, 2021). Chinese media and social media users excoriated H&M, alleging that the brand had spread malicious lies and smeared the reputation of China. These angry sentiments were amplified in social media's echo chambers, especially with firewalls blocking the global coverage of the same matter. Weibo posts containing the hashtag "I support Xinjiang Cotton" amassed more than 4 billion views (He & Westcott, 2021).

Through the local media, China rejected the complaints of abuse and maintained its integrity over the cotton industry in Xinjiang. Chinese media also further unearthed past history of how H&M had exploited labor in Southeast Asia and Bangladesh and were themselves involved in unfair practices such as paying suppliers below the cost of production (Al Jazeera, 2023). Using the Chinese idiom "Zei Han Zhuo Zei" (贼喊捉贼), Chinese social media imply that H&M had the audacity to slander China for misdeeds they themselves had committed (Sohu, 2021).

The catalyst that resulted in the widespread negative sentiments toward H&M can be attributed to the CCYL's post, which Big Vs and netizens took its cue from. Chinese netizens, frustrated with ongoing accusations by the West on supposed human rights violations in China, vented its anger on H&M. Since CCYL is a representative of the Chinese government, its stance on the feud on social media was hence deemed legitimate. Within a day, H&M's businesses from e-commerce platforms to navigation and ride-hailing apps disappeared from the Internet in China (Canales, 2021).

Throughout the controversy, H&M did not take any remedial steps to apologize instead issuing a statement on its dedication to regain the trust and confidence of the Chinese consumers. The company simply reiterated that China was a very important market, and it was making forward-looking strategies, and actively working on the next steps regarding raw material sourcing (Teh, 2021). However, no Chinese mainstream media picked up H&M's statement. According to Baidu search, other state-owned media such as People's Daily, CCTV continued to stoke anti-sentiments with headlines such as, "H&M maliciously accuse Xinjiang cotton over human rights." Given that H&M made no apology in the issued statement, and completely neglected the "face" element in the Chinese societal culture, it was to be expected that no social media picked up H&M's statement. This disconnected communication and gap in expectation resulted in a prolonged boycott by Chinese consumers.

Societal Culture

Although the Chinese Economic Reform brought about the perception of a new age of Chinese openness to the outside world, traditional ideas of Confucianism and Communism are still deeply entrenched in societal norms (Pier, 2022). With reference to Hofstede's cultural dimensions, China has high power distance (80), low individualistic-collectivistic orientation (20), and low uncertainty avoidance (30) (Hofstede Insights, 2021). We will use these dimensions to analyze the impact of culture on H&M's crisis communication in China. Group benefits are prioritized over individual benefits and the Chinese see national cooperation and unity as crucial foundations for social harmony and stability. The strong emphasis on collective harmony means it is the norm to consider one another's feelings or "面子" (pronounced as mianzi) in interpersonal relations. "面子" which means "face" refers to one's reputation in the eyes of others. Not losing face is similar to protecting one's dignity, and reputation is paramount to the Chinese (Huang et al., 2016) and they felt that H&M had not given them face and had disrespected them with the boycott, and as such they were deeply offended.

The Chinese believe that everyone should conform to defined hierarchical roles in society – a clear sign of high power distance accompanied by deference to authority. The Chinese government sees itself as the ultimate authority, and people or organizations should not overstep their low rank (Earnhardt, 2017). By commenting on the politically sensitive issue of the Muslim Uyghurs, H&M as an external party was deemed to have crossed the line in questioning China's internal affairs and was seen as a direct challenge to China's sovereignty (W. Wang, 2021). Nationalistic sentiment seemed to fuel the seismic onslaught of Chinese backlash and subsequent commercial decoupling from H&M (W. Wang, 2021). As a show of support, top Chinese celebrities such as Wang Yibo, Huang Xuan, and Victoria Song cut ties with H&M, citing "the country's interests are above all" (Brant, 2021). This showed collectivism, especially when national pride is deeply rooted in Chinese culture. The collective national pride is the result of rising economic power as well as authoritarian political system.

As succinctly put forth by Hall (1960), "communication is culture and culture is communication," international brands operating in a foreign market should sensitize themselves to the local societal culture for long-term relationship building and business success. This is because culture often serves as the neglected, yet fundamental lens, through which the target audience perceive and interpret messages from the outside world. Thus, the lack of in-depth cultural awareness, sensitivity, and respect for the local Chinese culture, coupled with a mismatch of communication styles, led to the escalation of the H&M crisis.

Activism

Given the harmony and good neighborliness societal culture, activism has a negative connotation and is discouraged in China. However, Big Vs, the equivalent of activists in China, are given relative free reign for social-related issues with off-limit censorship. Big Vs often have command over a fanbase of millions on WeChat, Weibo, Douyin (sister app of TikTok), Xiaohongshu, and Bilibili. These activists are often below the age of 30, and they are primarily followed by Chinese Gen Zs and Millennials (Chi, 2021). Most fashion and luxury brands employ Big Vs for their marketing campaigns to build trust with Chinese consumers, as well as to create awareness for the brands (Gentlemen, 2023). For example, during the pandemic, cosmetic brand Perfect Diary turned makeup artists in 50 offline stores into online Big Vs. Together, they generated more than 140,000 live-streaming views and catapulted the brand straight into the top-listed cosmetic products on the online shopping platform Taobao (Chi, 2021). The Chinese KOL marketing industry was estimated at over RMB100 billion in 2018 and has only grown since. Over 80% of Chinese consumers follow at least one Big V; over 70% of Chinese Gen Z consumers reportedly prefer to shop via social media. As Chinese social media professionals, Big Vs are experts at standing out in the crowd, promoting and selling products, and expressing their views publicly.

With economic progress and increasing prosperity, the Chinese government and the public have changed their views of MNCs drastically, moving from reverence to scrutinization (Park & Vanhonacker, 2007). Nationalism has become increasingly important among young Chinese consumers and has inspired them to start 国潮 or Guochao, meaning the National Trend movement (Hallanan, 2020). They believe that China has the potential to become a leader in innovation and represent the revival of Chinese culture. The trend also reflected the country's rising cultural self-esteem and strengthened national identity (Lam, 2021). At the same time, the trend has given rise to a new generation of Chinese consumers with different needs and expectations. These consumers need brands to celebrate their culture (Ye, 2022). Data revealed that local consumer sentiments were driven by nationalistic fervor, and purchases of domestic apparel brands rose 137% on Baidu, the nation's largest search engine (Sun, 2021).

In the case of H&M's boycott of cotton produced in China, Chinese netizens led by Big Vs expressed their nationalism displaying outrage at what they characterized as a misstatement of the human rights issues in Xinjiang. H&M's initial announcement went by without much reaction from Big Vs. It was only after CCYL posted its stance on Weibo that Big Vs followed with an avalanche of posts to campaign for the boycott of the brand. Without understanding the five socio-cultural systems in China that is overarched by the political system and how media system works, it would be difficult to comprehend the silence and the subsequent explosive response from the Big Vs.

The sanctions strengthened nationalists' view of the West's double standards on human rights issues. H&M was trapped in a social media echo-chamber with the nationalistic Big Vs creating and sharing content reflecting their beliefs, such as the hashtag "I support Xinjiang cotton" (Koetse, 2021), which went viral. This echo chamber stimulated and further radicalized Chinese netizens and magnified the H&M crisis. The debacle did not end there. On October 2021, yet another fiasco raged and reverberated across social media platforms. This time, it involved China's live-streaming platform Douyu, which was blasted for allowing H&M's advertisement to appear on the opening page of Douyu App on National Day. Condemnation was unanimous, and without promptings from Big Vs this time, netizens criticized Douyu for compromising its values in the pursuit of profits. National pride led netizens to further express vendetta against MNCs like H&M – a form of personal release in a tightly controlled social media environment. Douyu immediately issued an apology and removed the advertisement (Global Times, 2021).

This phenomenon demonstrates that MNCs operating in China need to factor in the Big V ecosystem, as well as the total control by the CCP and its government. An MNC needs to rely on and partner with the Big Vs to effectively communicate its side of the story so that the application in the social spaces generated can help the company to better recover and regain its legitimacy, which is very much about aligning with the socio-cultural systems in China.

Conclusion

The events surrounding H&M's boycott in China are a complex interplay of geopolitics and socio-cultural environment. These include a deep-rooted mistrust of the West and vice versa, the ascent of China as a geo-economic force, and the simultaneous rise of strong nationalist sentiments in China spurred by the economic might of its consumers.

At the heart of this chapter, the question is whether H&M could have pursued its commitment toward promoting human rights without incurring the wrath of the Chinese government and Chinese consumers. Another way to look at it is whether any MNC could straddle the diverging views on human rights between the West and China, while pursuing economic opportunities in the second largest economy. MNCs often face different socio-cultural environments when doing business and need to bridge socio-cultural divides and maintain relationships with global stakeholders. This could only be made possible by being extremely sensitive to the interpretation of issues such as human rights. Like any foreign brand, H&M believed there is a universal standard for human rights based on European, Judeo-Christian, and/or Enlightenment heritage (Shaheed & Richter, 2018). Ostensibly under the old international norm, the crisis can be seen as an ethical dilemma for H&M. The company had to choose between highlighting the plight of the Uyghurs in an effort to be a responsible corporate citizen, while risk losing the world's second largest consumer market. Unfortunately, fueled by digital technology that has ushered in an era of nationalism and populism, MNCs are frequently challenged by well-heeled consumers. In this case, H&M learned that the number one survival rule of doing business in China is to build a cordial relationship with the Chinese government by supporting government events and initiatives, while being respectful and sensitive to the Chinese socio-political system.

Just like national security, the Western definition of human rights may not align with that China's. Any attempt to enforce these standards is viewed as a foreign intrusion that jeopardizes the livelihoods of local population. This perception gap is manifested in conflicts like the Hong Kong unrest in 2019 also and Xinjiang cotton controversy (Carter, 2021). The Chinese societal culture is based on values of Confucianism, which emphasize collective harmony and face-saving ideals which are further reinforced or reshaped by the coming together of its political, economic, and media systems. Foreign companies hoping to succeed in China need to understand that China's "modus operandi" runs contrary to Western liberal beliefs of individualism, openness, directness, and honesty – values stated on H&M's website. The concepts of face-saving and face-giving, in particular, should not be taken lightly by Western companies doing business in China. By publicly announcing their stand against forced labor involving minorities in Xinjiang, H&M had not given the Chinese government, its leader, and the Chinese people "face." Foreign organizations should adopt a more localized approach and pay attention to the confluence of these five sociocultural systems to do business successfully in countries like China.

References

Al Jazeera. (2023, January 11). Global fashion brands exploiting Bangladesh workers: Study. *Al Jazeera*. Retrieved August 21, 2023, from https://www.aljazeera.com/news/2023/1/11/fashion-brands-paid-less-than-production-cost-to-bangladesh-firms

Autor, D. H., Dorn, D., & Hanson, G. H. (2016). *The China shock: Learning from labor market adjustment to large changes in trade* (working paper 21906). National Bureau of Economic Research. https://doi.org/10.3386/w21906

Baidu. (2021, March 26) 抵制新疆棉, H&M只是傀儡：一场美国蓄谋一年之久的阴谋 https://baijiahao.baidu.com/s?id=1695285245337461517&wfr=spider&for=pc

Batyalova, V., & Bucht, A. (2015) Corporate Value Transfer in China — Cultural Challenges and Opportunities arising when using a Corporate Training Program: An exploratory case study of H&M Uppsala University. https://www.diva-portal.org/smash/get/diva2:823578/FULLTEXT01.pdf

BBC News. (2014, March 6). Why is there tension between China and the Uighurs? *BBC News*. https://www.bbc.com/news/world-asia-china-26414014

BBC News. (2019, August 12). The Hong Kong protests explained in 100 and 500 words. *BBC News*. https://www.bbc.com/news/world-asia-china-49317695

BBC News (2020, December 26). Chinese economy to overtake US "by 2028" due to Covid. BBC News. https://www.bbc.com/news/world-asia-china-55454146

BBC News. (2021, March 26). Xinjiang cotton: Western clothes brands vanish as backlash grows. *BBC News*. https://www.bbc.com/news/world-asia-china-56533560

BBC News. (2022, December 21) China media guide. *BBC News*. https://www.bbc.com/news/world-asia-pacific-13017881

Better Cotton. (2023, June 30). Our manifesto – Better Cotton. https://bettercotton.org/who-we-are/our-manifesto/

Brant, R. (2021, March 25). Nike, H&M face China fury over Xinjiang cotton 'concerns.' *BBC News*. Retrieved October 25, 2021, from https://www.bbc.com/news/world-asia-china-56519411.

Business & Human Rights Resource Centre. (2020a, March 1). China: 83 major brands implicated in report on forced labour of ethnic minorities from Xinjiang assigned to factories across provinces; Includes company responses. Retrieved February 25, 2023, from https://www.business-humanrights.org/en/latest-news/

china-83-major-brands-implicated-in-report-on-forced-labour-of-ethnic-minorities-from-xinjiang-assigned-to-factories-across-provinces-includes-company-responses/

Business & Human Rights Resource Centre. (2020b, April 7). *China: Better Cotton Initiative suspends activities in Xinjiang due to concerns over labour abuses*. https://www.business-humanrights.org/en/latest-news/china-better-cotton-initiative-suspends-activities-in-xinjiang-due-to-concerns-over-labour-abuses/

Canales, K. (2021, March 31) H&M was wiped from the Internet in China, sending a chilling warning to other retailers. *Business Insider*. https://www.businessinsider.com/hm-boycott-wiped-from-internet-china-2021-3

Carter, J. (2021) China and the western world at loggerheads over human rights. *South China Morning Post* https://www.scmp.com/economy/article/3124489/china-and-western-world-loggerheads-over-human-rights

Chi, R. (2021, October 14). China's KOL economy: Shaping the conversation for western brands. *The Drum*. https://www.thedrum.com/opinion/2021/10/14/china-s-kol-economy-shaping-the-conversation-western-brands

Deng, I., & Hu, M. H. (2021, January 25). China updates rules on social media accounts, increasing the already high cost of moderation. *South China Morning Post*. https://www.scmp.com/tech/policy/article/3119134/china-updates-rules-social-media-accounts-increasing-already-high-cost

Dwyer, A. M. (2005). *The Xinjiang Conflict: Uyghur identity, language policy, and political discourse*. Retrieved June 29, 2022, from https://www.files.ethz.ch/isn/26109/PS015.pdf

Earnhardt, M. P. (2017, October 30). The successful expatriate leader in China. *Graziadio Business Review*. Retrieved October 25, 2021, from https://gbr.pepperdine.edu/2010/08/the-successful-expatriate-leader-in-china/

Fuller, G. E., & Starr, S. F. (2004). *The Xinjiang problem — ETH Z*. The Xinjiang Problem. Retrieved June 29, 2022, from https://www.files.ethz.ch/isn/30301/01_Xinjiang_Problem.pdf

Gentlemen. (2023, February 9). Top 10 Chinese fashion influencers & KOLs — Fashion China. *Fashion China*. https://fashionchinaagency.com/top-10-chinese-fashion-influencers-kols-in-2020/

Global Times. (2021, October 10). Chinese live streaming platform apologizes, removes ads from H&M after public outrage. https://www.globaltimes.cn/page/202110/1235885.shtml

Gonzalez-Rodriguez, A. (2021, August 24). Shein becomes the world's largest online-only retailer. *Fashion United*. https://fashionunited.com/news/business/shein-becomes-the-world-s-largest-online-only-retailer/2021082341718

Hall, E. T. (1960). The silent language in overseas business. *Harvard Business Review*, *38*(3), 87–96.

Hallanan, L. (2020, January 7). 5 Chinese marketing terms you must know in 2020. *Forbes*. https://www.forbes.com/sites/laurenhallanan/2020/01/07/5-chinese-marketing-terms-you-must-know-in-2020/?sh=20a581db39c6

He, H., & Lee, A. (2021, September 22). China's millennials embrace local brands as fast fashion giants like H&M face changing tastes. *South China Morning Post*. https://www.scmp.com/economy/china-economy/article/3149569/chinas-millennials-embrace-local-brands-fast-fashion-giants

He, L., & Westcott, B. (2021, March 26). H&M and Nike are facing a boycott in China over Xinjiang cotton statements. *CNN Business*. https://edition.cnn.com/2021/03/25/business/hm-nike-xinjiang-cotton-boycott-intl-hnk/index.html

He, Q. (2004). Media control in China. *China Rights Forum*, *1*(2004), 11–28.

Hofstede Insights. (2021, June 21). Country comparison. Hofstede Insights. Retrieved October 25, 2021, from https://www.hofstede-insights.com/country-comparison/china/.

Hu, S., Hu, L., & Wang, G. (2020). Moderating role of addiction to social media usage in managing cultural intelligence and cultural identity change. *Information Technology & People*, *34*(2), 704–730. https://doi.org/10.1108/ITP-10-2019-0518

Huang, Y. H. C., Wu, F., & Cheng, Y. (2016). Crisis communication in context: Cultural and political influences underpinning Chinese public relations practice. *Public Relations Review*, *42*(1), 201–213.

Javidan, M., Dorfman, P. W., de Luque, M. S., & House, R. J. (2006). In the eye of the beholder: Cross cultural lessons in leadership from project GLOBE. *The Academy of Management Perspectives*, *20*(1), 67–90. https://doi.org/10.5465/AMP.2006.19873410

Kemp, S. (2020). Digital 2020: China — DataReportal — Global Digital Insights. *DataReportal — Global Digital Insights*. https://datareportal.com/reports/digital-2020-china

Koetse, M. (2021, June 27). "Support Xinjiang Mianhua!" — China's social media storm over Xinjiang cotton ban. What's on Weibo. Retrieved June 30, 2022, from https://www.whatsonweibo.com/support-xinjiang-mianhua-chinas-social-media-storm-over-xinjiang-cotton-ban/

Lam, N. (2021, June 4). Global luxury brands stand a better chance of weathering China's nationalistic consumer fervour, says Credit Suisse. *South China Morning Post*. https://www.scmp.com/business/money/wealth/article/3133535/global-luxury-brands-stand-better-chance-weathering-chinas

Leibold, J. (2016). Preferential policies for ethnic minorities in China. In *Handbook on ethnic minorities in China* (pp. 165–188). Edward Elgar Publishing.

Li, X. (2022). The global meaning of the pluralistic Chinese cultural tradition. *Journal of Cultural Interaction in East Asia*, *13*(1), 15–28. https://doi.org/10.1515/jciea-2022-0005

Ministry of the Foreign Affairs of the People's Republic of China. (2013, June 27). *Foreign Minister Wang Yi on major-country diplomacy with Chinese characteristics*. Retrieved February 26, 2023, from https://www.fmprc.gov.cn/mfa_eng/wjb_663304/zzjg_663340/zcyjs_663346/xgxw_663348/201307/t20130701_493942.html

Ministry of the Foreign Affairs of the People's Republic of China. (2021, December 24). *Foreign Ministry spokesperson's statement on US' signing of the so-called Uyghur forced labor prevention act*. Retrieved February 26, 2023, from https://www.fmprc.gov.cn/mfa_eng/xwfw_665399/s2510_665401/2535_665405/202112/t20211224_10475191.html

Mitter, R. (2020). *China's good war: How World War II is shaping a new nationalism*. Belknap Press.

Mitter, R., & Johnson, E. (2021) What the West gets wrong about China. *Harvard Business Review* https://hbr.org/2021/05/what-the-west-gets-wrong-about-china

Park, S. H., & Vanhonacker, W. R. (2007, July 1). The challenge for multinational corporations in China: Think local, act global. *MIT Sloan Management Review*. https://sloanreview.mit.edu/article/the-challenge-for-multinational-corporations-in-china-think-local-act-global/

Pier. (2022). Chinese culture. Cultural Atlas. Retrieved June 29, 2022, from https://culturalatlas.sbs.com.au/chinese-culture/chinese-culture-core-concepts

PR Newswire. (2017, October 6) Media landscape in China: Social media as the most important source of collecting information. https://en.prnasia.com/blog/2017/10/media-landscape-in-china-social-media-as-the-most-important-source-of-collecting-information/

Rankin, K. N. (2004). *The cultural politics of markets: Economic liberalization and social change in Nepal* (Vol. 27). University of Toronto Press.

Reddy, S. K., Wang, Z. Z., & Dong, D. H. (2015). China's digital landscape: Breaking barriers to innovation. *Asian Management Insights*, *2*(2), 18–23. https://ink.library.smu.edu.sg/cgi/viewcontent.cgi?article=5760&context=lkcsb_research

Reuters. (2023, January 27). H&M highlights fast-fashion gloom as luxury takes hit in China. *Reuters*. https://www.reuters.com/business/retail-consumer/hm-highlights-fast-fashion-gloom-luxury-takes-hit-china-2023-01-27/

Shaheed, A., & Richter, R. P. (2018, October 17). Is "Human Rights" a Western Concept? *IPI Global Observatory*. https://theglobalobservatory.org/2018/10/are-human-rights-a-western-concept/

Smil, V. (1999). China's great famine: 40 years later. *BMJ (Clinical Research Ed, 319*(7225), 1619–1621. https://doi.org/10.1136/bmj.319.7225.1619

Sogou, B. (2021, March 25) H&M 岂能吃中国人的饭、砸中国人的碗 https://baike.sogou.com/appeal/snapshot?link=3Veun_MYT42-HSDoqy56_E9pIwJMOICNMZ4MMbkXjl7r0PAaOFAZ0ZyNOOqo0INNOk7wXA4prZFUr-OqRiqLpiFPXG&originRef=https%3A%2F%2Fmp.weixin.qq.com%2Fs%2FAo0orhRx-hKjtJ2Se_mMZw&lid=203079093&title=%5Bobject%20HTMLHeadingElement%5D

Sohu. (2021, March 26). 揭露H&M黑历史, 长期虐待女工雇童工, 发家史背后令人震惊. https://www.sohu.com/na/457368637_120866502

Sriramesh, K., & Vercic, D. (Eds.). (2009). *The global public relations handbook*, Revised and Expanded Edition: *Theory, research, and practice* (2nd ed.). Routledge. https://doi.org/10.4324/9780203889374

Sriramesh, K., & Verčič, D. (2020). *The global public relations handbook: Theory, research, and practice*. Routledge.

Sun, N. (2021, August 27) Nationalist consumption boosts Chinese fashion industry. *Nikkei Asia*. Retrieved from https://asia.nikkei.com/Business/Business-Spotlight/Nationalist-consumption-boosts-Chinese-fashion-industry

Tan, C. K. (2021, March 29). H&M shops in China forced to close amid Xinjiang backlash. *Nikkei Asia*. https://asia.nikkei.com/Business/Retail/H-M-shops-in-China-forced-to-close-amid-Xinjiang-backlash

Teh, C. (2021, March 31) H&M releases new statement following Xinjiang controversy, says China is a very important market. *Insider*. https://www.insider.com/hm-releases-new-xinjiang-statement-says-china-very-important-market-2021-3

Textor, C. (2023, April 12) Gross domestic product (GDP) per capita in current prices in China from 1985 to 2022 with forecasts until 2028. *Statista.com*. https://www.statista.com/statistics/263775/gross-domestic-product-gdp-per-capita-in-china/

The State Council Information Office The People's Republic of China. (2023, June 16). 4th volume of "Xi Jinping: The Governance of China" enhances global understanding of China. Retrieved June 22, 2023, from http://english.scio.gov.cn/governanceofchina/2023-06/16/content_87720135.htms

Thomala, L. L. (2021, July 19) Media industry in China – statistics & facts. *Statista*. https://www.statista.com/topics/1679/media-in-china/#dossierKeyfigures

United States Department of State. (2021, May 12*). China (Includes Tibet, Xinjiang, Hong Kong, and Macau)*. United States Department of State. https://www.state.gov/reports/2020-report-on-international-religious-freedom/china/

Wang, M. (2021, February 27). *Chinese consumers are changing. Foreign MNCs must keep track and adapt*. LinkedIn. Retrieved August 21, 2023, from https://www.linkedin.com/pulse/chinese-consumers-changing-foreign-mncs-must-keep-track-dr-mei-wang

Wang, W. (2021). Multinationals must learn hard lesson of respecting local consumers. *Global Times*. Retrieved October 25, 2021, from https://www.globaltimes.cn/page/202104/1220506.shtml.

Wei, D., Hong, J., Saito, Y., & Leung, A. (2022, March 13). China canceled H&M. Every other brand needs to understand why. *Bloomberg.com*. https://www.bloomberg.com/graphics/2022-china-canceled-hm/

Xu, V. X., Cave, D., Leibold, J., Munro, K., & Ruser, N.. (2020, March 1). *Uyghurs for sale*. Australian Strategic Policy Institute. Retrieved March 26, 2023, from http://www.aspi.org.au/report/uyghurs-sale

Yan, X. (2018). Chinese Values vs. liberalism: What ideology will shape the international normative order? *The Chinese Journal of International Politics*, *11*(1), 1–22. https://doi.org/10.1093/cjip/poy001

Ye, K. (2022, June 28). What is 'Guochao' this emerging trend in China?: Hi-com. HI. Retrieved June 30, 2022, from https://www.hicom-asia.com/what-is-guochao-this-emerging-trend-in-china/

Zhao, Z., (2023, June 5). H&M shuts Beijing Sanlitun district store a year after closing Shanghai shop. *South China Morning Post*. https://www.scmp.com/business/china-business/article/3223034/hm-shuts-flagship-store-beijings-sanlitun-district-year-after-closing-covid-hit-shanghai-shop

8

INDONESIA

Diversity Versus Ideology: Muslims Demand Starbucks Boycott Over LGBTQ+ Stance

Rahmatina Widyarini, Himesh Sharma, Ivan Chan, and Subhas Gopalakrishnan

Introduction

Today's world may be globalized, but the world still must be looked at through culturally nuanced lenses. "Two persons, sitting at the same table, having the same meal, may be worlds apart" (Misner, 2021), in terms of their perspectives and opinions driven by culture. Thus, corporate leaders must be able to strike a balance in their messaging, between the corporation that they work for and the society they live in. In a globalized world, the impact of a crisis is rarely limited to one geographical location, and if not handled decisively, may negatively impact their business across borders. Understanding the society and being cognizant of the political realities in which the business operates in (Boyles, 2022) is vital, as people increasingly believe companies should act as good citizens in society (Mohit, 2024).

In 2013, Howard Schultz, chief executive of Starbucks told a shareholder at the coffee chain's annual meeting: "…we want to embrace diversity. Of all kinds…if you feel, respectfully, that you can get a higher return than the 38% you got last year…you can sell your shares in Starbucks and buy shares in another company" (Allen, 2013). Schultz's and Starbucks' open support of the LGBTQ+ (lesbian, gay, bisexual, transgender, queer) community was applauded at a time when the world was slowly opening up to the LGBTQ+ community. Four years later, due to the rise in LGBTQ+ activism across the globe, Fahira Idris, an Indonesian politician and senator from Jakarta, and Anwar Abbas, leader of the Muhammadiyah Society, a non-governmental Islamic organization that has 30 million members, watched the 2013 video on Howard Schultz's comments and Starbucks' support for the gay community (Chan, 2017). This prompted

DOI: 10.4324/9781003411802-9

Idris to call for a boycott of the beverage giant and urged the Indonesian government to revoke Starbucks' operating license (Rizki & Damiana, 2017). Abbas stated that the authorities needed to revoke Starbucks' license as the company was "no longer in line" with the nation's ideology (Rizki & Damiana, 2017). He added that, "If Starbucks is only doing business, it's not a problem. But don't bring ideology here," implying that expressing certain ideologies in this context could lead to a negative reception from the locals who were culturally different. The situation escalated so quickly that a day later and across the border from Indonesia, Malay rights group Pribumi Perkasa Malaysia, also urged Malaysian Muslims to boycott Starbucks as it was "not in line" with the nation's ideology (Mail, 2017). These calls set in motion a crisis for Starbucks in the Muslim Archipelago of Southeast Asia.

A Brief Overview Indonesia

Indonesia is a complex nation with a diverse cultural and religious makeup. Having transited to full democracy after the fall of the authoritarian regime of President Suharto in 1998 (Greenwalt, 2021), the country now has a young secular democratic system (Cox et al., 2023). Over the years, Indonesia has grown rapidly and with an increasingly important voice in world affairs (Cox et al., 2012). With a population of approximately 275 million people (Worldometer, n.d.), the world's fourth most populous (Cox et al., 2012) country has the world's largest Muslim population, with an estimated 87.2% Muslim majority (Central Intelligent Agency, 2022). Although Islam is the principal religion and plays a crucial role in politics and society, Indonesia is not an Islamic country as it is not governed by Islamic laws (Cox et al., 2023). The country-state ideology of Pancasila comprises five principles, namely monotheism, civilized humanity, national unity, deliberative democracy, and social justice (Greenwalt, 2021). These principles were formulated in 1945, following the end of World War II, to unite the country, allowing greater freedom for all religions and communities. Under the rule of President Suharto, these principles were upheld with an iron fist and ideology supremacy were suppressed (Greenwalt, 2021). However, after the fall of President Suharto, rightwing parties started to impose their conservative views more forcefully (Wirawan, 2016).

Current President Joko Widodo has prioritized the combating of the rising tide of Islamism (Greenwalt, 2021) as certain hardcore Muslim groups have been able to influence judicial and political decisions through the threat of violence (Cox et al., 2023). Based on rightwing ideologies, some militant Islamist groups have attacked the public activities of the LGBTQ+ community such as stopping or forcing the cancellation of previously scheduled events (John, 2017; Knight & Harsono, 2023). In addition to such violence, LGBTQ+ individuals also face legal challenges. Attempts have been made in the Constitutional Court to criminalize extramarital sex and LGBTQ+ relationships (Wirawan, 2016). In Aceh province where Sharia (Islamic law) is fully implemented, same-sex sexual relationships are punishable by 100 public lashings (Knight & Harsono, 2023). Officials in the province have expressed anti-LGBTQ+ sentiments and view the community as a potential threat. Some Indonesians are of the view that LGBTQ+ activism is encroaching on their personal space, imposing their beliefs, and undermining local ethnic and religious traditions (Wirawan, 2016).

The Starbucks Indonesia Crisis

The crisis Starbucks Indonesia faced in 2017 was a significant lesson on why businesses and its leaders should be cognizant of the social fabric and political dynamics in the market they operate in. The controversy sparked by Schultz's 2013 advocacy stance to embrace diversity and the LGBTQ+ activism movements highlighted the complex intersection of religion, politics, and culture in Indonesia and how it impacts corporations that embrace ideologies that may run "against the grain" of the business social environment. Prior to the boycott calls on Starbucks, the social environment in the country in 2016 was already brewing with attacks on minority groups (Cho, 2019). Anti-LGBTQ+ sentiments from rightwing groups were most prominent and publicized (Cho, 2019), leading to an increase in harassment and violence against the LGBTQ+ community.

In 2016, Muhammad Nasir, Indonesia's Minister of Research, Technology and Higher Education, stated that LBGTQ+ groups should be barred from campus as a university is a moral safeguard. He made these statements when he learnt that an Indonesian university offered counseling for LGBTQ+ students (Davies, 2016). This anti-sentiment set off an "Anti-LGBTQ+ Moral panic" (Davies, 2016), increasing homophobia and transphobia sentiments in Indonesia (Tang, 2016). The brewing environment on anti-LBGTQ+ sentiments exacerbated the brewing Starbucks crisis, creating a challenging landscape for the company to navigate (Voss, 2017).

In reacting to CEO Schultz's 2013 advocacy for LGBTQ+ rights, Abbas and Idris perceived his statement as contrary to the nation's ideology of Pancasila, which emphasizes respect for God's moral standards, and the nation's core values (Putri, 2017; Rizki & Damiana, 2017). Despite Starbucks' emphasis on diversity, there was no deliberate attempt to publicly address the controversy surrounding their support for LGBTQ+ rights in Indonesia. In fact, Starbucks Indonesia kept a low profile and remained silent for as long as they could (Chicago Tribune, 2017). The statement from PT Sari Coffee Indonesia (which holds the license to run the Starbucks chain in Indonesia) about not being affiliated with political or ideological groups, may suggest a reluctance to engage in discussions about controversial social issues (Anya, 2017). When prominent companies, such as Starbucks, remain silent in the face of a national controversy, it could lead to a larger and potentially more damaging situation. This lack of response may cause speculation, frustration, and loss of trust among stakeholders, potentially leading to an escalation or reawakening of the crisis (Le et al., 2018). The Starbucks crisis was further magnified by the company's failure to navigate the complex web of Indonesian media, religion, politics and culture. The growing anti-LGBTQ+ sentiment from right-wing groups, calling for the criminalization of homosexuality, fueled an increase in harassment and violence against the LGBTQ+ community (Voss, 2017). Unintentionally, Starbucks became a convenient "whipping boy" against the perception that Western ideologies were being imposed in Indonesia. Although the impact on consumer patronage was minimal at Starbucks in Indonesia over this issue (Chan, 2017), damage in the longer term inflicted by other stakeholder groups could not be immediately established. Starbucks presence in Indonesia, after all, is important for the company's global standing because (1) Indonesia's emerging middle class was proactively driving consumption; (2) the growing and resilient Indonesian economy (Global Coffee Report, 2014); and (3) Indonesian as a coffee-producing nation (Walton & Scott, 2021).

Starbucks entered the Indonesian market in 2002 and quickly became a popular beverage chain for the country's growing middle class. Starbucks Indonesia expanded with more than 480 outlets and more than 4,000 partners across 36 cities (Starbucks, 2022). In 2019, the organization had a dominant share of the coffee market in Indonesia with 44.5%, while its closest rival Excelso Café had just 11.2% (Nurhayati-Wolff, 2022). The increase in the number of coffee shops in urban areas had also created new job opportunities for young people and contributed to the growth of the service sector, while the rise of coffee culture in Indonesia had been driven by lifestyle changes that accompany urbanization and economic development (Mergonoto, 2014). The Starbucks-style coffee culture had been systematically and massively cultivated among Indonesia's middle class (Purnomo et al., 2021) through social media and popular culture, creating a symbol of a new lifestyle and as a place for hanging out and relaxing (Purnomo et al., 2021).

As an agrarian society, Indonesia has over 1.24 million hectares of coffee plantations, with 933 hectares and 307 hectares of robusta and arabica plants, respectively, and it is the world's fourth largest producer of coffee (Walton & Scott, 2021). According to Badan Pusat Statistik (or Central Statistical Agency), Indonesia produced 742 thousand tons of coffee in 2019, with smallholder coffee plants contributing 98.6% of the total production (731.6 thousand tons), while huge state farms producing 0.8% (5.6 thousand tons), and large private plantations producing 0.6% (4.4 thousand tons) (Purnomo et al., 2021).

Following the call for a ban on the chain by Islamic groups, the company's share prices fell from Rp3,000 to Rp2,200 in July 2017, and the company stock prices continued to decline even after the issue had cooled, indicating the extent of the damage to the company's reputation and financial performance. However, the global share prices of Starbucks did not see a major impact, with only a minor dip in mid-July 2017; this was followed by a steady recovery (Anya, 2017).

The controversy surrounding the company's support for LGBTQ+ rights amid Indonesia's religious and cultural sensitivities highlighted the importance of effectively managing potential crises in diverse environments. Starbucks' communication strategy, while the social situation was brewing and subsequent lack of response during the crisis, demonstrated the risks of remaining silent. Although in this case study, there was little evidence of a significant boycott from consumers, and with the crisis lasting for only about a few months, it could have potentially worsened the already negative perceptions, and even escalated very quickly beyond borders. The crisis died down after a while and there was a lack of an effective response from Starbucks Indonesia in clarifying their position. The case study offers valuable insights for businesses operating in similar contexts, emphasizing the significance of addressing sensitive issues with transparency, cultural sensitivity, and timely communication.

Case Analysis

We will use the Global Public Relations Framework (Sriramesh & Verčič, 2020) discussed in Chapter 1 to analyze how the five socio-cultural elements described in Chapter 1 impacted the crisis that Starbucks faced in Indonesia. We examined the role that Indonesian politics and media played in shaping public opinion and looked at how cultural and religious factors influenced the boycott of Starbucks. We further discussed the role of activism and social media in amplifying the crisis and the implications for multinational corporations (MNCs) operating in Indonesia. Overall, this case study highlights the challenges and opportunities of conducting crisis communication in a complex, culturally diverse, and politically sensitive socio-political environment such as Indonesia.

Political System

As a democratic country with a Muslim majority in population, Indonesia's political system has been shaped by many factors, including its colonial history, vast geographic size, and the significant influence of religion on society and politics (Jibiki, 2020). The Indonesian constitution guarantees freedom of religion to all individuals in the country, allowing everyone to practice their own religion or belief system (Indonesia Investments, 2023). However, the state itself is built on the principle of belief in a single God, forming the foundation of Pancasila, the Indonesian state philosophy introduced by the first president, Soekarno (Indonesia Investments, 2023). This dual nature of religious freedom for individuals and an underlying religious orientation of the state set the stage for a complex political landscape.

Historically, the political influence of Muslims has increased significantly. Under the autocratic regime of Suharto, the second president, the political power of Muslims was curtailed to prevent the rise of fundamentalism (Jibiki, 2020). However, after Suharto's fall in 1998, democratic norms replaced military rule, leading to a surge in political Islam. Conservative Islamic groups gained increasing influence in shaping public opinion and policy, leading to the rise of political Islam. This shift in the political landscape is evident in instances like the Jakarta governor election in 2017, where incumbent Basuki Tjahaja Purnama, a Christian of Chinese descent was accused of being "anti-Muslim" during the campaign, resulting in his defeat to his Muslim opponent, Anies Baswedan (Lamb, 2017) In this political context, religious leaders have also assumed significant roles in the government. Vice President Ma'ruf Amin, who served as the former chairman of MUI (Majelis Ulama Indonesia), Indonesia's top Islamic scholar body, and Nahdlatul Ulama (NU), an influential Islamic organization, exemplified the integration of religious leaders into key positions within the government (Hasyim, 2021).

The Starbucks controversy in Indonesia further highlighted the intersection of politics and economics in the country. The demand for a boycott of Starbucks from politician and Senator Idris underscored how corporate spaces had become political arenas in Indonesia (Putri, 2017). Chief Executive Howard Schultz, when speaking to shareholders in the annual meeting in the United States (US) in 2013, should have been more mindful with his corporate messages and values that he wants Starbucks to represent even though the setting appeared to be within a certain geographical boundary. Highly cognizant and knowing very well that Starbucks is a global conglomerate with worldwide presence in the 21st century, he failed to craft his messages to better align with social sensitivities in the different markets that Starbucks operated in. A company like Starbucks ought to have avoided messages that could be interpreted as offensive or inappropriate within that cultural context (Sriramesh & Verčič, 2003). Furthermore, whenever possible, the company should have involved local spokespeople who understood cultures across different markets and to get them to interpret the group corporate message from headquarters while resonating with local audiences. This approach could help convey that Starbucks aimed to coexist harmoniously within the existing cultural fabric rather than seeking to alter the established norms. Indonesia's overarching Islamic religious views are deeply entrenched as social-political norms and a way of life, making it crucial for MNCs to navigate the complex sociopolitical landscape sensitively. As a democratic republic with many political parties, Indonesia's political system is made up of the President of Indonesia, who serves as both head of state and head of government, and the bicameral People's Consultative Assembly, vested with legislative power. The judiciary operates independently of the executive and legislature, contributing to a system of checks and balances (UN Office of the High Commissioner for Human Rights, 2017).

The Starbucks crisis demonstrated how various groups could add indirect pressure to the ruling party to ban organizations that do not support their stance (Chicago Tribune, 2017). The ruling party during the crisis was the Indonesian Democratic Party of Struggle, led by President Joko Widodo, whose government had to address the ramifications of the boycott and its potential implications on the nation's image and economy (UN Office of the High Commissioner for Human Rights, 2017). The influence of religious leaders in politics can make it challenging to enact progressive social and political reforms, as they may advocate for policies aligned with conservative interpretations of religious principles. However, it is essential to note that Indonesia is also a democratic country, and political dynamics can evolve over time. While conservative views may be deeply rooted, the political climate can change through the efforts of other political actors, civil society groups, and the engagement of the general public.

Drawing a parallel between a nation that shares close demographic, linguistic as well as cultural similarities to Indonesia is neighboring country Malaysia. The situation in Indonesia had some ripple effects in Malaysia. Perkasa, a group that advocated for a fundamentalist version of Islam and nationalism in Malaysia, urged its more than 500,000 members to avoid Starbucks (Chicago Tribune, 2017). In a statement, Perkasa urged the Malaysian government to cancel the trading permits granted to Starbucks and other businesses that promote same-sex marriage and LGBT rights, including the likes of technology giants Microsoft and Apple. The boycott, according to Gavin Bowring, a Malaysia analyst with risk management firm Eurasia Group, was unlikely to have much of an impact, but it did represent "a growing tendency toward conservatism and strict adherence to Islamic principles" (Chicago Tribune, 2017).

Furthermore, as a democratic nation with a majority-Muslim population, the influence of conservative Islamic groups can be significant in Indonesia's political and social landscape. This heightened influence of political Islam underscored the importance for companies, like Starbucks, to manage their corporate messages and approach their operations in the country with sensitivity by being cognizant of today's multicultural and polarized global audiences. In a context where corporate spaces have become political arenas, understanding, and respecting the religious sensitivities and cultural norms of the host country are essential for businesses to thrive in Indonesia's dynamic market.

Economic System

The Indonesian Republic currently thrives with a mixed economy of private liberties and centralized economic planning and government supervision. Indonesia's economic system has experienced steady growth in recent years, establishing itself as one of the most important economies in Southeast Asia. With a population exceeding 275 million, the country boasts a vast market for both domestic and foreign businesses (The World Bank, 2021). The economy primarily relies on trade and investment, and the government actively encourages foreign investments to bolster economic expansion (Verico & Pangestu, 2020 August). As a result, Indonesia has emerged as a thriving hub for international companies seeking to expand their presence in the region. With Islamic groups clamoring for a ban on Starbucks, it would seem that the coffee chain's business operations would be severely impacted; however as seen in a Reuters news report that was carried by a number of news organization including NBC and Newsweek, some consumers said they would continue to buy from Starbucks, and that the Muslim groups "should not make it such an issue that we have to boycott a company because of one small statement" (Newsweek, 2017). According to parent company, MAP Boga Adiperkasa (the holding group of Starbucks Indonesia), the coffee chain posted a dip in share prices "by 5.54 percent to Rp2,900 (US21 cents)" (Anya, 2017), but by 2018, it was projected "to expand 5.4 percent this year, the quickest pace of growth since 2013" (Dahrul & Suhartono, 2018).

The trade relationship between Indonesia and the US served as a testament to the country's significance on the global economic stage. In 2020, Indonesia was the US's 24th largest trading partner, with total goods trade amounting to US$27.6 billion. The trade balance featured US$7.4 billion in goods exports and US$20.2 billion in goods imports, resulting in a trade deficit of US$12.8 billion for the US (Office of the United States Trade Representation, n.d.). Indonesia's GDP reached an estimated US$1,186.09 billion in 2021, accounting for approximately 0.53% of the global total (Trading Economics, n.d.). The country has been successful in attracting foreign direct investment (FDI), experiencing an annual increase of 44.2% in 2022. Based on official calculations from the investment ministry, at an exchange rate of IDR14,350 to the dollar and excluded investment in the banking and oil and gas industries, Indonesia received FDI amounting to US$45.6 billion in the previous year (Suroyo, 2023). With 713 foreign conglomerates operating within its borders in 2020, Indonesia had solidified its status as an appealing investment destination (The Global Economy.com, n.d).

The Starbucks crisis in Indonesia emphasized the interconnectedness of the global economy and the importance of reputation management for MNCs operating in foreign markets. As a prominent international brand, Starbucks' image and financial performance were impacted by the crisis, shedding light on the significance of understanding, and adapting to local cultural and political sensitivities. However, Starbucks' global chief Schultz reiterated his support for the LGBTQ+ cause and said that this decision was not an economic one, rather, it was something he believed in deeply (Rizki, 2017).

The crisis also highlighted the importance of cultural intelligence and local engagement in global business operations. The Starbucks-style coffee culture has been widely cultivated among the middle class through social media and popular culture, and the coffee chain has become a symbol of modern lifestyle; it is also a popular place for people to socialize and relax (Purnomo et al., 2021). Many Indonesians in the middle class are open-minded, and their openness and willingness to embrace diverse influences contribute to the country's ability to navigate through difficulties and progress in the face of socio-political challenges.

In today's interconnected world, companies must recognize that their actions and decisions can have far-reaching consequences, especially in regions with diverse cultural and political contexts. Building a positive brand image and maintaining financial success necessitates a thorough understanding of the local markets, respect for cultural norms, and sensitivity to political dynamics. Furthermore, to mitigate the financial effects of such crises, corporations need to engage with local investors while aligning their strategies swiftly and accurately with religious and cultural values prevailing in the host country. By doing so, businesses can effectively manage potential risks, avoid controversies, and foster positive relationships with local communities, contributing to long-term success and sustainability in international markets like Indonesia (Team, 2023).

With this crisis, Starbucks faced significant challenges when Islamic groups called for a ban on its operations, resulting in a sharp decline in its stock prices in Indonesia and impacting its reputation and financial performance. Despite these localized challenges, the company's global share prices remained relatively unaffected, underscoring its resilience in international markets. The Starbucks crisis serves as a reminder of the importance of reputation management and cultural sensitivity for MNCs operating in Indonesia. The ability to navigate socio-political challenges while engaging with local investors and aligning strategies with religious and cultural values becomes crucial in a diverse and dynamic market like Indonesia. As Indonesia's economic prowess continues to grow, businesses that appreciate and adapt to its unique characteristics are likely to thrive. Embracing the open-mindedness and adaptability of the middle class, MNCs can forge enduring connections with the local community, thereby positioning themselves for success in this thriving market. The Starbucks experience highlights the need for companies to be responsive and adaptable while respecting the values and preferences of the Indonesian market, ensuring a harmonious and prosperous engagement with this dynamic nation.

Media System

The media system in Indonesia played a pivotal role in amplifying the Starbucks crisis, with both social media and traditional media influencing public perception. Indonesia's vast population contributes to one of the highest rates of social media usage globally, with approximately 160 million active social media users (Kemp, 2022). Platforms like Twitter, Facebook, and Instagram have become primary sources of news and information for many Indonesians, making them crucial channels for businesses and organizations to communicate with the public and internationally.

Even though this video was filmed in 2013, Schultz's statement in support of the LGBTQ+ community was spread on social media in 2017 and through the WhatsApp platform, reached a wide audience and fueled the boycott movement (Rizki & Damiana, 2017), while the hashtag #BoikotStarbucks gained traction on Twitter. A tweet criticizing the Arabic dress style with accompanying photos saw more than 577 reposts with 89 quotes, and another tweet had the caption #boikotstarbucks. We hypothesized that this Twitter post exacerbated the virality of the #boikotstarbucks movement. Social media further aided the call for a boycott in neighboring Malaysia, where a well-known Muslim group joined in demanding the boycott of the international coffee chain (Today Online, 2017).

Social media discussions and hashtags trended on Indonesian platforms and were further picked up by traditional media, demonstrating the interconnectedness between online and offline news sources. Social media has become a vital platform for expression and discussion, while influencer marketing has emerged as a key component of brand engagement strategies in Indonesia (Statista, 2021). The rise of multi-platform conglomerates is evident in the Indonesian media landscape, with media companies aligning their interests to support the agendas of their oligarch-owners (Tapsell, 2015). The media system in Indonesia is primarily driven by a free market, with public and readers influencing the news landscape.

There are two implications for this. First, even though the video was filmed and circulated in 2013, it traveled half the world, and four years later, it led Farida Idris to post the video on social media platforms in Indonesia. Senior management needs to be aware that cyberspace is an unforgiving medium where whatever is being said, good or bad, stays forever. Leaders will be held accountable for anything they say or have said in the past, since the virality of social media means that messages can be circulated globally anytime, anywhere. Second, the company missed an opportunity to engage with its stakeholders effectively through tailored social media strategies that addressed their concerns and values. By not considering the cultural and social context in which messages were received, Starbucks failed to connect with its audience and alleviate reputational damage. This highlights the importance for companies to understand the media landscape and adapt their communication strategies accordingly to achieve desired outcomes. In the era of new media, where messages are amplified and disseminated rapidly, the understanding and utilization of these platforms are crucial for successful brand management and crisis response. It underscores the significance of being aware of societal values, media preferences, and cultural sensitivities in the rapidly evolving media landscape to effectively navigate and address crises.

Societal Culture

Indonesia's conservative values are deeply rooted in its culture and religion, which plays a significant role in shaping the country's social norms and attitudes toward certain issues, including homosexuality (Pew Research, 2013). While Islam is the dominant religion in Indonesia, the country also has a significant Hindu, Buddhist, and Christian population, each with its own traditions and beliefs. These diverse religious and cultural influences have created a complex social landscape that can sometimes be at odds with contemporary Western values. Furthermore, Indonesia is a democratic country that values freedom of religion and expression (Pancasila), but it also faces challenges in balancing these freedoms with the need to maintain social harmony and prevent conflict while also adhering to Islamic conventions (Knight & Harsono, 2023). These internal dynamics explain why LGBTQ+ individuals often face persecution and discrimination in Indonesia, despite efforts by activists and civil society groups to promote greater inclusivity and tolerance.

Another critical factor shaping Indonesia's attitudes towards foreign brands is its diverse cultural and religious values. The country's societal culture is deeply influenced by its high power distance (77) and low individualism (14) score, making it a collectivist civilization (Hofstede, n.d.). In collectivist cultures like Indonesia, the priorities and needs of the community often supersede individual goals and preferences. Therefore, Indonesians may reject foreign brands that are perceived to violate their cultural or religious values, even if these brands are successful elsewhere in the world. Group harmony and avoiding conflict are highly valued, and this aspect greatly influences consumer behavior and perceptions of foreign companies.

The Starbucks crisis in Indonesia exemplified the impact of societal values and religious beliefs on the reception and success of foreign brands in the country. Although some Indonesians continued to patronize Starbucks despite the backlash (Rizki & Damiana, 2017), conservative Islamic groups took a strong stand against the company's support for LGBTQ+ rights, considering it conflicting with their religious and cultural beliefs. Led by influential Muslim leaders, these groups called for a boycott of Starbucks and even sought the revocation of the company's operating license in Indonesia. In Indonesia's socio-political landscape, these leaders wield significant authority and credibility, making them influential in shaping public opinion (Andriyan, 2017). The country's religious customs and conservative standards hold significant weight in its culture, particularly regarding issues related to social norms and values, which led to the opposition against Starbucks. This demonstrates how deeply ingrained cultural values can significantly impact the perception of foreign brands and their actions.

As Indonesia is the world's most populous Muslim country (Kettani, 2010), many Muslim sympathizers and activists viewed consumerism as potentially undermining their religious values (Berutu, 2020). Consequently, they urged fellow Indonesians to uphold Islamic values. According to Pew Research (2013), a majority of Indonesians (93%) believed that society should not accept homosexuality. Schultz's statement on supporting LGBTQ+ rights made at the annual shareholders' meeting clashed with the conservative values held by many Indonesians, particularly the more religious segments of the population. Starbucks Indonesia faced challenges in denying or distancing itself from Schultz's communication, as it was made on behalf of the company's global stance.

Indonesia's collectivistic culture places a high value on maintaining family lineage through children and following societal standards and norms (Hofstede, n.d.). Extramarital relationships, especially between same-gender individuals, are deemed contrary to social and religious values. The society encourages adherence to established in-groups and traditions. Failure to conform to these standards may lead to exclusion from the community or family. By aligning itself with values not fully embraced by mainstream Indonesian society, such as those espoused by the LGBTQ+ community, Starbucks found itself in a contentious position.

Starbucks CEO Schultz's individualist cultural background might have contributed to the oversight of how his stance on LGBTQ+ rights would be received in Indonesia's strong collectivistic culture. The coexistence of these diverse religious and cultural influences creates a complex social landscape that may not fully align with contemporary Western values. The Starbucks crisis in Indonesia underscores the significance of understanding and respecting the cultural and religious values of the country in shaping brand perception and reputation. For MNCs like Starbucks, effectively navigating the intricacies of Indonesia's societal culture and sensitively addressing cultural and religious considerations are essential for maintaining success and positive relations with their target audience.

Activism System

Activism in Indonesia has a rich history which is tied to social and political disengagement and reforms, and can be traced as far back to when Indonesia struggled for independence from the Dutch colonial rule. Prominent figures like Sukarno and Hatta led the movement, which eventually led to Indonesia's independence (Soekarno, 1963). In the 21st century, activism in Indonesia has evolved to be diverse and dynamic. For example, the types of activism in Indonesia in the modern era includes digital activism that use platforms like Twitter or Instagram to raise awareness of Indonesia's diverse religious and activist movements focused on preserving and challenging religious discrimination (Fealy & White, 2008). In the case of Starbucks's Indonesia crisis, activism was carried out both online and offline with strong advocacy seen primarily on Twitter, and newspaper reports. On Twitter, the emergence of the hashtag "boycott Starbucks" quickly gained traction and widespread attention, with prominent individuals linking news on the call for boycott. The influential personalities included the Deputy Chairman of the Committee III of the Indonesian Regional Representative Council (DPD RI), Fahira Idris, and the Central Board of Muhammadiyah (Putri, 2017). Twitter's user response which intimated that those who had coffee at a local cafe would be considered a man while those who patronized Starbucks were branded gays; hashtags #RejectingLGBT #StarbucksBoycott were included.

Offline, Politician and Activist, Fahira Idris urged the government to take a firm stance by revoking Starbucks' license in Indonesia. Furthermore, she stated that there should be a collective movement or synergy, especially among religious organizations supported by various communities, to campaign against buying Starbucks products due to their support for LGBT propaganda and same-sex marriage (Sudiaman, 2017). Previously, the Central Board of Muhammadiyah expressed a call to boycott Starbucks. The non-governmental Islamic organization is concerned about the potential impact on the Indonesian nation if the attitudes and lifestyle of the LGBTQ+ community were to proliferate in Indonesia (Asyari, 2017). Starbucks needed to be mindful that in the era of social media, past statements and actions may resurface at any time, impacting the company's reputation and brand image (Sriramesh & Verčič, 2003).

As Indonesia is an important market for Starbucks, the negative reaction from the Islamic Organization namely Muhammadiyah and MUI raised concerns among investors, potentially impacting the company's support. In response, PT Sari Coffee Indonesia, the licensee of Starbucks in Indonesia, emphasized its compliance with local regulations and respect for cultural values, attempting to deflect attention from the controversy and maintain a neutral stance (BBC News Indonesia, 2017). This situation highlighted the importance for MNCs to modify their communication strategies to be more inclusive and sensitive to cultural and religious sensitivities, without explicitly mentioning religious disputes (Tempo. Co., 2018). In 2018, Starbucks Indonesia shifted its focus to target the 18 to 35 age group, strategically opening outlets in universities, hospitals, and drive-throughs to tap into the growing middle-class economy (Tempo. Co., 2018). However, the company needs to take into account religious activism in its promotional and communication strategy if it wishes to rebuild its brand and reputation in Indonesia. This might involve engaging in religious and cultural immersion outreach exercises with the local Muslim population to salvage its reputation and demonstrate sensitivity to local values. While this approach may require additional time, effort, and investment, it is crucial to ensuring the company's success in Indonesia, a predominantly Muslim country.

Overall, understanding and engaging with the activism system, as well as respecting cultural and religious values, are essential for international corporations operating in foreign markets like Indonesia. By being proactive in addressing potential controversies and actively embracing cultural nuances, companies can build stronger relationships with their stakeholders and mitigate reputational risks. In a diverse and dynamic society like Indonesia, successful brand management must go beyond business operations and prioritize cultural understanding and adaptability.

Conclusion

The Starbucks crisis in Indonesia serves as a pertinent case study that highlights the intricate interplay of the various systems – political, economic, societal culture, media, and activism – in shaping the outcomes of a corporate crisis. The crisis originated in 2013 when Starbucks' CEO expressed support for LGBTQ+ rights in a video and escalated in July 2017 when local groups in Indonesia, led by the Indonesian Ulama Council (MUI), called for a boycott of the company. The crisis grew rapidly as the call for a boycott spread on social media, garnering around 25,000 mentions and gaining momentum in neighboring Malaysia as well.

The crisis seemingly tapered off when Starbucks Indonesia's parent company MAP Boga Adiperkasa's director Fetty Kwartati made a statement that highlighted its stance that it "does not affiliate itself with any political or ideological groups" (Anya, 2017) – a strategy some organizations used to distance themselves from the party that caused the problem in the first place (Sng et al., 2019). However, the lasting effects of the crisis were somewhat nuanced. The crisis also highlighted that certain sensitive issues might require decisive engagement and clarification, or it might keep re-erupting at the whims and fancies of political stakeholders. While the boycott and negative publicity initially had a significant impact on the company's image, Starbucks' global appeal and brand loyalty ultimately allowed it to rebound from the crisis. Over time, consumers gradually resumed their purchases, and the company regained its footing in the Indonesian market.

Throughout this crisis, various systems played crucial roles. The political system's complex intersection of religion, politics, and culture in Indonesia heightened the sensitivity of Starbucks' statements on social issues. The economic system's reliance on trade and investment made it vital for Starbucks to navigate the local market cautiously and respect cultural values to avoid financial harm. The societal culture, deeply rooted in collectivism and religious beliefs, influenced the negative reaction to Starbucks' perceived disregard for local values. Meanwhile, the media system, with its widespread social media usage, amplified the crisis and mobilized activists, demonstrating the power of social media in shaping public opinion. There was a missed opportunity to address, by issuing statements and immediate social media responses, to alleviate the pressure. This would have filled the information vacuum and increased the reputation by confidently addressing past issues, such as the old 2013 video. Such measures would have reassured stakeholders that Starbucks is committed to the religious diversity of all countries and all religions.

Lastly, the activist system, led by the MUI, showcased the importance of engaging with key stakeholders and understanding cultural memory to mitigate potential controversies. In retrospect, the Starbucks crisis in Indonesia underscored the importance of corporate messages articulated by leaders, and the significance of tailored communication strategies that account for cultural nuances and sensitivities in foreign markets. It also served as a warning that when diversity and ideology collide, a balancing act may not be possible as seen in the case of Starbucks Indonesia and as such, to avoid similar crises, MNCs must proactively engage with local communities, respect cultural values, and foster symbiotic communication with activists and stakeholders. By doing so, companies can build stronger relationships, build trust, and bolster their resilience to potential crises, ensuring their long-term success in diverse and sensitive markets like Indonesia.

References

Allen, F. E. (2013, March 22). Howard Schultz to anti-gay-marriage Starbucks shareholder: "You can sell your shares". *Forbes.com*. https://www.forbes.com/sites/frederickallen/2013/03/22/howard-schultz-to-anti-gay-marriage-starbucks-shareholder-you-can-sell-your-shares/?sh=415bd71b43fa

Andriyan, D. N. (2017, January 18). Kedudukan Dan fatwa MUI Dari Perspektif Ketatanegaraan. *detiknews*. https://news.detik.com/kolom/d-3398740/kedudukan-dan-fatwa-mui-dari-perspektif-ketatanegaraan

Anya, A. (2017, July 5). Starbucks Indonesia clarifies stance on LGBT rights following recent boycott. *The Jakarta Post*. https://www.thejakartapost.com/news/2017/07/05/starbucks-indonesia-clarifies-stance-on-lgbt-rights-following-recent-boycott.html

Asialink Business. (n.d.). Indonesia's economy. *Asialink Business*. https://asialinkbusiness.com.au/indonesia/getting-started-in-indonesia/indonesias-economy?doNothing=1

Asyari, Y. (2017, July 3). Reaksi keras Menag soal CEO Starbuck dukung LGBT. *Jawa Pos*. https://www.jawapos.com/humaniora/01139343/reaksi-keras-menag-soal-ceo-starbuck-dukung-lgbt

BBC News Indonesia. (2017, July 3). Seruan "Boikot Starbucks" diperbincangkan dari Indonesia sampai Malaysia. *BBC News Indonesia*. https://www.bbc.com/indonesia/trensosial-40477621

Berutu, I. S. (2020). Peran Majelis Ulama Indonesia (Mui) Dalam Meningkatkan Pemahaman Keagamaanmasyarakat Muslim Kabupaten Dairi. *Journal of Communication.* http://repository.uinsu.ac.id/10556/1/SKRIPSI%20IRFAN%20S%20BERUTU%20%28PMI%29.pdf

Boyles, M. (2022, July 19). *Understanding how politics can affect your business.* Havard Business School Online. https://online.hbs.edu

Central Intelligent Agency. (2022, August 30). *Indonesia.* Central Intelligence Agency-CIA https://www.cia.gov/the-world-factbook/countries/indonesia/#people-and-society

Chan, D. (2017, July 6). Muslim Groups in Malaysia, Indonesia Boycott Starbucks Over LBGTQ Support. *NBCNews*: https://www.nbcnews.com

Chicago Tribune. (2017, July 6). Malaysia, Indonesia Muslim groups call for Starbucks boycott. *Chicago Tribune.* https://www.chicagotribune.com/business/ct-malaysia-indonesia-muslim-groups-starbucks-boycott-20170706-story.html

Cho, C. (2019). *Indonesia's "fresh meat": LGBTQ activism amid political homophobia and transphobia.* IndepenCent Study Project (ISP) Collection. 3170.

Cox, M., Duituturaga, E., & Sholikin, N. (2012). *Indonesia Case study.* Australian Agency for International Development (AusAID), Canberra.

Cox, R., Schaar, R., Priyambada, R., Winardi, W., & Jamzuri, M. (2023). *Indonesia Investments.* http://www.indonesia-investments.com

Dahrul, F., & Suhartono, H. (Bloomberg). (2018, April 5). Starbucks Indonesia operator sees sales boost from spending. *The Jakarta Post.* https://www.thejakartapost.com/life/2018/04/05/starbucks-indonesia-operator-sees-sales-boost-from-spending.html

Davies, S. G. (2016, July 15). Indonesia's anti-LGBT panic. *East Asia Forum.* http://www.eastasiaforum.org

Fealy, G., & White, S. (2008). Expressing Islam: Religious life and politics in Indonesia. In *Institute of Southeast Asian Studies eBooks.* http://ci.nii.ac.jp/ncid/BA87520863

Global Coffee Report. (2014, March 17). *Global Coffee Report.* Starbucks in Indonesia. https://www.gcrmag.com

Greenwalt, P. (2021, March). *United States Commission on International Religious Freedom.* Indonesia's Pancasila. http://www.uscirf.gov

Hasyim, S. (2021). Commanding right and forbidding wrong: The Rising Influence of Muslim Mainstream Groups. *ISEAS Yusof Ishak Institute Perspective Issue, 2021(78)*, 1–7.

Hofstede Insight. (n.d.). *Country Comparison.* https://www.hofstede-insights.com/country-comparison/indonesia/

Indonesia Investments. (2023, March 7). *Religion in Indonesia. | Indonesia Investments.* https://www.indonesia-investments.com/culture/religion/item69#:~:text=Indonesia%20is%20a%20secular%20democratic,her%20own%20religion%20or%20belief

Jibiki, K. (2020, August 18). Indonesia's 75th anniversary highlights rise of political Islam. *Nikkei Asia.* https://asia.nikkei.com/Politics/Indonesia-s-75th-anniversary-highlights-rise-of-political-Islam

John, T. (2017, May 22). Indonesia arrested 141 men at an alleged gay sauna party. *Time.* https://time.com/4788057/indonesia-gay-sauna-arrests/

Kemp, S. (2022). *Special Report Digital 2022. wearesocial.* https://wearesocial.com/sg/blog/2022/02/digital-2022/

Kettani, H. (2010). Muslim population in Asia: 1950–2020. *International Journal of Environmental Science and Development, 1*(2), 143–153. http://www.ijesd.org/papers/28-D437.pdf

Knight, K., & Harsono, A. (2023, March 27). Permainan Politik Ini Menghancurkan Hidup Kami. *Human Rights Watch.* https://www.hrw.org/id/report/2016/08/11/292433

Lamb, K. (2017, April 19). Muslim candidate beats Christian in divisive Jakarta governor vote. *The Guardian World*. https://www.theguardian.com/world/2017/apr/19/divisive-campaign-for-jakarta-governor-sees-muslim-candidate-elected

Le, P. D., Teo, H. X., Pang, A., Li, Y., & Goh, C. (2018). When is silence golden? The use of strategic silence in crisis communication. *Corporate Communications: An International Journal*, *24*(1), 162–178. https://doi.org/10.1108/ccij-10-2018-0108

Mail, M. (2017, July 2). After Indonesia, Perkasa calls for boycott against Starbucks over 'pro-LBGT stand' (video). *Malay Mail*. https://www.malaymail.com/news/malaysia/2017/07/02/after-indonesia-perkasa-calls-for-boycott-against-starbucks-over-pro-lgbt-s/1412011

Mergonoto, K. (2014). Indonesia's coffee industry needs growth capital. *Global Business Guide*. http://www.gbgindonesia.com/en/agriculture/article/2014/indonesia_s_coffee_industry_needs_growth_capital.phpV

Misner, I. (2021, May 13). Choose the lens you see the world through. *Entrepreneur*. https://www.entrepreneur.com/living/choose-the-lens-you-see-the-world-through/369621

Mohit, M. (2024, June 10). The relationship between business and society. *Academia.edu*. https://www.academia.edu/6078716/The_relationship_between_business_and_society?auto=download

Newsweek. (2017, July 7). Gay rights: Muslim groups in Indonesia and Malaysia demand boycott on Starbucks for its LGBT support. *Newsweek*. https://www.newsweek.com/muslim-groups-malaysia-indonesia-call-starbucks-boycott-protest-lgbt-rights-633158

Nurhayati-Wolff, H. (2022, November 22). Share of market value of largest coffee chains in Indonesia in 2019. *Statista*. https://www.statista.com/statistics/1040920/indonesia-coffee-chains-market-share-value/

Office of the United States Trade Representation (n.d.). Indonesia. https://ustr.gov/countries-regions/southeast-asia-pacific/indonesia#:~:text=Economic%20and%20Trade%20Statistics&text=Indonesia%20is%20currently%20our%2024th,was%20%2412.8%20billion%20in%202020

Perigot, F., & De Rioja, D. F. (2005, May). *The Role of Business in Society*. International Organisation of Employers https://www.ioe-emp.org

Perigot, F., & De Rioja, D. F. (2005, May). *The Role of business in society*. International Organisation of Employers. https://www.ioe-emp.org

Pew Research. (2013, June 4). The global divide on homosexuality. *Pew Research Center's Global Attitudes Project*. https://www.pewresearch.org/global/2013/06/04/the-global-divide-on-homosexuality/

Purnomo, M., Yuliati, Y., Shinta, A., & Riana, F. D. (2021). Developing coffee culture among Indonesia's middle-class: A case study in a coffee-producing country. *Cogent Social Sciences*, *7*(1), 12.

Putri, E. (2017). Why Indonesians are being told to boycott Starbucks. *Culture Trip*. https://theculturetrip.com/asia/indonesia/articles/why-indonesians-are-being-told-to-boycott-starbucks/?amp=1

Rizki, N. (2017, July 1). Muslim leader urges Indonesians to boycott Starbucks over LGBT stand. *Reuters*. https://www.reuters.com/article/us-indonesia-starbucks-lgbt-idUSKBN19M36N

Sng, K., Au, T. Y., & Pang, A. (2019). Social media influencers as a crisis risk in strategic communication: Impact of indiscretions on professional endorsements. *International Journal of Strategic Communication*, *13*(4), 301–320. https://doi.org/10.1080/1553118X.2019.1618305

Soekarno. (1963). Nasionalisme, Islamisme dan Marxisme. *Jajasan Pembaruan eBooks*. http://ci.nii.ac.jp/ncid/BA75739590

Sriramesh, R., & Verčič, D. (2003). *The global public relations handbook: Theory, research, and practice* (1st ed.). Routledge.
Sriramesh, K., & Verčič, D. (2020). *The global public relations handbook: Theory, research, and practice* (3rd ed.). Routledge.
Starbucks. (2022, May 22). Starbucks celebrates 20 years in Indonesia by reinforcing its commitments to people, planet and coffee. *Starbucks*. https://stories.starbucks.com/asia/stories/2022/starbucks-celebrates-20-years-in-indonesia-by-reinforcing-its-commitments-to-people-planet-and-coffee/
Statista. (2021, August 24). Market share of social media platforms Indonesia 2021. https://www.statista.com/statistics/1256213/indonesia-social-media-market-share/#:%7E:text=Indonesia's%20social%20media%20landscape,Indonesia%20of%20about%2094%20percent.
Sudiaman, M. (2017, June 29). Fahira Idris ajak Ormas Keagamaan tolak Starbucks. *Republika Online*. https://news.republika.co.id/berita/osbdtx/fahira-idris-ajak-ormas-keagamaan-tolak-starbucks
Suroyo, S. S. (2023, January 24). Indonesia's FDI jumps in 2022, led by mineral processing. *Reuters*. https://www.reuters.com/markets/asia/indonesias-fdi-jumps-2022-led-by-mineral-processing-2023-01-24/#:~:text=Southeast%20Asia's%20largest%20economy%20received,of%2014%2C350%20to%20the%20dollar.&text=The%20data%20excludes%20investment%20in%20the%20banking%
Tang, A. (2016, March 9). Under attack, Indonesian LGBT groups set up safehouses, live in fear. *Reuters*. http://.www.reuters.com
Tapsell, R. (2015). Indonesia's media oligarchy and the "Jokowi phenomenon. *Indonesia*, *99*, 29–50. https://doi.org/10.5728/indonesia.99.0029
Team, T. I. (2023, January 30). How do brand image and marketing affect market share? *Investopedia*. https://www.investopedia.com/ask/answers/032615/how-does-brand-image-and-marketing-affect-market-share.asp
Tempo. Co. (2018, October 19). Starbucks Anothony Cottan: We try to be in different locations. https://en.tempo.co/read/503018/starbucks-anothony-cottan-we-try-to-be-in-different-locations
The Global Economy.com. (n.d.). Indonesia: Listed companies – data. *The Global Economy.com*. https://www.theglobaleconomy.com/Indonesia/Listed_companies/
The World Bank. (2021, October 25). The World Bank in Indonesia. The World Bank. https://www.worldbank.org/en/country/indonesia/overview#1
Today Online. (2017, July 3). After Indonesia, Malaysia's Perkasa calls for boycott against Starbucks over 'pro-LGBT stand'. *Today*. https://www.todayonline.com/world/asia/after-indonesia-malaysias-perkasa-calls-boycott-against-starbucks-over-pro-lgbt-stand
Trading Economics. (n.d.). Indonesia GDP – 2023 Data – 2024 Forecast – 1967–2022 historical. https://tradingeconomics.com/indonesia/gdp#:~:text=GDP%20in%20Indonesia%20averaged%20317.06,5.67%20USD%20Billion%20in%201967.
UN Office of the High Commissioner for Human Rights. (2017, February 20). Summary of stakeholders' submissions on Indonesia [Universal Periodic Review]: Report of the Office of the United Nations High Commissioner for Human Rights. *United Nations Digital Library System*. https://digitallibrary.un.org/record/861774?ln=en
Verico, K., & Pangestu, M. E. (2020, August). The economic impact of globalisation in indonesia. Discussion Paper series no. 338, 1–32. *The Economic Research Institute for ASEAN and East Asia (ERIA)*. https://www.eria.org/uploads/media/discussion-papers/The-Economic-Impact-of-Globalisation-in-Indonesia.pdf.
Voss, B. (2017, February 7). Muslim leader tells Indonesians to boycott Starbucks over LGBT support. *NewNowNext*. http://www.newnownext.com/indonesia-starbucks-lgbt-boycott/07/2017/

Walton, J., & Scott, G. (2021, August 18). The 5 countries that produce the most coffee. *Investopedia.* https://www.investopedia.com/articles/investing/091415/5-countries-produce-most-coffee.asp

Wirawan, G. B. (2016, October 10). Unbalanced wings of Indonesian politics. *The Jakarta Post.* https://www.thejakartapost.com/academia/2016/10/10/unbalanced-wings-of-indonesian-politics.html

Worldometer. (n.d.). Indonesia Population (2023). https://www.worldometers.info/world-population/indonesia-population/

9

THAILAND

FoodPanda Faces Boycott for "Terrorist" Comment

Jia Ning Neo, Isreya Liangkobkit, Natawan Panachuenvongsakul, Soe Honey Cho, and Lois Bastiaan

Introduction

The pen is mightier than the sword, and with it, one can possibly win a marketing war, or slay the competition. But, in the case of FoodPanda Thailand, it did not realize that its phrase "all types of terrorisms" to describe an ongoing political fracas would lead to a public outcry and cancellation of its delivery services. Located in the heart of Southeast Asia, Thailand, also known as "the land of smiles," is famed for its strong traditional values and richness in cultural ideologies. Buddhism and the monarchy have historically shaped Thailand's image of social order and stability, and they continue to serve as unifying symbols for the Thai people. However, due to globalization, the culture has adapted to modern customs and beliefs. This is evident in Bangkok, the country's capital, which is a bustling cosmopolitan metropolis with a mix of traditional and modern practices and views.

Thai people enjoy freedom of expression pertaining to various issues including social, political, and economic. However, the advent of social media has led to an increase in human rights activism and the call for freedom of speech (Ganjanakhundee, 2020). The accessibility of global information via social media empowers many Thais to become more interconnected among people, societies, and environments around the globe. Therefore, the 2014 coup d'état incident and the revival and obscurity of the lèse-majesté law to suppress anti-government protests have motivated many Thais, particularly the youth, to aspire for social equality, improved quality of life, and greater efficacy in the political system (Smith & Sumon, 2020). These rising demands portray the complexity of perspectives, values, and discourses in the

DOI: 10.4324/9781003411802-10

relationship between citizens and the state, as well as the legitimation of power and proper mode of governance. This phenomenon has created many layers of societal traction in Thai society and is intensifying the ongoing conflict as evident by the outrage, and blood-shed event between Thai protesters and the police against lèse-majesté law (Satienlerk & Kittisilpa, 2021). With the pandemic showing no signs of abating, Thailand's political climate became more divided as the government's handling of the crisis came under intense scrutiny and debate. At the same time, this political landscape is further impinged upon by pro-democracy' activists seeking a reduced role for the king in public life as the monarchy has been accused of overreaching its constitutional powers and interfering in politics. This situation is reminiscent of the crisis faced by Foodpanda Thailand, which highlighted issues related to political influence, labor rights, and inequality. This chapter will examine how the Foodpanda crisis during the Covid-19 pandemic provides insight into Thailand's intricate polarized political landscape.

COVID-19 Pandemic

When the COVID-19 pandemic struck, consumer behavior in Thailand rapidly shifted in response to the extensive nationwide lockdown and social restrictions, especially among middle-to-high-income urban consumers who reside in the major cities, are active Internet users and have substantial disposable income for leisure activities (Fitch Solutions, 2020). While many industries faced economic difficulties, the online food delivery industry, which largely targets this group of consumers, achieved impressive market growth (Leesa-Nguansuk, 2021). However, it also comes at the cost of intense competition and more complex stakeholder management. Thailand's food delivery industry is ranked the second largest in Southeast Asia, after Indonesia. With a number of players entering the market to keep up with increased demand (Li, 2021), GrabFood, Foodpanda, Get, and Line Man – the four main players in Thailand during the pandemic – used this opportunity to undertake massive capital investment. None made a profit as of November 2020 (Phoonphongphiphat, 2021); instead, they had a combined net loss of approximately 4.2 billion baht (US$130 million) (Fitch Solutions, 2020). Such a competitive business landscape generated aggressive actions to please and win consumers at all costs, hence eager attempts to nip every possible issue or potential crisis in the bud.

The Foodpanda Crisis

Launched in 2012, Foodpanda Thailand is a German-owned multinational company (MNC) and the second-largest player in the industry with a 23% market share as of 2020 (Hicks, 2011). The organization invested heavily in a strong hyper-localized business model, providing opportunities for local stakeholders and communities, specifically among its riders, restaurants, and retail partners, while offering a quick and convenient delivery service for consumers (Foodpanda, 2020). Since its establishment, Foodpanda has gained popularity and reputation among urban Thais.

Given the complexity and sensitivity of prevailing political issues in Thailand, and aggravated by the pandemic-related social changes, local attributes, and contexts must be taken into serious consideration for MNCs to effectively communicate with the local audiences. A fixed and standardized strategy will not satisfy the intricacies of a cross-cultural audience (Coombs & Claeys, 2019). The crisis that Foodpanda Thailand had to respond to is a perfect example that demonstrates the lack of knowledge on local crisis communication in a sensitive political, economic, media, societal and organizational culture, and activism.

In July 2021, Foodpanda Thailand was hit by a crisis related to the ongoing political instability, which drastically damaged its reputation and image. The main cause of the crisis was the lack of effectiveness in crisis communication and stakeholders' management. On the one hand, the company's hyper-localized business operation strategy could be effective in generating a win-win benefit for its stakeholders. On the other hand, within the realm of crisis communication, its localized strategy was without the synergy of local sensitivity and understanding. This displays a weak grasp and handling of unexpected crises relating to political issues that stem from polarized perspectives and hostile emotions among internal and external stakeholders. In this chapter, we use the Global Public Relations Framework presented by Sriramesh & Vercic (2020) to analyze the socio-cultural environment of the organization and the role it played in the origin and resolution of the crisis.

Foodpanda Thailand and Its Stakeholders

On July 18, 2021, Foodpanda Thailand faced its first Twitter social media crisis. One of their delivery drivers had participated in a pro-democracy demonstration and was seen burning the portrait of the King of Thailand – a serious crime in the country. In its eagerness to "correct the wrong" and to quickly please the public and government authorities, the company tweeted that they were "against violence and all types of terrorisms" and proceeded to terminate the delivery rider on the same day (Satienlerk & Kittisilpa, 2021).

The crisis for Foodpanda Thailand erupted when Twitter user Ton Patiwat (@tonpatiwat) shared two recorded videos of the incident. The first video showed a man with a surgical mask on his forehead, a red cover for his nose and mouth, and wearing a Line Man's (another food delivery provider) uniform (Patiwat, 2021a). The video described how protesters were burning the portrait of the Thai king and urged the police to go after them. The second video showed the protestor on his motorcycle with a delivery box emblazoned with the Foodpanda logo (Patiwat, 2021b). Patiwat tagged the Thai police account @CSDThailand, urging officials to prosecute the rider for his criminal act of burning the king's portrait (Rojanaphruk, 2021).

Foodpanda Thailand was aware of the incident because another Twitter user had tagged a screenshot of the videos to Foodpanda's account. In its eagerness to please supporters and to avoid breaking the law, Foodpanda was quick to respond with a tweet: "We will expedite the strict implementation of the company's rules by dismissing the rider from his service immediately. Please note that Foodpanda Thailand has a policy against all forms of violence and terrorism. We are willing to fully assist the authorities in the prosecution of criminals" (Masayuki, 2021).

While the quick action to fire the delivery driver for burning the king's photo ought to be lauded, the message triggered a backlash with the emergence of the #banfoodpanda hashtag in response to the firing. Although the employee's action was seen as disrespectful and offensive to the highly revered Thai monarchy, many Thai netizens felt sorry for the driver. A hashtag was subsequently created to express unhappiness over Foodpanda's decision to abruptly remove the employee (an internal stakeholder) as the fervor in wanting to please authorities and the public (external stakeholder groups) was perceived as unjust and showed a lack of empathy for the poorer segment of the population – an act that went against the social values in Thai culture.

Unfortunately, the hashtag created an online backlash for the MNC – #banfoodpanda became one of the highest trending hashtags in Southeast Asia, with more than 1.25 million retweets (Masayuki, 2021). A raging and vocal digital audience drastically impacted Foodpanda Thailand's reputation nationwide. In this crisis, Foodpanda Thailand's affected stakeholder groups can be divided into two groups: the primary stakeholders and the secondary stakeholders. The primary stakeholders were (1) the Foodpanda Thailand customers and franchisees of Foodpanda, (2) Foodpanda Thailand Employees, (3) Foodpanda Thailand [delivery] Riders, and (4) the government. The secondary stakeholders were (1) pro-democracy activists, (2) government supporters, and (3) monarchy supporters. The difference between the two groups is that the secondary stakeholders were involved for a short period of time during the crisis and were the ones who alerted the company about the issue. Foodpanda Thailand's initial response to the secondary stakeholders' alert did not ease the situation, but instead created a ripple effect that negatively impacted its primary stakeholders.

In response to the escalating public outcry, Foodpanda Thailand issued two apologies – both of which were poorly received. In the first apology posted on Twitter on July 18, 2021, the company did not bear any responsibility, instead shifting the blame onto the page administrator who had used the word "terrorism" in the tweet and had "acted without consent from Foodpanda" (Ragavan, 2021). The blaming strategy resulted in greater negative publicity for the organization as the onus was on them to manage their own social media accounts. Ultimately, it is the responsibility of the company to ensure that their brand image and reputation are not negatively impacted by the actions of their employees.

Within 24 hours of the first apology tweet, a second apology – an extended announcement – was shared across the organization's Twitter and Facebook platforms. This time, the tone and content of the message were devoid of any blame as they attempted to reassure the public of their belief that "freedom of speech and expression is not terrorism." They also added in the tweet that they had reversed the decision regarding the driver, stating that "the rider will not be dismissed" (Masayuki, 2021).

However, as the Internet had already triggered and facilitated the escalation of the crisis (Lambret & Barki, 2018), public furor did not abate despite the apologies. Foodpanda Thailand had to deal with the stakeholder repercussions that followed – the loss of over 2 million users who deleted their Foodpanda accounts and the exit of business partners – 90,000 restaurants and merchants who quit the platform (Li, 2021). These losses amounted to a staggering 4.7 billion baht (Leesa-Nguansuk, 2022), impacting the survivability of the business. To add fuel to the fire, the company's app experienced glitches and technical errors during the crisis, which prevented more users from deactivating or deleting their accounts (Coconuts Bangkok, 2021). This untimely incident resulted in more misunderstanding of the company's action as many felt that this was a ploy to stem the flow of users quitting their services. As the stakeholders' sentiments became more heated than ever before (Masayuki, 2021), Foodpanda Thailand's refusal to release any statement to clarify the situation led the public to believe that the technical fault was a barrier created by the company on purpose to prevent further losses.

Internally, the crisis caused a rift between the company and its riders (Rojanaphruk, 2021). The exodus of the company's users and partners created an internal rift with the riders whose livelihoods were affected. The rift was posted on Facebook by one of the riders. The rider had a #banfoodpanda hashtag, showing how bad the situation was for him and blaming Foodpanda Thailand for the crisis. The tweet went viral, attracting 40,000 likes, and was shared 16,000 times. In the context of Thailand's political situation, "pro-democracy" activists are seeking a reduced role for the king in public life. This is because the monarchy has been accused of overreaching its constitutional powers and interfering in politics. Another Foodpanda Thailand rider added to the discord by posting a picture of himself with a three-finger salute – a sign originally from the *Hunger Games* book series and later an anti-government reform symbol in Thailand – reaffirming his identity with the pro-democracy public and his willingness to go against the company he worked for to take a political stance (Bangkok Post, 2021a). The company did not issue any specific response to these social media posts, other than emphasizing how they would not dismiss their riders, presumably not to further aggravate the situation.

The incident of the Foodpanda Thailand driver attempting to burn a portrait of a member of the royal family was not directly related to the government. However, given the sensitive nature of the monarchy in Thailand, the company should have been more cautious in its actions to avoid any negative impact on its reputation as it had multiple polarized stakeholders to appease. The issue is based on the major divide in Thailand's political system – after many decades of being deferential to the king, many Thai citizens have lately been opposing the monarchy and seeking full democracy. With this as a push factor, MNCs such as Foodpanda Thailand, cannot offend the stakeholder groups with differing political viewpoints.

On August 3, 2021, Foodpanda Thailand CEO Alexander Felde had an online interview with *The Standard* (The Standard, 2021) – a local media agency popular among the younger generations for its domestic and international stories. During the interview, Felde answered every question with an emotional tone, tearing up at some point, including when talking about the disappearance of the delete button due to a technical glitch and the overall impact on Foodpanda Thailand's reputation. Felde's key message continuously focused on how the company had "a broader responsibility" for the Thai community that went beyond the brand image, reputation, and business. Felde's messages targeted Foodpanda Thailand's key stakeholders – the public, merchants, delivery riders, and their employees. These four stakeholder groups were crucial driving forces that could cushion the company's fall from grace (Wan-Kitpaiboon & Areepermporn, 2021).

After the interview was released on YouTube, the tension from the crisis subsided with less social media backlash. To further bolster its image, Foodpanda Thailand took to Instagram to showcase how they were active in giving back to the community through their Corporate Social Responsibility efforts. While the calls for a boycott of Foodpanda may have diminished on social media, the ongoing crisis continued to have a negative impact on the company's delivery riders – many of whom experienced a loss of orders, which in turn affected their livelihood during a time of economic and healthcare crisis (Li, 2021). As independent contractors, these riders are not entitled to the same labor rights as regular employees, which has led to concerns about the power imbalance between them and the company. These concerns have been a major factor in the ongoing crisis involving Foodpanda in Thailand, which led to protests, strikes, and calls for greater regulation of the gig economy. This underscores the importance of resolving the crisis in a timely and effective manner, not only for the sake of company's reputation but also for the well-being of its delivery riders.

As of 2023, Foodpanda continued to face significant challenges in its operations in Thailand and the broader Southeast Asian region – it laid off 50% and 20% of its workforce in Thailand and Malaysia, respectively (Deal Street Asia, 2023). The company's ongoing brand crisis and the impact of the COVID-19 pandemic on the food delivery industry have likely contributed to the need for cost-cutting measures, including workforce reductions. Line Man Wongnai's potential acquisition of Foodpanda Thailand could certainly impact the food delivery market in the country as it plans for a future stock-market debut (The Business Times, 2022).

Case Analysis

This crisis illustrates the profound lack of understanding by Foodpanda Thailand of the political, economics, media, culture, and activism system in which it operates. A single message posted on the social media platform negatively impacted the company's reputation within a day and lead to a deluge of criticism by tens of thousands of its customers. The company should not have been in the crisis to begin with but then failed to respond appropriately to the incident, indirectly harming their stakeholders with careless choice of words, and a lack of preparedness in their crisis response. This crisis is a great example to illustrate the nexus between crisis communication and the five socio-political factors offered as the Global Public Relation Framework by Sriramesh and Vercic (2020).

Political System

Thailand is the only Southeast Asian nation that has never been colonized – an achievement in itself. Its political system is that of a constitutional monarchy, with the king as head of state and the prime minister, elected by parliament, as the head of government. However, since it transitioned to constitutional monarchy, its political environment has never been stable. The country has faced 13 military coup-d'etat, with an equal number of aborted or failed coups between 1932 and 2014 (Ferrara, 2015). The roots of Thailand's current political polarization can be traced back to the 1932 revolution when the king's political role became a source of fierce political debate. The culturally constructed ideology of the king as the nation's soul and bearer of immense political power has established a fixed hierarchical social order and provided justification for socioeconomic inequalities (Sombatpoonsiri, 2020).

Throughout decades of political unrest, Thailand has had many public protests that challenged the political setup in the country. One of the more famous ones was the "Red shirt" movement in 2009–2010, when tens of thousands of Thai citizens in red shirts barricaded themselves in the heart of the commercial district of Bangkok for several weeks, demanding that the government of Abhisit leave calling for fresh parliamentary elections. This led to an armed response by the government that resulted in many deaths. The protests continued, however, resulting in victory for the protesters when new parliamentary elections were held a year later. In 2020, youth-led protests targeted the military junta government. There were two main circumstances that stirred up anger among the youth protesters. The first stemmed from the 2019 election, where the military-backed Palang Pracharath Party won a disputed general election and elevated former military general Prayut Chan-o-cha as prime minister. As a result, a pro-democracy group named Forward Party was banned and dissolved by the constitutional court (Peck & Blake, 2020). Another factor was the suspicion and negative perception of the prime minister and his party due to the numerous corruption scandals and poor management of public health and economic policies (Sombatpoonsiri, 2020).

The pandemic highlighted prevailing socioeconomic inequalities in Thailand that caused distrust and anger to grow in many anti-government crowds, many of whom are university and high school students. Their protest consisted of a list of three demands – the resignation of the prime minister, the amendment of the constitution, and the reformation of the monarchy (Peck & Blake, 2020). The last demand is the most controversial since the king and monarchy are seen as "sacred" (Chankaew, 2021) and are protected by Section 112 of the country's Penal Code: Whoever defames, insults, or threatens the king, the queen, the heir-apparent or the regent shall be sentenced three to 15 years in prison (Tanakasempipat, 2020). This law not only distances the monarchy from Thai citizens but also shadows the negative impression and attitude toward King Maha Vajiralongkorn due to his individualistic personality traits, the obscurity of his royal duties, and rumors surrounding him. Likewise, it is worth mentioning that his father, King Bhumibol Adulyatej (King Rama IX), was well-loved by most Thai citizens during his 70-year reign. In response, the king had attempted to solidify the power of the monarchy through the use of media as well as some government diktats; however, this has not been impactful, possibly due to the enduring image that Thais, especially among the youth, had of him through individual perception and their sense of social justice (Reuters Staff, 2019). This reflects the weakening of the foundation of the Thai political system, with polarization tensions intensified by social media through the facilitation of mass mobilization, which further creates partisan information bubbles and the reinforcement of taking action for their rights (Sombatpoonsiri, 2020).

The ongoing political unrest in Thailand, specifically the junta government and the detached monarchy, has penetrated every facet of Thai society, resulting in a cultural and ideological divide amongst the Thais regardless of age, gender, education, and societal level. In particular, the political issue has never been this sensitive in the business sector; companies operating in Thailand must stay neutral as much as possible in the face of intense pressure from external sources and stakeholders (Reed, 2020). Thus, MNCs operating in Thailand must understand the nuances and fragility to deploy appropriate communicative strategies in this unconventional political landscape.

In the case of Foodpanda Thailand, the rage among youth protesters stemmed from the misused linguistic term "terrorist" in their tweet, which led to the debate of the company's political stance. In crisis management, the speed of response is crucial, based on the concept of the "Golden Hour," which is to prevent information vacuum and reputational risks from occurring (Coombs, 2020). However, the Foodpanda Thailand case has shown that the speed of response can backfire without the accompaniment of adequate information and understanding of local attributes and contexts.

The role of communication practitioners in MNCs is critical in this pendulum – how can communication practitioners in MNCs strike a balance between organizational and national interest? With the many layers of political complexities within a country, there is a need for MNCs to invest more time and resources to upskill communication practitioners to be tenacious and multifaceted as a strategic communicator, critical thinker, and problem-solver in order to assist organizations through the peaks and troughs.

Economic System

The COVID-19 pandemic rattled global economies, resulting in a global recession that has affected most countries, including Thailand. In 2020, Thailand's GDP contracted by 6.1%, the worst since the 1997 Asian Financial Crisis (Deloitte, 2021) when it contracted by 7.6%. Thailand's economy registered a mere growth of 0–1% in 2021, mostly due to the drop in tourism – a principal driver of Thailand's economic growth and one of the worst-hit sectors during the pandemic. Concurrently, poverty rose to 6.4%, representing an additional 200,000 people falling into poverty as they lost jobs – many in the hospitality sector as tourism ground to a halt. The rate of poverty reduction has declined substantially over the past three decades, from 65.2% in 1988 to 6.2% in 2019.

According to Thailand's 20-Year National Strategy (2017–2036) that targets key economic and social reforms to end poverty and boost shared prosperity, the primary difficulty restricting Thailand's sustainable development and goal of becoming a high-income country is inequality (World Bank, 2021). The rise of inequality is interconnected with the emergence of the Thai middle class – made up of urban white-collar workers, professionals, and business owners – which grew dramatically from 15% of the workforce in 1960 to 34% in 2000.

The Modernization theory (Sripokangkul et al., 2019) suggests that this growing middle-class phenomenon will lead to democratization and broader political participation as they value social and economic self-interest over specific political characteristics and finding solace in the nationalistic and royalist imagery proffered by non-democratic regimes, especially in the semi-divine nature of the Thai king as a righteous Buddhist god-king.

Thailand's progress in executing its digital government policy "Thailand 4.0" would help to drive the country's overall economic competitiveness by accelerating the digitalization of the private sector and improving citizens' and businesses' access to public sector data (Bangkok Post, 2021b). Thailand's high Internet and mobile Internet penetration have fueled demand for data centers and cloud technologies, with individuals and consumers spending more time online, and businesses adjusting to new practices such as work-from-home and the gig economy (Bangkok Post, 2021b). While still in infancy, the food delivery and grocery delivery market in Thailand is growing rapidly. Additionally, all mobile phone users are expected to have access to the Internet by 2024, further increasing the lucrativeness of the market. Businesses and MNCs should capitalize on this uptrend and invest in this emerging e-commerce sector to boost Thailand's economic development.

Thailand's digital infrastructure offers every citizen access to the Internet but also magnifying any crisis – as was evident in the Foodpanda Thailand saga. All it took was a tweet of five lines that were interpreted as the organization's pro-government sentiments to cause Foodpanda Thailand's fortune to spiral downward overnight along with a loss of stakeholder goodwill. The nationwide Twitter campaign to boycott the company galvanized all stakeholders – including members of the public, partners, franchisees, riders, customers – and led to the loss of two million customers and the departure of 90,000 merchants from the delivery platform (Deepti, 2021) that translated to a total loss of 4.7 billion baht in 2021 (Leesa-Nguansuk, 2022). Riders were severely impacted as they experienced a significant loss of orders, further accentuating how the lower-income class suffered financially during the pandemic.

The success of food delivery services or companies, in general, is determined by the businesses' ability to strategically connect with these consumers, which was evidently lacking in the Foodpanda Thailand case. In today's complex business environment, companies need to reframe their strategies to look at the bigger, long-term picture to identify opportunities and gaps. This includes refining operational practices, maintaining and building honesty and transparency in their internal and external relations. These intangible assets are important pillars that will protect a company's image and reputation during crises. The role of communication practitioners in MNCs then has the strategic and influential ability to strengthen connections and align their communication chemistry within the community to ensure a smooth venture into the blossoming e-commerce sector to help boost Thailand's economic development.

Media System

Even though Thailand's 2007 constitutions restored freedom of expression guarantees were eliminated in the 2006 coup, lèse-majesté (crimes against the sovereign) laws, on the other hand, continue to prohibit both media and citizens from defaming, insulting, or opposing the monarchy (United Nations High Commissioner for Refugees, 2011).

However, Thailand's media sector is considered progressive compared to other Southeast Asian countries, despite the government and military's heavy control and regulation of both radio and television (Manakitsomboon, 2021a). In Thailand, television is the most popular form of media, and it is also the medium in which businesses spend the most money on advertisements (Advertising Association of Thailand, 2021). And in recent years, the consumption of newspapers or journals has shifted from print to mobile devices and tablets (Manakitsomboon, 2021b).

In parallel, Thailand has seen a proliferation of social media and Internet users, like many other countries with reliable ICT infrastructure that use virtual channels to serve their various communication needs. Facebook and YouTube are the most popular platforms in Thailand with 94% users of the population, among other platforms such as Line, Twitter, and Instagram. As of January 2021, Thailand ranked seventh worldwide, with 55 million monthly active social media users (Statista, 2021).

Communicating over the Internet will decentralize the information monopoly held by people with oppressive regimes. Not only does it enable a free and balanced flow of information, but it also allows every citizen to freely access information sources and even voice their own opinions, eliminating any unfair and unequal communication process (Kularb, 2007). Following the 2006 coup d'état, the Thai military government began to implement new Internet censorship mechanisms as social media is widely used to mobilize support for political purposes. The censorship is based on Singaporean laws, which include new Internet-specific laws as well as to tighten criminal provisions for lèse-majesté (Schaffar, 2016). Given that social media usage in Thailand is rapidly increasing year on year, the government is unable to monitor and control it. This is evident with the increasingly dissident videos and clips insulting both the king and the monarchy on YouTube despite existing rules and regulations (Schaffar, 2016).

Facebook has become not only a social media platform for communication but also a major online source for news, information, and even entertainment among Thai social media users and consumers. Twitter is the fifth most popular social media platform (Sinpeng, 2021), and it is an appealing platform for exploring controversial and political topics because it provides more anonymity than Facebook, where people can use fake photos and names more easily. In 2020, an estimated 55% of the online Thai population used Twitter, and the usage has grown rapidly since 2018, owing largely to uptake by Generation Z, those aged 16 to 24, who use it primarily to discuss entertainment interests, with Thai pop, K-pop, and fans of Thai evening soap operas dominating conversations and hashtags (Sinpeng, 2021). Since digital media has profoundly enhanced the diversity of voices, the Internet has fueled the rise of amateur journalism through the emergence of "middle" media such as alternative media and "micro" media – individuals with personal blogs and social media pages or accounts used for consumption and information sharing (Tangkitvanich & Wongkitrungruang, 2011). With the rise of "middle" and "micro" media, Foodpanda Thailand was heavily impacted by this crisis, with social media users rallying together to urge the company to take a stand in the political situation.

In this case study, Thais who support pro-democracy demonstrations sparked an Internet movement in 2020 to force large corporations to choose sides. Activists started using Twitter to persuade firms including Foodpanda, Burger King, and the Pizza Company, all of which are controlled by Bangkok-listed leisure group Minor International, to stop advertising on The Nation TV. As The Nation TV is a pro-government and pro-monarchy private media outlet, some businesses stopped using the medium for marketing. Seven of the station's newscasters resigned. Three months later, The Nation TV began reporting on the protests in a more nuanced manner before expanding its coverage of the protesters' demands on its channel and website (Reed, 2020).

With the surge of both online and offline activism, social media have become an increasingly sophisticated new battleground for democracy in Thailand. The Foodpanda Thailand crisis highlighted how strongly Thais with certain political beliefs felt about their cause and how quickly they reacted to defend what they perceived to be violations, such as when the "#banfoodpanda" hashtag went viral. Given that the protest movement is an ongoing and rapidly developing phenomenon, understanding this power play is crucial for a deeper analysis of the country's political situation and the pressure MNCs will constantly face. The advent of social media activism has put pressure on companies to take a stand, and this rising demand from protesters could be paramount to the survival and success of Thai companies.

As technology advancement inevitably creates more layers of communication complexity, communication practitioners play a role in ensuring that communication flows constantly in a circular rather than in a linear way (Argenti, 2017). This requires them to be eagle-eyed to distinguish key issues from background noise. They should be trained, proactive, and well-articulated in the convergence of modern communications of social media management, multimedia content creation, creativity, and data analysis.

When Foodpanda Thailand rushed to comment on the crisis, it elicited a strong reaction from the public that resulted in yet another crisis. The company reacted quickly to people's outrage by bringing out its top management and to sincerely apologize for the rushed statement on Twitter and its consequences to the primary stakeholders involved, such as the public on social media, riders, franchisees, and partners. Also, the company chose *The Standard*, a top local media outlet that resonates with its target audience, to conduct an exclusive interview with its CEO. The objective was to engage with younger audiences who had been actively condemning the company on social media through hashtag campaigns. This approach successfully resulted in reversing the younger segment's opposition to the company, as they started to change their perceptions of the company. In a similar vein, the company launched a program to support their partners and riders to express their appreciation during this difficult period, as it is a critical time for them to regain their reputation and repair their image following the crisis.

This study informs us that Thailand's social media culture has the power to make or break the reputation of organizations by amplifying the state of the crisis (Lambret & Barki, 2018). However, MNCs have the power to control the narrative and connect with stakeholders emotionally and psychologically (Pang et al., 2013) by understanding their external stakeholder emotions through social media analysis and tailor-make response strategies to address their specific concerns and regain their confidence (Jin & Pang, 2010).

Societal Culture

According to Hofstede's six cultural dimensions, Thailand has a high power distance with a strict chain of command and protocol through hierarchical order; a high level of collectivism that manifests in a close long-term commitment to the member group; high level of femininity with a nature of empathizing, giving back and supporting people; high uncertainty avoidance to control everything to eliminate or avoid the unexpected; and high level of long-term orientation exhibiting a high value on education, and emphasizing strong work ethic (Hofstede, 2001a). In the case of Foodpanda Thailand, we used the relevant dimensions of power distance, collectivism, uncertainty avoidance, and femininity to analyze the impact of these factors on the organization's crisis communication.

In Thai culture, status is extremely important, as many social interactions among Thai people consider another person's status related to oneself (i.e., age, income level, family connections, education, job), demonstrating a prominent level of power distancing (Gadavanij, 2020). People generally do not question the hierarchical system, preferring instead to follow the chain of command and accept social status discrepancies. Given Thailand's long history of monarchical rule, it is illegal to show disrespect for the king and royal family, and citizens are prohibited from engaging in behavior deemed to be in opposition of the royal family, which is also considered to be defamatory to the king (Scroope, 2016). Foodpanda Thailand appears to have acted quickly – in issuing a statement condemning the rider who had tried to burn the king's portrait – by considering the culture of power distancing while abiding by the laws to avoid friction with the government.

At the same time, Foodpanda Thailand overlooked the other cultural dimension of collectivism during this crisis in which a group of activists and young generation collectively protested against the government and monarchy. People in collectivistic cultures use social media more frequently to share ideas, influence each other's opinions, and guide purchase decisions (Goodrich & de Mooij, 2014). The company's debacle became a hot topic on social media because of the Thais' collectivistic culture of sharing posts or expressing their opinions to seek in-group support. In a collectivist society like Thailand, people rarely jeopardize the group's interests and frequently take responsibility for fellow members (Hofstede, 1984). As a result, Foodpanda Thailand was chastised and threatened for causing discontent by standing out from the crowd. People in a collectivist society are concerned about what others think of their actions, and they try to earn respect by acting in ways that meet the expectations of those around them (Pimpa, 2012). Given Thailand's collectivistic culture, the company attempted to correct its actions as soon as possible to please its customers and target audiences.

Furthermore, Foodpanda Thailand considered the Thai culture of high uncertainty avoidance by adhering to strict rules, laws, policies, and regulations to reduce the level of uncertainty associated with the crisis at the outset. However, it backfired on the company, exacerbating the crisis and directly impacting its business, resulting in the loss of customers. Finally, Thailand's low masculinity reflects a feminine society that values empathy, respect, charity, and support over assertiveness and competitiveness (Hofstede, 2001b). Even though the company's statement and use of the word "terrorism" was condemned, people tend to forgive and forget due to a culture of high femininity – believing that being a good person means giving back and showing care and empathy to everyone. As a result, Foodpanda Thailand took advantage of Thailand's high femininity culture to repair its image by launching a campaign to support riders and merchants during the pandemic, diverting the publics' attention by creating a new narrative to replace the crisis narrative.

Thai culture is very feminine in nature (Hofstede, 1980). Therefore, external stakeholders, especially consumers and media, are likely to prefer brands that support their stances, opinions, and preferences. However, as an MNC operating in a foreign country, it is difficult to avoid the pressures from various parties such as the government, investors, or regulators. These stakeholders stop MNCs from freely expressing their opinions and to take any stances. Therefore, MNCs should communicate and respond in a neutral tone that shows a sense of empathy and comfort. This will allow them to convey appropriate messages that elevate a strong sense of understanding and acceptance while bringing back confidence and trust among stakeholders. Additionally, MNCs need to maintain good relationships and collaborations with internal and external stakeholders including employees and suppliers, the government, public institutions, and local agencies as these groups have a better understanding of the local culture and context (Sriramesh and Vercic, 2020) and hold a latent power in supporting the organization during a crisis.

The Foodpanda Thailand controversy exemplified how multinational corporations' ignorance of cultural nuances can result in negative consequences such as market share loss, reputation damage, and missed opportunities such as partnerships and joint ventures. During the boycott, consumers deleted the company's app, resulting in a loss of market share. Its reputation, built over the course of years, was ruined in a matter of hours because of the company ignoring cultural nuances. Partners such as riders and merchants also joined the boycott essentially isolating the management.

Activism

In the past, traditional media channels dominated the dissemination of information and news in Thailand. Activists had limited access to these platforms and often faced censorship or biased reporting. However, social media has democratized access to information and given activists a global platform to reach a wider audience and engage with people from all walks of life, including those who may not have been previously exposed to their causes.

In the past, organizing protests and mobilizing people required significant planning and coordination through offline means. Now, activists use social media as a potent means to quickly disseminate information about events, share updates, and mobilize support. This has led to more spontaneous and impactful demonstrations that can quickly gain momentum, as is evident in this case study. With Thailand's ongoing political instability and civil strife, democracy is continually disrupted by a strong culture of military intervention and monarchical overreach. Against this backdrop, the country's political discourse is further fueled by the amplification of social media and digital activism (Beattie, 2020). Thailand has one of the world's youngest Internet markets (Statista, 2023), with youths accounting for the majority of the web population – children as young as six use the Internet. A highly globalized environment with high social media penetration and user engagement rate (Leesa-Nguansuk, 2018) are factors that shape the younger generations' thinking, influencing them to express their political stance daringly and fearlessly.

The power asymmetry between protesters and authorities is reduced and transformed in the digital sphere. Authorities are unable to operate on social media platforms where they do not have full control – social media channels are the ultimate arbiters. The online dynamics of protest movements are thus fundamentally different from their offline component, although both can complement and influence one another (Beattie, 2020).

The youth-led pro-democracy movements in both the streets and digital space have undoubtedly increased tensions in Thailand's politically polarized society. Aside from the fundamental demands, students have their own concerns and proposals for reforming Thailand's educational system. The youth protesters call themselves "Bad Students" because they refuse to adhere to traditional Thai education standards of expecting children to accept and follow commands blindly; they seek to demolish the harassment aimed at pro-democracy students and repeal outdated and harsh school regulations (Phasuk, 2020 as cited in Chankaew, 2021).

Young activists have been using a combination of humor and creativity to showcase the absurdity and disproportionality of the political unrest in Thailand (Ratcliffe, 2020). The non-violent protests leverage art as a creative forefront to capture the attention of the international media. For example, a giant inflatable rubber duck was used as a pro-democracy symbol to mock the authorities for blocking the entrance to the parliament building where constitutional changes were being debated, and protesters joking that the only way in was to send rubber ducks down the river (Ratcliffe, 2020). Protest artworks also emerged online, portraying the ducks as superhero figures and muscled fighters protecting the students (Ratcliffe, 2020).

Additionally, the youth protesters have adopted a range of pop cultural symbols, from the three-fingered salute from the dystopian *Hunger Games* novels during morning assemblies in schools, to singing the revolutionary "Do you hear the people sing?" from the musical *Les Misérables*, and Harry Potter dress-ups to make a stand against "He Who Shall Not be Named" (Handley, 2020). While the imagery was not intentional in appealing to Western audiences specifically, they often resonated with international observers.

Conclusion

Thailand seems to be a polarized country with different worldviews and beliefs vis-à-vis the role of corporations in society as well as the role of government and the monarchy. However, the country has also come a long way from its traditional approach to the role of government and monarchy, which was evident in the way the protesters opposed a company's perceived support of governmental and monarchy privilege in politics (Abuza, 2021). MNCs are unable to take an accommodative stance (Pang et al., 2020) as it will lead to huge societal conflicts between inter-generations and pro-monarchy groups. With the government turning to repressive means to curb the protests, it suggests unsettling insecurity as the ongoing student movements are dependent on the characteristics of the social environment that they seek to change (Chankaew, 2021). With each side blaming the other for invoking violence and no compromise in sight, the situation could become extremely dangerous if it further escalates.

Our analysis of the Foodpanda Thailand crisis using the Global Public Relation Framework (Sriramesh & Vercic, 2020) also outlined in Chapter 1 has shed light on the importance of crisis management and communication taking into account various nuances of the cultural and societal dimension in a society such as a divergence in political opinion, changes in societal ideology toward equality, high ambiguity towards governance standard and legal system, the fluctuation and instability of economic performance, and the reliance on social media. These factors showcase the intricacies of what Thai culture is built on, further stressing the need for communication practitioners to bridge the gaps in such a polarized environment. MNCs should embark on a public-centered continuum focusing on restoring and building confidence not only from outside in (external audiences) but also from inside out (internal audiences), as confidence is a future predictor of the publics' crisis responses relating to behaviors, emotions, and reputational impact (Pang et al., 2020).

References

Argenti, P. A. (2017). Strategic communication in the C-suite. *International Journal of Business Communication*, *54*(2), 146–160.

Abuza, Z. (2021). Thailand's Constitutional Dictatorship Weathers the Storm. *The Diplomat*. https://thediplomat.com/2021/09/thailands-constitutional-dictatorship-weathers-the-storm/

Advertising Association of Thailand. (2021). Distribution of advertising expenditure in Thailand in 2021, by medium [Graph]. In *Statista*. https://www-statista-com.libproxy.smu.edu.sg/statistics/586789/thailand-ad-spend-medium-share/

Bangkok Post. (2021a). Foodpanda bashed after 'terrorism' tweet. https://www.bangkokpost.com/thailand/general/2151347/foodpanda-bashed-after-terrorism-tweet

Bangkok Post. (2021b). Thailand's transformation boots data industry. *Bangkok Post*. https://www.bangkokpost.com/business/2142475/thailands-digital-transformation-boosts-data-industry

Beattie, T. (2020). The power dynamics of Thailand's digital activism. *The Strategist*. https://www.aspistrategist.org.au/the-power-dynamics-of-thailands-digitalactivism/

Coconuts Bangkok. (2021). #BanFoodpanda: Outrage after delivery giant vows to fire protester for 'terrorism.' *Coconuts*. https://coconuts.co/bangkok/news/banfoodpanda-outrage-after-delivery-giant-vows-to-fire-protester-for-terrorism/

Chankaew, P. (2021). Child protection practitioners' perceptions of working with children whose rights were violated due to their participation in the protests in Thailand in the year 2020 (Master's thesis, University of Stavanger). https://uis.brage.unit.no/uis-xmlui/handle/11250/2787111

Coombs, W. T. (2020). Conceptualizing crisis communication. In *Handbook of risk and crisis communication* (pp. 99–118). Routledge.

Coombs, W. T., & Claeys, A. S. (2019). Global crisis communication. In *The global public relations handbook* (pp. 217–225). Routledge.

Deal Street Asia. (2023). People Digest: Foodpanda lays off staff in SE Asia; Eight Roads hands out promotions in China unit. *Deal Street Asia*. https://www.dealstreetasia.com/stories/foodpanda-lay-offs-malaysia-thailand-330140

Deepti, S. (2021). Foodpanda Thailand reportedly loses over 2 million users after social media debacle. *Tech in Asia*. https://www.techinasia.com/foodpanda-thailand-reportedly-loses-2m-user-accounts-after-social-media-outburst

Deloitte. (2021). Respond, Recover, Thrive: An evolving perspective on the economic impacts of COVID-19. https://www2.deloitte.com/th/en/pages/about-deloitte/articles/thailand-economic-outlook.html

Fitch Solutions. (2020). Thai Food Delivery Market Taking Off. *Bangkok Post*. https://www.bangkokpost.com/business/2019015/thai-food-delivery-market-taking-off.

Ferrara, F. (2015). *The political development of modern Thailand*. Cambridge University Press.

Foodpanda. (2020). *Foodpanda announces nationwide coverage in Thailand*. Foodpanda. https://www.foodpanda.com/2020/11/foodpanda-announces-nationwide-coverage-in-thailand-the-first-food-delivery-platform-to-operate-across-all-77-provinces/.

Ganjanakhundee, S. (2020). Social Media and Thailand's Struggle over Public Space.

Gadavanij, S. (2020). Contentious polities and political polarization in Thailand: Post-Thaksin reflections. *Discourse & Society*, *31*(1), 44–63. https://doi.org/10.1177/0957926519877695

Goodrich, K., & de Mooij, M. (2013). How "social" are social media? A cross-cultural comparison of online purchase decision influences. *Journal of Marketing Communications*. *20*, 103–116. https://doi.org/10.1080/13527266.2013.797773

Handley, E. (2020). Why Thai students use rubber ducks, dinosaurs and three-finger salutes as protest symbols. *ABC News*. https://www.abc.net.au/news/2020-11-24/thai-protests-rubber-duckies-dinosaurs-three-finger-salute/12911494

Hicks, W. (2011). Rapid Shopping via Pandamarts. *Bangkok Post*. https://www.bangkokpost.com/business/2066351/rapid-shopping-via-pandamarts

Hofstede, G. (2001a). *Culture's consequences: Comparing values, behaviors, Institutions and organizations across nations*. Sage.

Hofstede, G. (2001b). *Culture's consequences: Comparing values, behaviors, institutions and organizations across nations*. Sage.

Hofstede, G. (1980). Culture's consequences: International differences. In *Work-Related Values*. Sage.

Hofstede, G. (1984). National cultures revisited. *Asia Pacific Journal of Management*, *2*, 22–28. http://dx.doi.org/10.1007/BF01732507

Jin, Y., & Pang, A. (2010). Future directions of crisis communication research: Emotions in crisis–the next frontier. In *The handbook of Crisis Communication* (pp. 677–682). Wiley-Blackwell. https://ink.library.smu.edu.sg/cgi/viewcontent.cgi?article=7036&context=lkcsb_research

Kularb, P. (2007). *Communicating to the Mass on Cyberspace: Freedom of Expression and Content Regulation on the Internet*. © Institut de Recherche Sur l'Asie Du Sud-Est Contemporaine, 2007 Terms of Use: http://www.openedition.Org/6540. https://books.openedition.org/irasec/385?lang=en

Lambret, C. V., & Barki, E. (2018). Social media crisis management: Aligning corporate response strategies with stakeholders' emotions online. *Journal of Contingencies and Crisis Management*, *26*, 295–305.

Leesa-Nguansuk, S. (2018). *Thai Social Media Use Deepens*. Bangkok Post. https://www.bangkokpost.com/business/1576478/thai-social-media-use-deepens.

Leesa-Nguansuk, S. (2021). *Food Delivery Sector Enjoys Hike In Orders*. Bangkok Post. https://www.bangkokpost.com/business/2109811/food-delivery-sector-enjoys-hike-in-orders.

Leesa-Nguansuk, S. (2022). *On-demand app struggle poised to intensify in 2023*. Bangkok Post. https://www.bangkokpost.com/business/2437867/on-demand-app-struggle-poised-to-intensify-in-2023

Li, S. P. (2021). *Foodpanda is facing a brand crisis in Thailand, but delivery riders bear the brunt*. KrASIA. https://kr-asia.com/foodpanda-is-facing-a-brand-crisis-in-thailand-but-delivery-riders-bear-the-brunt

Manakitsomboon, H. (2021a). *The digitalization in the media in Thailand — statistics & facts*. Statista. https://www.statista.com/topics/7152/the-digitalization-in-the-media-in-thailand/#dossierKeyfigures

Manakitsomboon, H. (2021b). *The digitalization in the media in Thailand — statistics & facts*. Statista. https://www.statista.com/topics/7152/the-digitalization-in-the-media-in-thailand/#dossierKeyfigures

Masayuki, Y. (2021, July 20). Foodpanda faces backlash after calling Thai protest "terrorism." *Nikkei Asia*. https://asia.nikkei.com/Business/Food-Beverage/Foodpanda-faces-backlash-after-calling-Thai-protest-terrorism

Pang, A., Kim, H.-J., & Chaidaroon, S. (2013). Dealing with emotions of stakeholders during crises: Why should leaders care? In *Handbook of Research on Crisis Leadership in Organizations* (pp. 129–132). Edward Elgar Publishing. DOI: https://doi.org/10.4337/9781781006405.00015

Pang, A., Jin, Y., Kim, S., & Cameron, G. T. (2020). Contingency theory: Evolution from a public relations theory to a theory of strategic conflict management. In F. Frandsen, & W. Johansen (Eds.), *Crisis communication* (pp. 141–164). De Gruyter Mouton.

Patiwat, T. (2021, July 18 a). มีผู้ชุมนุมบางราย … ฝาก จนท. พิจารณาดำเนินคดีด้วย @CSDThailand #ไปม๊อบไปเมรุ. Twitter [@tonpatiwat]. Retrieved August 10, 2023, from https://twitter.com/tonpatiwat/status/1416708778934738951

Patiwat, T. (2021, July 18 b). เบาะแสผู้ก่อเหตุ ตั้งใจมาทำเรื่อง ถอดป้ายทะเบียนรถออก. Twitter [@tonpatiwat]. Retrieved August 10, 2023, from https://twitter.com/tonpatiwat/status/1416709364908318723

Peck, G., & Blake, C. (2020). Thai Student-Protesters Aim for Ambitious Political Change. *AP News*. https://apnews.com/article/virus-outbreak-bangkok-thailand-prayuth-chan-ocha-crime-e0ea7336b54513bac59930fb9f45a85d

Phasuk, S. (2020, September 17). Thailand's 'Bad Students' are rising up for democracy and change. *The Washington Post*. Retrieved from https://www.washingtonpost.com/opinions/2020/09/17/thailands-bad-students-arerising-up-democracy-change/

Phoonphongphiphat, A. (2021). Thai food delivery sector still hungry despite business boom. *Nikkei Asia*. https://asia.nikkei.com/Business/Food-Beverage/Thai-food-delivery-sector-still-hungry-despite-business-boom

Pimpa, N. (2012). Amazing Thailand: Organizational culture in the Thai public sector. *International Business Research*, *5*(11). https://doi.org/10.5539/ibr.v5n11p35

Ragavan, S. (2021, July 29). *Foodpanda's botched comms strategy amid Thailand crisis*. PR Week. Retrieved October 22, 2021, from https://www.prweek.com/article/1723386/foodpandas-botched-comms-strategy-amid-thailand-crisis

Ratcliffe, R. (2020). Giant rubber ducks become symbol of Thai pro-democracy rallies. *The Guardian*. https://www.theguardian.com/world/2020/nov/20/giant-rubber-ducks-become-symbol-of-thai-pro-democracy-rallies

Reed, J. (2020). Thai protesters turn their anger on country's big businesses. *Financial Times*. https://www.ft.com/content/0b3a7448-da9e-457e-a774-b534d067e5a7

Reuters Staff. (2019, May 2). Thailand's King Rama X — from pilot prince to powerful monarch. *Reuters*. https://www.reuters.com/article/us-thailand-king-vajiralongkorn-profile-idUSKCN1S8114

Rojanaphruk, P. S. S. W. (2021, July 19). Foodpanda faces boycott after calling anti-gov't protester 'terrorist.' *Khaosod English*. https://www.khaosodenglish.com/news/crimecourtscalamity/2021/07/19/foodpanda-faces-boycott-after-calling-anti-govt-protester-terrorist/

Satienlerk, V., & Kittisilpa, J. (2021, July 18). Thai protesters clash with police near Government House. *Reuters*. https://www.reuters.com/world/asia-pacific/thai-youth-activists-go-ahead-with-protest-despite-gatherings-ban-2021-07-18/

Scroope, C. (2016). *Thai Culture — Core concepts*. Cultural Atlas. https://culturalatlas.sbs.com.au/thai-culture/thai-culture-core-concepts#thai-culture-core-concepts

Schaffar, W. (2016). New social media and politics in Thailand: The emergence of fascist vigilante groups on Facebook. *Austrian Journal of South-East Asian Studies*, *9*(2), 215–234.

Sinpeng, A. (2021). Hashtag activism: Social media and the #FreeYouth protests in Thailand. *Critical Asian Studies*, *53*(2), 192–205. https://doi.org/10.1080/14672715.2021.1882866

Smith, P., & Sumon, N. (2020, November 25). Young Protesters in Thailand Risk Much to Demand Change from Military, Monarchy. *NBC News*. Retrieved October 25, 2021, from https://www.nbcnews.com/news/world/young-protesters-thailand-risk-much-demand-change-military-monarchy-n1248807

Sripokangkul, S., Draper, J., Crumpton, C.D., & Muangming, A. (2019). Understanding the social environment determinants of student movements: A consideration of student activism in Thailand and the Thai "social cage." *International Journal of Asia Pacific Studies*, *15*(1): 59–96. https://doi.org/10.21315/ijaps2019.15.1.3

Sriramesh, K., & Vercic, D. (2020). *Global Public Relations Framework: Theory, Research, and Practice*. Routledge. https://doi.org/10.4324/9781315173290

Statista. (2021). Number of social network users in Thailand from 2017 to 2020 with a forecast through 2026 (in millions) [Graph]. In *Statista*. https://www-statista-com.libproxy.smu.edu.sg/statistics/489230/number-of-social-network-users-in-thailand/

Statista. (2023). Share of internet users in Thailand as of the 4th quarter of 2022, by age group. https://www.statista.com/statistics/1294833/thailand-share-of-internet-users-by-age-group/#:~:text=As%20of%20the%20fourth%20quarter,and%20older%20used%20the%20internet

Sombatpoonsiri, J. (2020). *Two Thailands: Clashing political orders and entrenched polarization*. Carnegie Endowment for International Peace. https://carnegieendowment.org/2020/08/18/two-thailands-clashing-political-orders-and-entrenched-polarization-pub-82438

Tanakasempipat, P. (2020, August 4). *Explainer: Thailand's Lese Majeste Law*. Reuters. Retrieved October 25, 2021, from https://www.reuters.com/article/us-thailand-protests-monarchy-explainer-idUSKCN2501Q1

Tangkitvanich, S., & Wongkitrungruang, W. (2011). *Mapping Digital Media: Thailand*. The Open Society Foundations. https://www.refworld.org/pdfid/4e324f1c2.pdf

The Business Times. (2022). GIC-backed unicorn in talks to acquire Foodpanda in Thailand. *The Business Times*. https://www.businesstimes.com.sg/companies-markets/gic-backed-unicorn-talks-acquire-foodpanda-thailand

The Standard. (2021). *เปิดใจครั้งแรกหลังกระแส #แบนfoodpanda* (Video). YouTube. Retrieved August 10, 2023, from https://www.youtube.com/watch?v=Dzp368w38vE&t=1s

United Nations High Commissioner for Refugees. (2011). *Refworld | Freedom in the World 2011 –Thailand.* Refworld. https://www.refworld.org/docid/4e4518e311.html

Wan-Kitpaiboon, N., & Areepermporn, P. (2021, August 3). Interview Session: First time interview with CEO after the backlash #แบนfoodpanda. *The Standard.* https://thestandard.co/foodpanda-apology-after-banning-trend/

World Bank. (2021). *The World Bank in Thailand.* https://www.worldbank.org/en/country/thailand/overview#2

10

SOUTH KOREA

Ignoring History Imperils Uniqlo's Business

Kritika Gupta, Quelle Audris Loo, Zi Xiang Phoon, Jotham Tobiah Lim, and Ju Young Yoon

Introduction

In October of 2019, Japanese fashion giant Uniqlo faced intense criticism and backlash by South Korean consumers for a new advertisement the brand had released in the country. Uniqlo, one of Asia's biggest apparel retailers, was founded in Yamaguchi, Japan, in 1949, and is wholly owned by Fast Retailing Co (Uniqlo, n.d.). A company that belongs to Japanese billionaire Tadashi Yana, Nikkei Asia calls him "the man who clothes Asia" (Okumura & Okutsu, 2020). Uniqlo is also known to appeal to younger consumers who enjoy the range of colors and materials the brand offers (Roxburgh, 2023). For many South Koreans, the advertisement was controversial and upsetting, and it was eventually withdrawn from the country after consumers took to the streets to protest and boycott the brand (Al Jazeera, 2019). In fact, the crisis spiraled to a point where Uniqlo's sales were greatly impacted in the region, even leading to closure of some of its key stores in the market (Bloomberg, 2020).

In recent years, South Korea has been at the forefront of global "pop culture," commonly known around the world as the "Korean Wave." The development of the Korean wave, pronounced "hallyu" in the Korean language (Lee, 2011), is driven by the popularity of the country's pop bands, its fashion, television, food and more, assimilating all the aspects of cultural globalization (Chen, 2011). The world's growing interest in Korean popular culture has also acted as a catalyst for foreign tourists visiting the locations where their favorite dramas and acts were filmed (Kim, 2013). Capitalizing on the rise of Korean culture (or K-culture), the Korean government introduced a five-year "Visit Korea" plan, in a bid to attract 30 million tourists (Park, 2022) annually. In particular, at

DOI: 10.4324/9781003411802-11

the heart of Hallyu is the ever-growing popularity of K-pop, which is short for Korean pop music (Romano, 2018). K-Pop at a global scale has directly contributed to the growth of the South Korean economy, as the foreign market for South Korean music and pop culture roughly doubled from $5.7 billion in 2015 to $10 billion in 2019. Overall, it has also had a profound impact on domestic and foreign politics, demonstrating its importance for South Korean diplomacy (Bartlett, 2022).

However, less is known about other important aspects of Korea's history and culture. For example, Japan's colonial rule over the Korean Peninsula from 1910 to 1945 continues to roil sentiments and politics on both sides of the strait to date (Lee, 2018). Furthermore, Korea has a complex culture of protests that has, in more ways than one, shaped the country's social fabric for decades. Separated from North Korea after World War II, protests have always been a part of political participation in South Korea (Chang, 2018). South Korea has had many social movements beginning with the April Revolution in the 1960s, which were led by students and young people in the country as a response to autocratic rule. Citizens have since started several social movements, symbolic of its collectivistic values, which have deeply impacted Korean society (Chae, 2016; Jung, 2022; Lee, 2005).

Tensions between South Korea and Japan

South Korea and its neighbor Japan have shared a complicated military history since the 7th century. In 1910, Japan successfully annexed Korea and colonized the nation. During World War II, Koreans were forcibly enlisted into the Japanese military. Over 200,000 girls and women, a significant proportion of whom were Korean, were forced to work in brothels run by the Japanese military before and during World War II as "Comfort women." This issue continues to be seen as unresolved by the South Korean government and citizens. For nearly three decades, Koreans both young and old have regularly gathered in front of the Japanese embassy in central Seoul to demand that the Japanese government apologize and compensate the female victims. The younger generation of South Koreans remains acutely aware of the painful stories of the victims, and views it as a much larger issue of women's rights (Banks, 2017; Bemma, 2017). In 1965, two decades after Japan was defeated, South Korean President Park Chung-Hee agreed to normalize relations and diplomatic ties with Japan, in exchange for loans and grants of approximately US$800m (BBC, 2019). However, the problems between the two nations remained far from resolved as sentiments between the citizens of the two nations continued to be hostile.

In 2013, six million South Korean merchants and mom-and-pop store owners joined a nationwide campaign to boycott Japanese products to protest Japan's claim over a disputed set of islands in the East Sea known in Korea as the Dokdo but in Japan as Takeshima. The protest targeted Japanese products ranging from Nikon cameras to Uniqlo clothes, and Toyota and Honda cars (Rahn, 2013; Song, 2013). Relations between the two countries slumped to their lowest in decades after a 2018 ruling by South Korea's top court ordering Japanese firms such as Mitsubishi, Nippon Steel, and Sumitomo, to compensate wartime forced laborers (Shin & Lee, 2018). Resentment between the two nations was further aggravated when in July 2019, the Japanese government announced restrictions on semiconductor and chemical exports to South Korea. While Japan cited "national security reasons" for the curb, this was the beginning of a trade war between the two countries – which eventually led to a boycott of Japanese products amongst the South Korean public in 2019, in what came to be termed as the #NoJapan movement. On August 2, 2019, Tokyo further escalated the trade dispute by removing South Korea from its "whitelist" of trusted trading partners. Within weeks, South Korea had removed Japan from its own "whitelist" in obvious retaliation (Deacon, 2022; Stangarone, 2020).

In the following section, we describe and then present our analysis of the Uniqlo crisis of 2019 in South Korea, including a discussion of the key stakeholders involved, how the crisis impacted the firm's reputation, position, and financial performance in the country, and the sentiments of South Korean consumers toward the apparel brand.

The Uniqlo Crisis

Boycott movements against Japan and Japanese products had been ongoing in South Korea (Lee & Chon, 2021) and acted as a precursor for the current crisis. It is noteworthy to mention that consumers' anger toward Japan continued to smolder, especially as young Koreans kept up the momentum through social media. A report by South Korean digital marketing firm eMFORCE suggested that the boycott was largely driven by people in their 20s and 30s (Suzuki, 2019). After Japan had already tightened controls on exports of three key high-tech materials to South Korea (Cha, 2019), an intersection of both the Korean culture of protest and Japan-Korean tensions came to the fore on October 21, 2019. A new commercial released in the country by Uniqlo was perceived by South Korean consumers as mocking the victims of forced labor and the comfort women of World War II (McCurry, 2019).

Until 2019, Uniqlo owned about 190 stores in South Korea (Dolan et al., 2019). The commercial by the brand featured fashion icon Iris Apfel chatting with critically acclaimed designer Kheris Rogers, who is 85 years her junior. In the advertisement, Apfel was asked how she used to dress when she was a teenager, to which she responded: "Oh my god, I can't remember that far back." However, Uniqlo's Korean department translated and subtitled its version of the advertisement a little differently. It read, "Gosh! How can I remember something that goes back 80 years?" (Cha, 2019). The specific reference to "80 years" immediately angered South Koreans, both old and young, for to them, it hinted at the dark history of colonization. To this day, South Koreans are still bitterly resentful toward Japan for its occupation of the country from 1910 to 1945 (Song & Inagaki, 2019).

Backlash against the commercial spread quickly, setting off a series of protests around the country and calls for a boycott of Uniqlo. The organization failed to address the boycott in a dialogical manner, even as protesters took to the streets demanding an official apology from the brand (Cha, 2019). Reportedly, an anonymous Uniqlo official was quoted by newswire Reuters in Seoul, saying: "There was no intention to touch on the issue of comfort women or the South Korea-Japan dispute" (Cha, 2019).

Local and Global Media Reporting

Journalists shape audience interpretations of issues and events by structuring their stories around certain frames (Pan & Kosicki, 1993) with trigger words that elicit reactions. Thus, it is essential to analyze how local and international media framed and reported on the issue. Most of the South Korean media reported the incident using keywords such as "sparking outrage," "controversial ad," "defaming," and "ridicule sexual slavery" (Kim, 2019; Ock, 2019). The tonality of headlines published by the local Korean press was largely negative and accusatory toward the brand, which may have acted as a catalyst to existing resentment among readers. In the international news media, the headlines were more subdued in nature, describing the incident using keywords such as "mistranslation" and "South Korean objections" (Lothian-McLean, 2019; Pike, 2019). However, none of the reporting helped Uniqlo's case, as the brand continued to deny any ill-intention behind the commercial (AFP, 2019).

Consumer Sentiments

The Uniqlo advertisement crisis reportedly worsened consumer sentiments toward Japanese products, especially since the controversial advertisement was released during the #NoJapan boycott movement that had begun three months earlier as a result of the ongoing trade dispute between the two nations.

The phrase "Uniqlo comfort women" – in reference to the euphemism commonly used to describe the victims of sexual slavery during Japan's pre-1945 occupation of Korea – became among the most-searched terms on Naver, South Korea's largest online platform (Al Jazeera, 2019). Tensions between South Korean consumers and Uniqlo escalated when a YouTube video created by a local student parodying the ad went viral. Gaining more than 101,000 views in just two days, the video depicted South Korean college student Youn Dong-hyeun standing with Yang Geum-deok, a 90-year-old forced laborer for Japan's

Mitsubishi during World War II. In the parody, Youn, asked how hard it was for Yang when she was young, to which she responded: "It is impossible to ever forget that awfully painful memory" (Cha, 2019). Students began demonstrating in front of Uniqlo stores around the country, and rallied on the streets demanding an official apology from the brand. Park Young-Sun, South Korea's minister for small and medium enterprises, also told a parliament committee that the advertisement controversy was "very upsetting" (Cha, 2019). Four days later, Uniqlo pulled the advertisement from South Korea.

By August 2020, the year-long boycott had resulted in the closure of nine Uniqlo stores in South Korea, bringing the number of stores down to 165 from its peak of 187 in August 2019. By January 2021, Uniqlo's flagship store in Myeong-Dong was also shuttered amid the pandemic, when tourism fell, and business continued to plummet due to the boycott (Arnold, 2020). The term "Shy Uniqlo" surfaced in relation to the boycott movement in which consumers were conscious when entering Uniqlo stores, as they felt they were being scrutinized and even had to hide the goods they had bought from the company (Lee & Kim, 2019).

Financial Impact on Uniqlo

Due to the crisis, the company suffered a sharp decline in revenue and sales, and posted an operating loss in the first quarter of fiscal year 2020 (Fast Retailing Co, 2020). South Korea was deemed an important market for Uniqlo's business, accounting for 8% of the company's sales (Ando, 2019) and had the second-largest number of Uniqlo stores overseas after China (Du, 2020). South Korea's weakened performance significantly impacted Uniqlo's International's overall sales and profit. For the first quarter of 2020, Fast Retailing Co. Ltd. reported a fall of 3.6% year-on-year in sales and a drop of 27.8% year-on-year in its profit for its international segment (Du, 2020). In addition, despite offering discounts to attract Korean customers, Uniqlo sales showed no signs of recovery (Kang, 2019).

Case Analysis

Uniqlo's crisis in South Korea suggests a failure of the brand to consider the five socio-cultural variables discussed in Chapter 1. We next discuss the socio-cultural variables of South Korea and their impact on how the Uniqlo crisis played out in the country.

Political System

At the outset of the 20th century, Japan, China, and Russia were vying for control over the Korean Peninsula, before Japan emerged the victor, occupying the peninsula in 1905 and annexing it five years later (Jun, 2018). This, undoubtedly, was the beginning of animosity between the two countries.

After Japan's surrender in 1945, South Korea was introduced to the concept of liberal democracy under the United States (US) occupation, from 1945 to 1948. When the peninsula was divided in August 1948, the pro-US Republic of (ROK or South Korea) was established in Seoul. During this period, the Americans allowed press freedom and free speech, which led to the formation of numerous new political groups and communities. However, the road to democracy and economic freedom did not happen overnight. South Korea struggled to shake off its authoritarian heritage as the history of a Confucian social religion and the hangover of the Japanese colonial rule continued to hinder its progress toward democracy. Forty years of trial and error ensued in South Korea before a bona fide democratic system was established (Heo & Hahm, 2014). During this time, South Korea's political system underwent many changes beginning with the declaration of independence in 1950. Soon after, North Korea invaded the South leading to the loss of two million lives in the Korean War. This was followed by a military coup in 1961, which was followed by rapid industrialization and economic development. The country also witnessed a presidential assassination (Kamiya, 1980), and ultimately, the formation of a new constitution in 1986, which allowed for the direct election of a president. A notable moment in South Korea's political history came when democracy was restored in 1987, led primarily by student unrest (Jun, 2018). In fact, by the late 1980s, the student movement had become the driving force for the country's transition from an authoritarian military regime to a parliamentary democracy (Lee, 2007). Today, South Korea is an established presidential democracy, and a leading consolidated democracy in Asia. The Economist Intelligence Unit (2020) listed it as one of five full democracies in the Asia and Australasia region (Lee, 2022).

South Korea and Japan are both allies of the US, with a democratic system backed by market economies. However, their relationship is deeply strained by the legacy of Tokyo's 20th-century expansionism (Al Jazeera, 2019). Although government structuring has empowered the business landscape as an open market, South Korea continues to grapple with cultural and social traits rooted in traditional authoritarian rule. This defensive stance was exacerbated in the 2019 Japan-South Korea Economic war when the Japanese government removed South Korea from its list of preferential trading partners for violating trade agreements by exporting goods to North Korea (Ezell, 2020). This incensed South Koreans who were already averse to, and skeptical about Japanese brands. The underlying historical tensions have led to Japanese firms facing immense scrutiny by the South Korean public, which could also be seen during the #NoJapan movement that began in 2019.

In the case of Uniqlo, Takeshi Okazaki, director of Uniqlo's holding company, Fast Retailing Co. Ltd., remarked that the boycott of Japanese goods in South Korea "would not last long" (Reidy, 2019). His initial response avoided direct mention of the issue and failed to implement three accommodative strategies:

Apology, compensation, and corrective action (Sriramesh et al., 2020). This diversionary tactic and crisis response created a double crisis in which Uniqlo had to issue a second response indicating that they did not deliver that "sincerity properly" and apologized for "disturbing many customers" (Nam, 2019). Despite the second attempt toward an apology, Uniqlo avoided addressing the fundamental issue of the countries' shared political history and sensitivities, choosing to classify the South Korean public as "customers" while highlighting their incompetence in delivering sincerity, instead of focusing on their failure of integrity. It also must be noted that the backlash Uniqlo faced in South Korea over the advertisement, occurred against the backdrop of the country's democratic regime, where citizens are known to express their dissent openly.

Economic System

As mentioned in Chapter 1, the economic and political systems of countries are usually closely interlinked. When Korea gained independence from Japan in 1945, few thought that the Republic of Korea would become one of the world's most dynamic economies. One notable characteristic of the country's rapid economic growth was strong economic nationalism, which first grew because of residual negative feelings against foreign regimes, and then, by the desperate need for economic survival (Lee & Lee, 2015).

After 1945, fierce anti-Japanese sentiments continued to dominate, and economic relations remained restrained. However, trade relations between the two nations re-emerged in 1965 during General Park Chung-hee's regime, when he embraced the economic benefits of exchange with Japan even as major political questions of reconciliation remained (Vekasi & Nam, 2019). The emergence of South Korea as a modern industrial society in the 1980s from a traditionally agricultural nation in the 1960s was primarily due to rapid economic development; Japan's also contributed to its economic development when President Park Chung-hee normalized relations with Tokyo in 1965. In fact, Japan was a major foreign investor in South Korea, second only to the US (Seth, 2017), in spite of heated objections from Koreans who feared a return of Japanese dominance.

During Korea's industrial evolution, a strategic group of contributors was the Chaebols – from the Korean words "chae" (wealth) and "bol" (clan) – massive, mostly family-owned business conglomerates which had porous boundaries between them and the government (Albert, 2018; Pae, 2019). After 1961, the South Korean government began working closely with Chaebols to achieve economic development goals, leading to some even dominating the economy. Many South Koreans feared that the domination of the economy by a few huge Chaebols such as Lotte and Samsung were stifling many smaller startups in the country, in addition to having too much influence on public policy. (Seth, 2017). Between 1988 and 2019, South Korea achieved remarkable success in combining rapid economic growth with significant poverty reduction, resulting in real gross domestic product (GDP) growth averaging 5.45% annually (World Bank, 2022). In 1996, the country joined the Organization for Economic Cooperation and Development, being internationally recognized as a "developed state" (Seth, 2017).

In 2005, one of South Korea's leading Chaebols, Lotte Shopping, partnered with Japan's Fast Retailing Co. Ltd (FRL). The latter invested US$19.7 million to establish FRL Korea to operate Uniqlo – where they introduced the fast-fashion trend to the South Korean market and successfully settled in the country (Kim, 2017). According to the director of Fast Retailing Co. Ltd., Tadashi Yanai, Uniqlo's main reason for entering South Korea (the fourth largest Asian economy) was to gain a foothold in the Asian Market.

During the Uniqlo crisis, information on the financial losses sustained by Uniqlo following the boycott was withheld by the company's representatives. They adopted a "no comment" response, a frequently deployed strategy in Asia when attempting to conceal matters relating to crisis (Huang et al., 2016). Moreover, they continued in the tradition of face-saving in front of their out-group counterparts, South Koreans (Wen et al., 2012). Uniqlo could have addressed the importance of solid business relationships with South Korea and emphasized that their customers were their utmost priority. This would have driven the focus to their efforts toward maintaining a good working relationship with the country and avoid exacerbating complicated political history. As can be seen from the history of South Korea's economic system, resentment toward Japan, which began during colonization, has also seeped into the country's economic framework.

Media System

The media system of South Korea, which has evolved in the past few decades, also played a part in amplifying the Uniqlo crisis in 2019. The size of South Korea's media industry has expanded in both breadth and depth since the 1980s. There has been a shift from traditional mass media to new media with an emphasis on social media. South Korea has the fastest Internet connection speed globally (Ang, 2021) and a high Internet penetration rate of 97% (Kemp, 2021). It comes as no surprise that online news consumption has surpassed television (TV) news – with online news access primarily controlled by giant domestic platforms such as Naver and Daum (Newman, 2020). However, TV news consumption continues to be influential and South Korea's major terrestrial networks, including market leaders KBS and MBC, command the biggest audiences. Most South Koreans subscribe to digital cable, satellite, or Internet TV (BBC, 2023). In addition to this, there are over 100 national and local newspapers in the country, many of which are controlled by industrial conglomerates (BBC, 2023). Given their influence with the government, Chaebols are known to often assert influence over the media and are amongst the highest paying media advertisers in the country (Kim & Kim, 2016; Seoulz, 2023).

After World War II and during the authoritarian rule of the Chun Doo-hwan government in the 1980s, the majority of the news media were state-run, resulting in censorship of print and broadcast media. However, 1987 was the turning point when South Korea transitioned to a democratic country, and Roh Tae-woo of the Democratic Justice Party was elected President. This was when the South Korean government reorganized its media policy and introduced freedom of the press (Kim, 2018).

From the 1990s to the 2000s, the media landscape in South Korea became fiercely competitive with the government recognizing the global influence of the media industry. This established the sector as the nation's critical strategic area influenced by globalization and modernization. However, some measures of government censorship over the Internet and the press are practiced in every country. In South Korea, in particular, there continues to be a contradiction between the democratic values of the country and the level of media censorship by the government (Yoon, 2017). Furthermore, criminal defamation laws, including imprisonment and fines (Human Rights Watch, 2022), have had a chilling effect on media reporting in the country,

When the Uniqlo advertisement went viral in South Korea, Uniqlo first responded via a phone interview with Joongang Tongyang Broadcasting Company (JTBC), denying the allegations and blaming South Koreans for "distorting the meaning of the advertisement" (Kim, 2019). Uniqlo used a sub-optimal response strategy to avoid crisis responsibility (Claeys & Coombs, 2020). Four days later, with no sign of public fury abating, Uniqlo pulled the advertisement from its official YouTube account and public broadcast in South Korea. As a form of damage control, Uniqlo released another statement claiming that the advertisement was part of its global campaign and was designed to target 24 countries where the company sells its products. Subsequently, Uniqlo changed its stance from advocacy to partial accommodation (Pang et al., 2010) due to negative public sentiments and public backlash from their first statement.

Furthermore, as a country with advanced technological infrastructure, South Korea has a high social media usage of 85%. It has the third highest rate of active social media users globally as of January 2019 (Chan, n.d.). The social media landscape in South Korea is unique as it has its own domestic set of social platforms like Naver, Daum, and KakaoTalk, which were initially more popular than Google, Facebook, or WhatsApp in the country. Although these domestic social media apps continue to be sought-after among the younger generations of South Koreans, Facebook has now raced into the lead, with over 60% of South Koreans using it and 39% using Instagram (Chan, n.d.). This change suggests a shift in consumption from domestic social apps to international social apps, capable of amplifying a regional crisis to a global audience. This was indicated clearly in the Uniqlo crisis, as the commercial first began garnering criticism online. At the same time, a YouTube video by a South Korean student parodying the Uniqlo ad went viral, garnering over a hundred thousand views in just a few days, and mobilizing online attack against the brand. On October 19, 2019, a Twitter user's screenshots of the phrases "mockery, comfort women" and "Uniqlo ad" were among the most searched terms on Naver when the advertisement was released.

Today, with the rise of new media technologies, brands like Uniqlo must understand the dual capabilities of social media. While online and social platforms provide brands with a host of opportunities, these platforms have also made them more vulnerable to attacks, criticism, trolls, and public dissent. Companies now have less control of communication while various constituencies, competitors, and the general public have greater access to information (Argenti, 2005). As Uniqlo continued to face consumer backlash online, it would have been prudent for the brand to adopt a proactive, assertive response strategy toward the criticism it was facing. It is known that assertive response strategies can be successful when companies are faced with social media firestorms (Scholz & Smith, 2019). Furthermore, the adoption of a two-way, dialogical communication approach with consumers would have been effective in perhaps lessening the degree of damage to their reputation amongst the public.

Societal Culture

The nuances of societal culture in South Korea play a pertinent role in shaping public sentiment and attitude in the controversial Uniqlo commercial. The country is unique given its rich culture and complex history. However, this has also made it challenging for foreign companies to enter and establish their brands in the market.

With South Korean's nationalistic sentiments driving loyalty for homegrown brands and local-based enterprises dominating the market, multi-national companies (MNCs) have low market share and power and are often seen exiting the country for various reasons. Prominent MNCs that had entered the South Korean market failed due to a lack of understanding of the culture of the consumers, including Walmart, Nokia, Nestle, and Yahoo (Hun, 2006). As seen from these brands that exited South Korea, it is imperative for others to understand the cultural nuances of the country if they wish to succeed in the market. Especially for global brands looking to penetrate the region, they must make a steadfast effort to embrace and adapt to the local culture and community. It is also pertinent for MNCs to understand that Korean culture, to date, continues to be influenced by various elements of the nation's past. Brands must make a conscientious effort to understand the country's history and how it impacts values and perspectives of citizens in present times. In other words, when it comes to South Korea, they cannot view the world as a homogenous market while developing their strategies for internationalization.

South Koreans value their culture and heritage, especially considering its importance and intersection with the country's political history. During Japan's colonization, there was a concerted effort by the Japanese to erase and alter Korean culture from the peninsula. Schools and universities were not allowed to use the Korean language, as Japanese became the primary language. It was even a crime to teach history from non-approved texts, and Japanese authorities burned over 200,000 Korean historical documents, essentially seeking to wipe out the historical memory of Korea (Blakemore, 2020).

A present analysis of South Korean culture using Hofstede's Cultural Dimensions (Lee, 2020) shows that South Korea has a Power Distance Index (PDI) above the average, is a hierarchical society and accepts societal and organizational inequalities (Hofstede Insights, 2019). In countries with a high PDI index, people tend to accept and follow a hierarchical norm that has been set for them in society, accepting that each person has a certain "role" and "place." Influenced by Confucian heritage, South Korean culture emphasizes respect for authority. Even amongst organizations, it follows a hierarchical structure with a top-down management approach. This is a pattern in South Korean companies – bosses at the top of the ladder usually only adopt one-way communication channels. This contrasts with Uniqlo which has a flat organizational hierarchy with a decentralized management approach that focuses on teamwork, open communication, and a sense of ownership (Aaker, 2014). This decentralized flexibility in business strategies may have contributed to the Uniqlo crisis, due to a possible communication gap between the marketing and public relations (PR) departments regarding the contents of the controversial advertisement. Better integration between Uniqlo's marketing and PR strategies, a robust communications team to filter sensitivity in messaging, and a better understanding of each specific culture to ensure that all public messages consider the first two stages of the Strategic Crisis Management across the Life Cycle framework – environmental scanning and understanding stakeholder emotions (Diers-Lawson & Pang, 2021), would be advised.

While South Korea remains a competitive society in general, the country has gradually shifted from its masculine past. South Korea is considered a fairly feminine society, that is, a country that is relationship-oriented and values the quality of life and people. In feminine countries, the focus is on "working in order to live" – a trait that can be seen stemming from South Korea's history of "survival." Caring for the weak is a common trait of feminine societies. Hence, it makes sense for South Koreans to stand in solidarity to stage a non-violent boycott of Uniqlo after the controversial advertisement that seemingly targeted the comfort women of World War II (Lee, 2020). Another important trait of South Korean society is their level of long-term orientation. According to Hofstede Insights (2021), South Korea's score of 100 pegged it as one of the most pragmatic, long-term-oriented societies. This essentially means that people in Korea live their lives guided by virtues. Furthermore, South Korea remains a highly collectivistic society that places high emphasis on long-term relationships and focuses on responsibility and commitment for their groups, families, and extended families. Loyalty is an inherent quality in collectivistic societies – and this can be seen clearly in South Koreans' attitudes toward their families, organizations, fellow citizens, and by extension, toward the nation. South Korea's protest and boycott of Japanese products at the expense of their economy ascertained their collectivistic characteristics, coupled with their deep-rooted nationalistic sentiments.

Activist Culture

South Korea's history of activism and widely prevalent activist culture have greatly impacted the aftermath of the release of Uniqlo's advertisement, which eventually led to the commercial being pulled. In 1960, the student movement for democracy in South Korea brought down the Rhee Syngman regime. Syngman, the first president of the Republic of Korea (ROK), replaced the democratic presidential system with an authoritarian system by amending the constitution to secure his power (Lee, 2021). What came to be known as the April 19 Revolution of 1960, became a seminal historical event that would come to define the contours of activism in the country (Kim, 2017). In 1980, a dawning of democracy began in the southwestern city of Gwangju in South Korea, when the region was engulfed in protests against martial law (Kingston, 2014). Then came the nationwide uprising of June 1987, which ended President Chun Du-Hwan's regime and opened a new chapter in South Korea's contemporary history (Paik, 2007). Even during South Korea's post-democratic era, the country experienced a rise of social activism movements. In 2004, in a first for the country, President Roh Moo-Hyun was impeached by the National Assembly on charges of illegal campaigning. This led to outcry and anger amongst citizens. Tens of thousands of citizens poured into the streets Saturday night in support of the president, who was later reinstated and cleared of charges (Demick, 2004; Len, 2004). This is just another example of how powerful activism and social movements have been in bringing about change in South Korea. The most recent social movement in South Korea is the 2016–2017 candlelight vigils against then-President Park Geun-Hye, who was accused of corruption and abuse of power. The protests eventually led to Park being stripped of presidential powers, making her the first president in the country's history to be removed from office (The Economist, 2017).

South Korean citizens' desire and capacity for political participation have intensified in the 21st century, driving many to the public stage and act on issues that matter (Shin, 2020). The advent of the Internet has also promoted interpersonal interactions among activists, allowing the disaffected and like-minded to band together to organize protest activities more easily (Lee & Fu, 2019). Given the slew of social networking platforms available, it has fostered a new generation of young activists and laid the foundation of social movements. As of 2019, 85% of South Koreans use social media, far ahead of the US (70%) (Chan, n.d.). In the past two decades, there have been multiple instances of digital activism in South Korea. In 2002, candlelight vigils were held for two 13-year-old girls killed in a roadside accident by a US military vehicle, with youths going online to commemorate their "sisters and friends" (Kang, 2017). In 2008, protests sparked against a US beef import deal and the policies of the new president, Lee Myung-Bak. Technologically, young Koreans have built a collective on the Internet based on a shared fear of contaminated beef being from the US, and a critique of Lee's neoliberal policies (Herskovitz, 2008; Kang, 2017).

The Uniqlo crisis sparked a massive outcry amongst citizens in South Korea. Protestors, including university students, took to the streets to criticize the Uniqlo advertisement and called for the brand to apologize (Cha, 2019). A 22-year-old student was among those who campaigned outside a Uniqlo store in Seoul and held a sign reading, "colonial rule 80 years ago — we remember!" (Cha, 2019). According to King (2021), activists are important stakeholders, and they have the power to spotlight a particular company's actions and influence the larger community. If activists are not well engaged, they have a huge ability to tarnish a company's reputation. They also pose a threat to a company's broader reputation and have the ability to jeopardize the company's relationships with both customers and its own employees (King, 2021). In Uniqlo's case, its lack of effort to engage in dialogic communication with activists and ease the situation affected its reputation among stakeholders. Particularly in South Korea, Uniqlo must understand that activists are a very influential group of stakeholders they must actively engage, especially during crises. Compared to older generations, millennials and Gen Zs actively turn to social media to speak up about social or political issues. Given the active role shareholder activism plays in South Korea, this requires companies such as Uniqlo to be more proactive and utilize two-way symmetrical communication to understand and foster mutually beneficial relationships with its activists.

Conclusion

Despite Uniqlo's success in many Asian markets, its negligence and insensitivity toward South Korea's culture and history fueled the ongoing trade dispute between South Korea and Japan. South Korea's collectivistic society, coupled with

Uniqlo's crisis history in the country, intensified the reputational threat of the current crisis (Coombs, 2004), making its recovery in the market challenging.

It is pertinent to view the crisis through the perspective of the five socio-cultural variables, to understand their interplayed impact on the Uniqlo crisis. The country's dark political history concerning the Japanese colonization, the ongoing economic trade war between the two nations, and feelings of economic nationalism amongst citizens of the country, have together, most definitively played a role in respectively framing and worsening consumer sentiments against Japanese apparel brand Uniqlo. It is also important to note here that given the social media consumption patterns amongst South Koreans, the backlash against Uniqlo first began online, in turn spreading like wildfire and inciting demonstrations on-ground. The boycott against the brand was primarily led by its deep-seated societal aspects and the country's existing thriving activist culture, catalyzed by high levels of nationalistic and collectivistic sentiments prevalent in the country.

Considering these aspects and overall Asian communication cultures, the crisis could have been handled better if the brand had timely adopted, softened, and provided apologetic responses, instead of deploying an ambiguous, non-confrontational approach. Moving forward, Uniqlo could ponder upon adopting a global citizenry approach and balance its Japanese interests with the international community.

References

Aaker, D. (2014, October 6). 6 reasons why Uniqlo is winning. *Prophet*. https://www.prophet.com/2014/10/6-reasons-why-uniqlo-is-winning/

AFP. (2019, October 21). Japan's Uniqlo pulls ad after South Korean fury. *The Straits Times*. https://www.straitstimes.com/asia/east-asia/japans-uniqlo-pulls-ad-after-south-korean-fury

Al Jazeera. (2019). Uniqlo ad pulled in South Korea over wartime sexual slavery row. https://www.aljazeera.com/economy/2019/10/21/uniqlo-ad-pulled-in-south-korea-over-wartime-sexual-slavery-row

Albert, E. (2018, May 4). South Korea's chaebol challenge. *Council on Foreign Relations*. https://www.cfr.org/backgrounder/south-koreas-chaebol-challenge

Ando, R. (2019). Japan's fast retailing likely hit by South Korea boycott; succession plans in focus: Analysts. *Reuters*. https://www.reuters.com/article/us-fast-retailing-results-preview-idUSKBN1WO08V

Ang, C. (2021, September 29). Mapped: The Fastest (and slowest) Internet speeds in the world. *Visual Capitalist*. https://www.visualcapitalist.com/mapped-the-fastest-and-slowest-internet-speeds-in-the-world/

Argenti, P. A. (2005, April 15). The Strategic Communication Imperative. *MIT Sloan Management Review*. https://sloanreview.mit.edu/article/the-strategic-communication-imperative/

Arnold, M. (2020, September 4). Uniqlo South Korea closes more outlets amid boycott. *Inside Retail*. https://insideretail.asia/2020/08/04/uniqlo-south-korea-closes-more-outlets-amid-boycott/

Banks, G. (2017, September 28). South Korea: New generation joins 'comfort women' fight. *Breaking News, World News and Video from Al Jazeera*. https://www.aljazeera.com/features/2017/9/28/south-korea-new-generation-joins-comfort-women-fight

Bartlett, J. (2022, June 28). Domestic and global political impacts of K-Pop: BoA, BTS, and beyond. *The Diplomat*. https://thediplomat.com/2022/06/domestic-and-global-political-impacts-of-k-pop-boa-bts-and-beyond/

BBC (2023, January 24). South Korea media guide. https://www.bbc.com/news/world-asia-pacific-15291415

BBC (2019, December 2). South Korea and Japan's Feud explained. https://www.bbc.com/news/world-asia-49330531

Bemma, A. (2017, September 8). South Korea: World's longest protest over comfort women. *Breaking News, World News and Video from Al Jazeera*. https://www.aljazeera.com/news/2017/9/8/south-korea-worlds-longest-protest-over-comfort-women

Blakemore, E. (2020, July 28). How Japan took control of Korea. *History Channel*. https://www.history.com/news/japan-colonization-korea

Bloomberg (2020, January 10). Uniqlo suffers worst overseas sales drop in decade on Hong Kong protests, South Korea boycott. *South China Morning Post*. https://www.scmp.com/business/article/3045473/uniqlo-suffers-worst-overseas-sales-drop-decade-hong-kong-protests-south

Cha, S. (2019). Uniqlo ad sparks protest, parody as South Korea-Japan dispute flares. *Reuters*. https://www.reuters.com/article/us-southkorea-japan-uniqlo-idUSKBN1X106Q

Chae, Y. H. (2016, December 24). South Koreans protest for ninth straight weekend for Park to step down. *Reuters*. https://www.reuters.com/article/cnews-us-southkorea-politics-idCAKBN14D04H

Chan, J. (n.d.). Explained: The Unique Case of Korean Social Media. https://www.linkfluence.com/blog/the-unique-case-of-korean-social-media

Chang, P. Y. (2018). The origins and legacies of South Korean protest culture. *Cross-Currents: East Asian History and Culture Review*, *27*, 155–162, https://cross-currents.berkeley.edu/e-journal/issue-27/chang.

Chen, J. D. (2011). The globalizing effect of Korean pop culture. *Mountaineer Undergraduate Research Review*, *3*(1), 7.

Claeys, A., & Coombs, W. (2020). Organizational crisis communication: Suboptimal crisis response selection decisions and behavioral economics. *Communication Theory*, *30*, 290–309. https://doi.org/10.1093/ct/qtz002

Coombs, W. T. (2004). Impact of past crises on current crisis communication: Insights from situational crisis communication theory. *Journal of Business Communication*, *41*(3), 265–289. https://doi.org/10.1177/0021943604265607

Deacon (2022). (Re)producing the "history problem": Memory, identity and the Japan-South Korea trade dispute. *Pacific Review*, *35*(5), 789–820. https://doi.org/10.1080/09512748.2021.1897652

Demick, B. (2004, March 14). Thousands of South Koreans protest Roh's impeachment. *Los Angeles Times*. https://www.latimes.com/archives/la-xpm-2004-mar-14-fg-roh14-story.html

Diers-Lawson, A., & Pang, A. (2021, February 8). 11 strategic crisis management: State of the field, challenges and opportunities. In C. Valentini (Ed.), *Public Relations* 27, 195–216. De Gruyter. https://doi.org/10.1515/9783110554250-011

Dolan, D., Ando, R., Gallagher, C., Coates, S., & Pullin, R. (2019). South Korea boycott hitting sales of Japan's Uniqlo, company says. *Reuters*. https://www.reuters.com/article/us-southkorea-japan-labourers-fast-retai-idUSKCN1UY2X7

Du, L. (2020). Uniqlo sees worst drop in overseas sales in decade amid Hong Kong unrest and South Korea row. *Bloomberg*. https://www.bloomberg.com/news/articles/2020-01-09/uniqlo-sees-worst-overseas-sales-drop-in-decade-amid-asia-unrest

Ezell, S. (2020, January 16). Understanding the South Korea-Japan trade dispute and its impacts on U.S. foreign policy. https://itif.org/publications/2020/01/16/understanding-south-korea-japan-trade-dispute-and-its-impacts-us-foreign

Fast Retailing Co. (2020). First quarterly results announcement for the three months ended 30 November 2019. https://www.fastretailing.com/eng/ir/library/pdf/tanshin202008_1q_eng.pdf

Huang, Wu, F., & Cheng, Y. (2016). Crisis communication in context: Cultural and political influences underpinning Chinese public relations practice. *Public Relations Review*, *42*(1), 201–213. https://doi.org/10.1016/j.pubrev.2015.11.015

Henry, H. (2019). Uniqlo Pulls Ad Accused of Mocking South Korea's 'Comfort Women.' *Branding in Asia Magazine*. https://www.brandinasia.com/uniqlo-pulls-ad-in-korea/

Heo, U., & Hahm, S. D. (2014). Political culture and democratic consolidation in South Korea. *Asian Survey*, *54*(5), 918–940. https://doi.org/10.1525/as.2014.54.5.918

Herskovitz, J. (2008, July 5). South Koreans protest against beef and Lee. *Reuters*. https://www.reuters.com/article/us-korea-protest-idUSSEO26305920080705

Hofstede Insights. (2019). The dimensions of National Culture. https://hi.hofstede-insights.com/national-culture

Hofstede Insights. (2021, June 21). Country Comparison. https://www.hofstede-insights.com/country-comparison/japan,south-korea/

Human Rights Watch. (2022). World Report 2022: South Korea. https://www.hrw.org/world-report/2022/country-chapters/south-korea

Hun, C. S. (2006, May 23). Wal-Mart selling stores and leaving South Korea. *The New York Times*. https://www.nytimes.com/2006/05/23/business/worldbusiness/walmart-selling-stores-and-leaving-south-korea.html

Jun, C. S. (2018). South Korea. *History Channel*. https://doi.org/https://www.history.com/topics/asian-history/south-korea

Jung (2022). Anti-authoritarian attitudes after democratic movements: Evidence from the June struggle of 1987 in South Korea. *Asian Journal of Comparative Politics*, *7*(4), 1115–1126. https://doi.org/10.1177/20578911221103641

Kamiya (1980). The Korean peninsula after Park Chung Hee. *Asian Survey*, *20*(7), 744–753. https://doi.org/10.1525/as.1980.20.7.01p01792

Kang (2017). Internet activism transforming street politics: South Korea's 2008 "Mad cow" protests and new democratic sensibilities. *Media, Culture & Society*, *39*(5), 750–761. https://doi.org/10.1177/0163443717709444

Kang, H. (2019). Uniqlo Sales Plunge Despite Special Discounts. http://koreabizwire.com/uniqlo-sales-plunge-despite-special-discounts/147049

Kemp, S. (2021, February 11). Digital in South Korea: All the Statistics You Need in 2021. *DataReportal – Global Digital Insights*. https://datareportal.com/reports/digital-2021-south-korea

Kim, C. R. (2017). *Youth for nation: Culture and protest in Cold War South Korea*. University of Hawaii Press. https://doi.org/10.1515/9780824855970

Kim, D. (2018). *Media governance in Korea, 1980–2017*. Palgrave Macmillan.

Kim, H. B. (2019, October 20). Uniqlo halts ad after being accused of defaming sex slave victims. *Korea Times*. https://m.koreatimes.co.kr/pages/article.amp.asp?newsIdx=277402

Kim, Y. (Ed.). (2013). *The Korean wave: Korean media go global*. Routledge.

Kim, D., & Kim, S. (2016). Media ownership and concentration in South Korea. *Who owns the world's media?* Oxford University Press. https://doi.org/10.1093/acprof:oso/9780199987238.003.0027

King, B. (2021). Why Companies Should Engage with Activists. *Kellogg School of Management at Northwestern University*. https://insight.kellogg.northwestern.edu/article/why-companies-should-engage-with-activists

Kingston, J. (2014, May 17). Dying for democracy: 1980 Gwangju uprising transformed South Korea. *The Japan Times*. https://www.japantimes.co.jp/news/2014/05/17/asia-pacific/politics-diplomacy-asia-pacific/dying-democracy-1980-gwangju-uprising-transformed-south-korea/

Lee (2005). Law, politics, and impeachment: The impeachment of Roh Moo-hyun from a comparative constitutional perspective. *The American Journal of Comparative Law*, *53*(2), 403–432. https://doi.org/10.1093/ajcl/53.2.403

Lee. (2007). *The making of minjung democracy and the politics of representation in South Korea*. Cornell University Press. https://doi.org/10.7591/9780801461699

Lee, E.-J. (2021). The 1960s in South Korea: *Modernisation, nationalism and the pursuit of democratisation. International Quarterly for Asian Studies*, *52*(3–4), 187–205. https://doi.org/10.11588/iqas.2021.3-4.16181

Lee, & Lee, K. T. (2015). Economic nationalism and globalization in South Korea: A critical insight. *Asian Perspective*, *39*(1), 125–151. Https://doi.org/10.1353/apr.2015.0012

Lee, S. (2020, December 1). Analyzing Korean customers with Hofstede's Four Cultural Dimensions. *Brand2Globa*l. https://www.brand2global.com/korean-customers-hofstede-four-cultural-dimensions/

Lee, S. J. (2011). The Korean wave: The Seoul of Asia. *The Elon Journal of Undergraduate Research in Communications*, *2*(1), 85–93.

Lee, S. J. (2022). The contentious state of South Korean democracy: Pitfalls and hopes. *Council on Foreign Relations*. https://doi.org/https://www.cfr.org/blog/contentious-state-south-korean-democracy-pitfalls-and-hopes

Lee, Y. (2018, December 12). South Korea's 100-year grievance with Japan still isn't settled. *Bloomberg*. https://www.bloomberg.com/news/articles/2018-12-11/how-wwii-still-stirs-tension-in-south-korea-and-japan-quicktake?leadSource=uverify%20wall

Lee, Y., & Chon, M. G. (2021). "Don't go, Don't buy": Understanding the motivations of the anti-Japan boycott movement in South Korea during an international conflict. *Negotiation and Conflict Management Research*, *15*(1), 6–31.

Lee, S. H., & Fu, K. (2019). Internet use and protest politics in South Korea and Taiwan. *Journal of East Asian Studies*, *19*(1), 89–109. https://doi.org/10.1017/jea.2018.25

Lee, Y. J., & Kim, H. K. (2019, October 10). Order online and wear at home… Fashion "Shy Uniqlo" also appeared. *Maeil Business News*. https://www.mk.co.kr/news/business/view/2019/10/817463/

Len, S. (2004, March 13). President's impeachment stirs angry protests in South Korea. *The New York Times*. https://www.nytimes.com/2004/03/13/world/president-s-impeachment-stirs-angry-protests-in-south-korea.html

Lothian-McLean, M. (2019, October 23). Uniqlo advert accused of mocking sexual slavery victims pulled from South Korea. *The Independent*. https://www.independent.co.uk/life-style/uniqlo-advert-japan-south-korea-world-war-two-japan-brothel-sex-a9167666.html

McCurry, J. (2019). Uniqlo accused of mocking wartime sexual slavery victims. *The Guardian*. https://www.theguardian.com/world/2019/oct/21/uniqlo-accused-mocking-wartime-sexual-slavery-victims-south-korea

Nam, H.-woo. (2019, July 22). Consumers unimpressed by Uniqlo's 2nd apology. *The Korea Times*. https://www.koreatimes.co.kr/www/tech/2019/07/694_272688.html

Newman, N. (2020, May 20). South Korea. *Reuters Institute Digital News Report*. https://www.digitalnewsreport.org/survey/2018/south-korea-2018/

Ock, H. J. (2019, October 20). [Newsmaker] Uniqlo pulls controversial ad. *The Korea Herald*. https://www.koreaherald.com/view.php?ud=20191020000244

Okumura, S., & Okutsu, A. (2020, October 14). The man who clothes Asia: Uniqlo chief Tadashi Yanai. *Nikkei Asia*. https://asia.nikkei.com/Spotlight/The-Big-Story/The-man-who-clothes-Asia-Uniqlo-chief-Tadashi-Yanai

Pae, P. (2019, August 29). South Korea's Chaebol. *Bloomberg*. https://www.bloomberg.com/quicktake/republic-samsung

Paik, N. C. (2007). Democracy and peace in Korea twenty years after June 1987: Where are we now, and where do we go from here? *Asia-Pacific Journal-Japan Focus*, *5*(6), 1–9.

Pang, A., Jin, Y., & Cameron, G. T. (2010). Contingency theory of strategic conflict management: Directions for the practice of crisis communication from a decade of theory development, discovery and dialogue. In W. T. Coombs, & S. J. Holladay (Eds.), *Handbook of crisis communication* (pp. 527–549). Wiley Blackwell.

Pan, Z., & Kosicki, G. M. (1993). Framing analysis: An approach to news discourse. *Political Communication*, *10*(1), 55–75. http://www.tandfonline.com/doi/abs/10.1080/10584609.1993.9962963

Park, C. K. (2022, December 15). South Korea lures K-pop lovers, digital nomads in plan to become 'tourism powerhouse'. *South China Morning Post*. https://www.scmp.com/week-asia/lifestyle-culture/article/3203444/south-korea-lures-k-pop-lovers-digital-nomads-bid-become-tourism-powerhouse

Pike, A. (2019, October 22). Uniqlo pulls ad after South Korean objections. *Japan Today*. https://japantoday.com/category/business/japan%27s-uniqlo-pulls-ad-after-south-korean-fury

Rahn, K. (2013, July 25). Merchants to boycott Japanese products. *The Korea Times*. https://www.koreatimes.co.kr/www/tech/2022/07/419_131118.html

Reidy, G. (2019). Uniqlo Maker apologizes for saying Korea boycott won't last long. *Bloomberg*. https://www.bloomberg.com/news/articles/2019-07-22/uniqlo-maker-apologizes-for-saying-korea-boycott-won-t-last-long?leadSource=uverify%20wall#xj4y7vzkg

Romano, A. (2018, February 26). How K-pop became a global phenomenon. *Vox*. https://www.vox.com/culture/2018/2/16/16915672/what-is-kpop-history-explained

Roxburgh, H. (2023, July 21). *Uniqlo in China: New threads*. CKGSB Knowledge. https://english.ckgsb.edu.cn/knowledges/article/uniqlo-in-china-new-threads/

Sriramesh, & Verčič, D. (2020). *The global public relations handbook: Theory, research, and practice*. Taylor & Francis Group. https://doi.org/10.4324/9781315173290

Scholz, J., & Smith, A. (2019). Branding in the age of social media firestorms: How to create brand value by fighting back online. *Journal of Marketing Management*, *35*(11–12), 1100–1134. https://doi.org/10.1080/0267257x.2019.1620839

Seoulz. (2023). The South Korean media and newspapers — a full breakdown. https://www.seoulz.com/the-south-korean-media-and-newspapers-a-full-breakdown/

Seth, M. J. (2017). South Korea's economic development, 1948–1996. In *Oxford Research Encyclopedia of Asian History*. https://doi.org/10.1093/acrefore/9780190277727.013.271

Shin, J.-W. (2020). Changing patterns of South Korean social movements, 1960s–2010s. Testimony, firebombs, lawsuit and candlelight. In *Civil society and the state in democratic East Asia* (pp. 239–268). Amsterdam University Press. https://doi.org/10.1515/9789048551613-011

Shin, H., & Lee, J. (2018). South Korean court angers Japan with order to compensate wartime laborers. *Reuters*. https://www.reuters.com/article/us-japan-forcedlabour-southkorea-idUSKCN1NY05D

Song, J. A. (2013, February 25). S Korean grocers threaten Japan boycott. *Financial Times*. https://www.ft.com/content/3a8e6114-7f31-11e2-89ed-00144feabdc0

Song, J., & Inagaki, K. (2019, October 21). Japan's Uniqlo under fire in South Korea over TV commercial. *Financial Times*. https://www.ft.com/content/86c5a0f2-f3cd-11e9-b018-3ef8794b17c6

Sriramesh, K., Verčič, D., Coombs, W. T., & Claeys, A.-S. (2020). Global crisis communication. In Sriramesh, K., & Vercic, D. (eds.), *The global public relations handbook: Theory, research, and practice* (pp. 217–225). essay, Routledge.

Stangarone, T. (2020, January 24). Parsing the economic damage from the Japan-South Korea dispute. *The Diplomat.* https://thediplomat.com/2020/01/parsing-the-economic-damage-from-the-japan-south-korea-dispute/

Suzuki, S. (2019, October 28). Boycott Japan: How young South Koreans keep the anger alive. *Nikkei Asia.* https://asia.nikkei.com/Spotlight/Comment/Boycott-Japan-How-young-South-Koreans-keep-the-anger-alive

The Economist. (2017, March 10). South Korea's president is permanently stripped of her powers. https://www.economist.com/asia/2017/03/10/south-koreas-president-is-permanently-stripped-of-her-powers

The Economist Intelligence Unit. (2020). Democracy Index 2020: In sickness and in health? https://www.eiu.com/n/campaigns/democracy-index-2020/

Uniqlo. (n.d.) *About Uniqlo.* Retrieved March 30, 2023, from https://www.uniqlo.com/uk/en/company/

Vekasi, & Nam, J. (2019). Boycotting Japan: Explaining divergence in Chinese and South Korean economic backlash. *Journal of Asian Security and International Affairs*, *6*(3), 299–326. https://doi.org/10.1177/2347797019886725

Wen, W.-C., Yu, T., & Benoit, W. L. (2012). The failure of "scientific" evidence in Taiwan: A case study of international image repair for American beef. *Asian Journal of Communication*, *22*(2), 121–139. https://doi.org/10.1080/01292986.2011.642393

World Bank. (2022, March 11). *The World Bank in Republic of Korea.* https://www.worldbank.org/en/country/korea/overview

Yoon, J. (2017). South Korea and internet censorship. *University of Washington.*

EPILOGUE

Su Lin Yeo

In an age of hyperconnectivity, values drive business. The medium of this era with its digital networked structures has not only connected the globe and enabled innovation and economic growth; it has also established channels for individuals to connect across social systems. More than 60 years after McLuhan (1964) predicted that modern communication technologies would bring together every tribe and culture in the world to exchange information and experiences without the need to be physically present, the ever-accelerating technological progress has since brought this "global village" to a whole new different level. Now into the 21st century, the exponential growth in digital technology has not only banded individuals from every corner of the globe together in lightning speed but also transformed the way humans connect, communicate, and engage with one another. Through virtual platforms, i.e., social media, individuals equipped with a digital device can literally carry out conversations with anyone on this planet. Notably, it allows everyone to speak out without the need for a face or identity, alongside the ability to control personal narratives by creating content for social platforms (Yang & Liu, 2017).

While independent cultures like those in North America and Western Europe celebrate having another communication platform and democratic space to speak out and advance ideologies and social causes, interdependent cultures like many in Asia never quite had that "space." The Western concept of a marketplace of ideas (i.e., maintaining that truth will emerge from unrestrained debates, transparent exchanges, and discourse) is foreign to many Asians. Individual opinions are not similarly valued, and influential elites or leaders usually take the lead in shaping, creating, and interpreting public sentiments that often resonate with cultural norms and national identity. High in power distance, many Asian societies adhere tightly to hierarchies and deference to authority. This applies to every stratum in society, within families, schools, organizations, and governments. Overt expression of ambition that challenges views and decisions taken by those higher in the packing order is deemed inappropriate, annoying, and unwelcome. As such, Asians' overnight access to social media was received with delight and uneasiness. It gives everyone a voice but also threatens to remove all societal structures as individual opinions from every layer of the social hierarchy can now be heard reverberating over networks across the globe in seconds (Yeo, 2021).

The transformative force of social media is ultimately a double-edged sword. While some democracies are optimistic that autocracies can finally be eradicated as the world unites and people become closer, social spaces are also used to echo and strengthen control, thereby ushering in new cultural norms as differing human values and behaviors offline are ported over and amalgamated online. It may have pooled together multiple groups of like-minded individuals who share similar values and motivations, but such "diverse unities" have also polarized the world. The divide is so great that we are witnessing not only cross-cultural clashes but also major splits within cultures.

As a result, it is short-sighted for businesses to focus on being enticed solely by the boundless opportunities to reach out to and engage with global customers. Although digital spaces have certainly let organizations save costs, streamline processes, and increase productivity in addition to facilitating cultural exchanges, organizations have never had to thrive in such a volatile business environment weighed down by endless issues and crises. In the past, companies only had to deal with crises relating to products or those inflicted by economic and financial meltdowns. Today, regardless of size, market share, or market capital, they are confronted daily by value-ladened crises. Be it racism, nationalism, religious discrimination, bullying, sexism, animal rights, or climate change, social advocacy has never threatened companies' immediate and long-term survivability like the way our digitalized globe is capable of inflicting. The technological designs of the medium are characterized by interactivity, participation, openness, and connectedness, and the anonymity, speed, and amplification that social media affords essentially means that if businesses do not prioritize strategizing its communication efforts with polarized audiences over profits, the medium which allows companies to capitalize on to make profits overnight can also wipe off billions of dollars from their coffers instantly.

Consequently, it is imperative that organizations must recognize that the battle fields for operating in the digital landscape have changed drastically. Given the many faces of influence, business competitors are not the only threats to corporate reputation. Individuals who have large following or small-scale opponents can sometimes wreak greater damage to brands and take down even the largest of corporations considering that "today anyone armed with a hundred-dollar digital camera and a connection to the Internet is a potential Spielberg or Riefenstahl" (Collings & Rohozinski, 2009, p. 77). This is particularly acute in Asia, where the concept of collectivism is prevalent across the continent. Guided by social values that emphasize the principle of placing greater importance of the group, individuals are to forego his or her personal interests for the sake of the larger community to ensure progress and unity. Hence, it only takes one voice to mobilize a contingent of millions to either support or undermine the organization. We read of individual voices calling for large-scale national boycotts when values clash in our chapters on China, Vietnam, India, Indonesia, and South Korea.

The eclectic nature of every country in Asia with its own unique interplay of politics, economics, media, culture, and activism makes it necessary for foreign companies to familiarize themselves with the complex communicative environment before establishing their presence or expanding their operations in this hugely diverse continent. The Global Public Relations Framework provides an essential roadmap and is a "must have" playbook to better "diagnose" and understand corresponding best practices in stakeholder engagement and communication in the Far East. Without such a playbook, foreign conglomerates may be setting themselves up for no-win situations as all it takes is for one communication miscue owing to cultural incompatibility to trigger a crisis and misplaced trust. As the chapters in this book have attested, such an unfortunate oversight can be costly even to the most reputable global brands.

Given the multitude of contradictions that can negatively impact businesses, it is almost obligatory for foreign firms to embrace "local multi-culturalized mindsets" and be highly cognizant that there is no "one-size fits all" approach or narrative when managing communication with stakeholder groups in any one Asian market. We know that different country markets have different requirements but for Asia, one country can account for different markets, and they can be contra distinctive from one another. This is a key differentiator for doing business in Asia. We see this in the case of McDonald's in India, where the simple act of ensuring excellent customer service to one consumer group is abhorrent to another. Such an aberration in Asian societies suggests that the slightest unconscious communication oversight, even if it is "business as usual" for the organization, can result in long-term damage and needless reputation miring of brands operating in Asia. Hence, adopting a conceptual map that can flexibly comprehend Asian stakeholders' perceptions, which are influenced by the interactions of factors that exist in the larger nuanced social and structural environment, is vital if global brands hope to win the hearts and minds of diverse publics in the new tribal age.

References

Collings, D., & Rohozinski, R. (2009). *New media and the warfighter: An analytical synthesis and workshop report*. Bullets & Blogs.

McLuhan, M. (1964). *Understanding media: The extensions of man*. McGraw-Hill.

Yang, J. H., & Liu, S. (2017). Accounting narratives and impression management on social media. *Accounting and Business Research*, *47*(6), 673–694.

Yeo, S. L. (2021). Commentary: Strategic communication in Asia. In Crawshaw, S., Fitzsimmons, A., McCorkindale, T., Pang, A., Thomas, S. & Yeo, S.L. (Contributors), *The 2021 IPR future of communications in Asia report*. Institute of Public Relations. https://instituteforpr.org/2021-foc-asia-report/

INDEX

Made in the USA
Monee, IL
14 September 2026

62978588R00125